LANGUAGE!®

The Comprehensive Literacy Curriculum

Reading

Writing

Spelling

Vocabulary

Grammar

Speaking

Jane Fell Greene, Ed.D.

Sopris West®

Sopris West®
EDUCATIONAL SERVICES

A Cambium Learning Company

BOSTON, MA • LONGMONT, CO

10 11 12 13   RRDJEFMO   15 14 13 12

Authors:
Jane Fell Greene, Ed.D.
Nancy Chapel Eberhardt

Quicksilver is a registered trademark of Marvel Characters, Inc. New York Times is a registered of The New York Times Corporation. Tony Awards is a registered trademark of American Theatre Wing, Inc. Grammy Awards is a registered trademark of the National Academy of Recording Arts & Sciences, Inc. Muppets is a registered trademark of The Muppets Holding Company, LLC. Sesame Street is a registered trademark of Children's Television Workshop. Mister Rogers is a registered trademark of The McFeely-Rogers Foundation. Arthur is a registered trademark of Marc Brown. Juilliard is a registered trademark of The Juilliard School Corporation. Silk Road Project is a registered trademark of The Silk Road Project, Inc. The New Yorker is a registered trademark of Advance Magazine Publishers Inc. Scotch Tape is a registered trademark of the Minnesota Mining and Manufacturing Company. Rubik's Cube is a registered trademark of Seven Towns Ltd. Corp. Tetris is a registered trademark of the Elorg Corporation. Toyota is a registered trademark of Toyota Motor Corporation

For acknowledgement of permissioned materials, see Sources, page 215.

ISBN 13: 978-1-60218-694-1
ISBN 10: 1-60218-694-4
170000/6-11

Printed in the United States of America

Published and distributed by

Cambium
L E A R N I N G®
Sopris West®

4093 Specialty Place • Longmont, CO 80504 • (303) 651-2829
www.voyagerlearning.com

Table of Contents · Handbook

Table of Contents • Handbook

Unit 19

Go With Speed

Independent

Build Knowledge
Use Text Features
Interpret Visual
   Information
Fluency

Instructional

Build Knowledge
Predict
Identify Character
   Traits
Identify Setting
Connect and Clarify
   Ideas
Literary Terminology

Challenge

Build Knowledge
Predict
Build Vocabulary
Clarify Meaning

Unit
20

Play On

Independent
Build Knowledge
Interpret Visual
  Information
Fluency

Instructional
Build Knowledge
Predict
Identify Character
  Traits
Connect and Clarify
  Ideas
Literary Terminology

Challenge
Build Knowledge
Predict
Build Vocabulary
Clarify Meaning

Unit
21
Join the Family

Independent
Build Knowledge
Interpret Visual Information
Fluency

Instructional
Build Knowledge
Predict
Connect and Clarify Ideas
Literary Analysis

Challenge
Build Knowledge
Predict
Build Vocabulary
Clarify Meaning

Unit

22

Solve the Puzzle

Independent

Build Knowledge

Interpret Visual
Information

Fluency

Instructional

Build Knowledge

Predict

Connect and Clarify
Ideas

Literary Analysis

Challenge

Build Knowledge

Predict

Build Vocabulary

Clarify Meaning

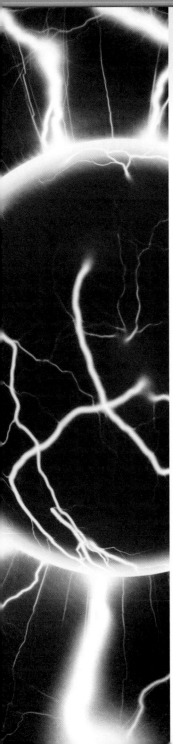

Unit
23
Power Up!

Independent

Build Knowledge
Interpret Visual
  Information
Fluency

Instructional

Build Knowledge
Predict
Connect and Clarify
  Ideas
Literary Analysis

Challenge

Build Knowledge
Predict
Build Vocabulary
Clarify Meaning

Table of Contents • Text Selections

Unit 24
Have a Dream

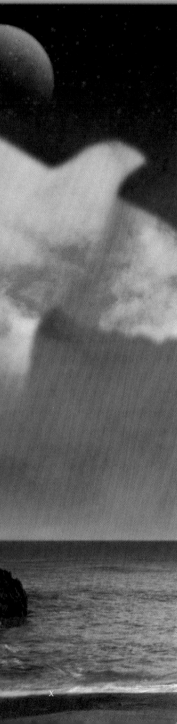

Independent
Build Knowledge
Use Text Features
Interpret Visual Information
Fluency

Instructional
Build Knowledge
Predict
Identify the Speaker
Literary Analysis
Literary Terminology

Challenge
Build Knowledge
Predict
Build Vocabulary
Clarify Meaning

Table of Contents · Resources

Handbook

Handbook

How to use the Table of Contents and Index

To find information in this Handbook, you can use the Handbook Table of Contents, pages xix–xx, or the Handbook Index, pages 208–214. Below are some tips for using both features.

Table of Contents

A table of contents lists **general** topics in the order they are presented in a book. Use a table of contents when you are looking for a general topic.

general topic

page numbers

Index

An index lists **specific** topics in alphabetical order.

Use an index when you are looking for a specific topic.

specific topics

page numbers

Phonemic Awareness and Phonics

Consonants and Vowels (Unit 1)

Languages have two kinds of sounds: **consonants** and **vowels**.

- **Consonants** are closed sounds. They restrict or close the airflow using the lips, teeth, or tongue.

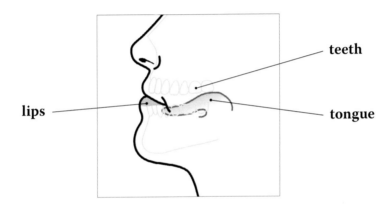

- **Vowels** are open sounds. The air doesn't stop.

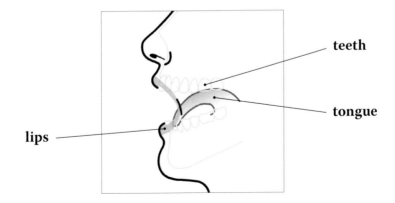

English Consonant Chart

(Note the voiceless/voiced consonant phoneme pairs)

Mouth Position

	Lips (Bilabial)	Lips/Teeth (Labiodental)	Tongue Between Teeth (Dental)	Tongue Behind Teeth (Alveolar)	Roof of Mouth (Palatal)	Back of Mouth (Velar)	Throat (Glottal)
Stops	/p/ /b/			/t/ /d/		/k/ /g/	
Fricatives		/f/ /v/	/th/ /<u>th</u>/	/s/ /z/	/sh/ /zh/		/h/[1]
Affricatives					/ch/ /j/		
Nasals	/m/			/n/		/ng/	
Lateral				/l/			
Semivowels	/ʰw/ /w/[2]			/r/	/y/		

(Type of Consonant Sound)

1 Classed as a fricative on the basis of acoustic effect. It is like a vowel without voice.

2 /ʰw/ and /w/ are velar as well as bilabial, as the back of the tongue is raised as it is for /u/.

English Consonant Chart based on Bolinger, D. 1975. *Aspects of Language* (2nd ed.). Harcourt Brace Jovanovich, p. 41.

Consonant Letter Combinations (Units 8, 11)

di = 2
graph = letter

Digraphs are two letters that represent one sound.

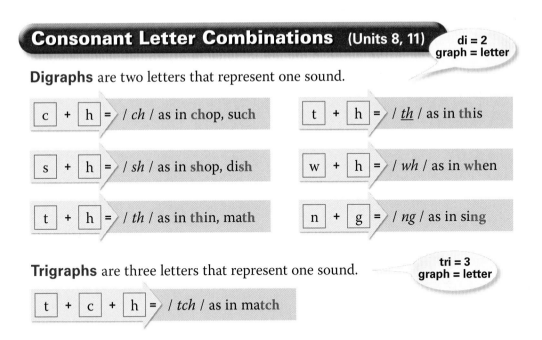

| c | + | h | = | / ch / as in chop, such |

| t | + | h | = | / th / as in this |

| s | + | h | = | / sh / as in shop, dish |

| w | + | h | = | / wh / as in when |

| t | + | h | = | / th / as in thin, math |

| n | + | g | = | / ng / as in sing |

Trigraphs are three letters that represent one sound.

tri = 3
graph = letter

| t | + | c | + | h | = | / tch / as in match |

Blends are consonant sound pairs in the same syllable. The consonants are not separated by vowels. In blends, each consonant is pronounced.

> **Initial blends** are letter combinations that represent two different consonant sounds at the beginning of a word.

l blends: <u>bl</u>-, <u>cl</u>-, <u>fl</u>-, <u>gl</u>-, <u>pl</u>-, <u>sl</u>-	black
r blends: <u>br</u>-, <u>cr</u>-, <u>dr</u>-, <u>fr</u>-, <u>gr</u>-, <u>pr</u>-, <u>shr</u>-, <u>thr</u>-, <u>tr</u>-	brick
s blends: <u>sc</u>-, <u>sk</u>-, <u>sm</u>-, <u>sn</u>-, <u>sp</u>-, <u>st</u>-	scare
w blends: <u>dw</u>-, <u>sw</u>-, <u>tw</u>-	dwell

> **Final blends** are letter pairs that represent two different consonant sounds at the end of a word.

-<u>mp</u>, -<u>nd</u>, -<u>sk</u>, -<u>st</u>, -<u>ct</u>, -<u>lk</u>, -<u>lt</u>, -<u>sp</u>	band

Clusters consist of three or more consonants in the same syllable. The consonants are not supported by vowels. Each consonant is pronounced.

<u>scr</u>, <u>spl</u>, <u>spr</u>, <u>str</u>	spray

English Vowel Chart

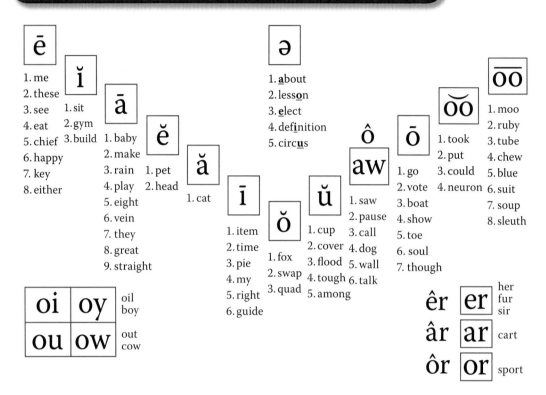

Note: *The order of spelling examples reflects the relative frequency of incidence for that spelling of the phoneme.*

ē
1. me
2. these
3. see
4. eat
5. chief
6. happy
7. key
8. either

ĭ
1. sit
2. gym
3. build

ā
1. baby
2. make
3. rain
4. play
5. eight
6. vein
7. they
8. great
9. straight

ĕ
1. pet
2. head

ă
1. cat

ī
1. item
2. time
3. pie
4. my
5. right
6. guide

ŏ
1. fox
2. swap
3. quad

ŭ
1. cup
2. cover
3. flood
4. tough
5. among

ə
1. about
2. lesson
3. elect
4. definition
5. circus

ô / aw
1. saw
2. pause
3. call
4. dog
5. wall
6. talk

ō
1. go
2. vote
3. boat
4. show
5. toe
6. soul
7. though

o͝o
1. took
2. put
3. could
4. neuron

o͞o
1. moo
2. ruby
3. tube
4. chew
5. blue
6. suit
7. soup
8. sleuth

oi	oy	oil / boy
ou	ow	out / cow

êr	er	her / fur / sir
âr	ar	cart
ôr	or	sport

Vowel Chart based on Moats, L.C. (2003). *LETRS: Language Essentials for Teachers of Reading and Spelling*, Module 2 (p. 98). Adapted with permission of the author. All rights reserved. Published by Sopris West Educational Services.

Vowel Sounds

The same vowel letter can represent different sounds.

Diacritical mark:
The breve (˘) signals short vowel sounds.

Short sounds

Letter	a	e	i	o	u
Sound	/ ă /	/ ĕ /	/ ĭ /	/ ŏ /	/ ŭ /
	cat	egg	sit	fox	up

Long sounds

The long vowel sound for **a**, **e**, **i**, and **o** is the same as the name of the letter that represents it. The long vowel sound for **u** can be pronounced two ways.

Diacritical mark:
The macron (¯) signals long vowel sounds.

Letter	a	e	i	o	u	
Sound	/ ā /	/ ē /	/ ī /	/ ō /	/ o͞o /	/ yo͞o /
	cake	Pete	bike	nose	tube	cube

Sounds of y as a vowel   (Unit 17)

The letter **y** represents three different vowel sounds. The position of the letter in the syllable determines the sound it represents.

Letter	y	y	y	y	y
Sound	/ ī /	/ ī /	/ ī /	/ ē /	/ ĭ /
	sky	deny	type	happy	gym
Syllable type	end of a one-syllable word (an open syllable)	end of a two-syllable word, when the second syllable is stressed	final silent **e** syllable	end of a two-syllable word, when the second syllable is unstressed	closed syllable

Syllable Types

Words are made up of **syllables**, words or word parts that have one vowel sound.

Syllable Type	Pattern	Vowel Sound	Diacritical Mark
Closed (Unit 13)	A syllable that ends with a consonant sound. **dig, trans-mit**	The vowel sound is short.	ă
r-controlled (Unit 14)	A syllable that has a vowel followed by **r**. **car, mar**-ket	The vowel sound is r-controlled: / âr /, / ôr /, or / êr /.	âr
Open (Unit 15)	A syllable that ends with a vowel. **she, my, o**-pen	The vowel sound is long.	ā
Final Silent e (Unit 16)	A syllable that ends in a final silent **e**. de-**fine**, ath-**lete**	The vowel sound is long.	ā
Vowel Digraph (Unit 19)	A syllable that contains a vowel digraph. **rain, see, boat**	The vowel sound is usually long.	ā
Final Consonant + le (Unit 22)	A syllable pattern that is only at the end of multi-syllable words. a-**ble**, ea-**gle**, puz-**zle**	The vowel sound is schwa / əl /.	ə
Vowel Diphthong (Unit 23)	A syllable that contains a vowel diphthong. **oi**l, b**oy**; **out**, c**ow**	The vowel sound is a glide, sounding like two sounds.	oi, ou

Conditions of schwa

Stress in words and the **schwa** go together. Stress is the emphasis that syllables have in words.

Unstressed syllable in a two-syllable word	Words beginning or ending with **a**	Multi-syllable words
If a syllable is not stressed, the vowel is usually reduced to schwa. lesson = /les'ən /	An **a** that begins or ends a word is often reduced to schwa. alike = / ə-līk /	In a multi-syllable word, the second syllable is often reduced to schwa. multiply + / mul'-tə-pli /

STEP 2

Word Recognition and Spelling

Building Words from Sounds and Letters   (Unit 1)

We put vowels and consonants together to make words.

Two words in English are made of just one vowel.

All other words combine consonants and vowels.

Syllables

> For more about **Syllable Types**, see Step 1, page H8.

What is a Syllable?

Words are made up of parts we call **syllables**.

- Some words have just one syllable.
- Every syllable has one vowel sound.
- A syllable may or may not be a word by itself.

	How many syllables?		
	1	2	3
map	map		
bandit	ban	dit	
inhibit	in	hib	it

When a syllable has a vowel followed by at least one **consonant,** the vowel sound (v) is usually short.

ĭ<u>t</u>	mă<u>p</u>	bĕ<u>nd</u>
vc	vc	vcc

Syllable Patterns

Note the pattern of vowels (**v**) and consonants (**c**).

VC/CV Pattern   (Unit 3)

> **ban** + **dit** = **bandit**
>
> vc   cv = vc/cv

atlas	sudden
basket	problem
random	traffic

Some two-syllable words have a different pattern.

VC/V Pattern   (Unit 5)

> **rob** + **in** = **robin**
>
> vc   v = vc/v

finish	solid
lemon	melon
seven	rapid

V/CV Pattern   (Unit 15)

> **si** + **lent** = **silent**
>
> v   cv = vcv

legal	acorn
moment	equip
music	secret

VR/CV Pattern   (Unit 14)

If the first vowel is followed by an **r**, the syllable is **r**-controlled.

> **mar** + **ket** = **market**
>
> v   cv = v/cv

corner	target
current	orbit
perhaps	harvest

V/V Pattern   (Unit 15)

> **ne** + **on** = **neon**
>
> v   v = v/v

diet	poem
fuel	quiet
lion	poet

Compound Words

For more about **Compound Words**, see Step 3, page H27.

What Is a Compound Word?   (Unit 3)

A **compound word** is made up of two or more smaller words.

In a compound word, both words have to be real words that can stand on their own.

| sand | + | bag | = | sandbag |

Prefixes and Suffixes   (Units 13, 17)

We can build longer words and change their meaning by adding prefixes and suffixes.

Prefixes are word parts added to the beginning of words.

| un | + | lock | = | unlock |

Unit 19	fore-, mid-, mis-, over-	Unit 22	dis-, pro-
Unit 20	de-, ex-	Unit 23	per-
Unit 21	con-, in-		

Suffixes are word parts added to the ending of words.

| quick | + | ly | = | quickly |

Unit 19	-en, -er, -ful, -ist, -less, -ment, -ness	Unit 22	-able, -ous
Unit 20	-y	Unit 23	-ate, -ize
Unit 21	-or		

Roots (Unit 20)

We can build words using roots. We usually attach a prefix or suffix to make it a word. Roots carry the most important part of the word's meaning.

| ex | + | tract | = | extract |

Unit 20	form, port, tract	Unit 22	dic/dict, spect
Unit 21	duc/duct, scrib/script	Unit 23	fac/fact/fec/fic, ject

Contractions

For other uses of an **Apostrophe**, see Step 4, page H35.

Contractions are two words combined into one word. One or more letters are left out and are replaced by an **apostrophe** (').

Contraction with **not**   (Unit 7)

is + n̸ot = isn't

The letter **o** in **not** is replaced by the apostrophe (').

Contractions with **would**   (Unit 9)

I + ~~woul~~d = I'd

The letters **woul** in **would** are replaced by the apostrophe (').

Contractions with **will**   (Unit 10)

it + ~~wi~~ll = it'll

The letters **wi** in **will** are replaced by the apostrophe (').

Contractions with <u>am</u>, <u>is</u>   (Unit 13)

I + ǝm = I'm

The letter <u>a</u> in **am** is replaced with the apostrophe (').

she + ɨs = she's

The letter <u>i</u> in **is** is replaced with the apostrophe (').

I'm	she'll	he's	it's

Contractions with <u>are</u>   (Unit 14)

they + ǝre = they're

The letter <u>a</u> in **are** is replaced with the apostrophe (').

we're	you're	they're

Contractions with have   (Unit 15)

they + h̶a̶ve = they've

The letters <u>ha</u> in **have** are replaced with the apostrophe (').

I've	we've	you've	they've

Contractions with had or has   (Unit 16)

you + h̶a̶d = you'd

she + h̶a̶s = she's

The letters <u>ha</u> in **had** or **has** are replaced with the apostrophe (').

had: I'd, you'd, he'd, she'd, it'd, we'd, you'd, they'd
has: he's, she's, it's

Abbreviations

An **abbreviation** is a shortened form of a word.

Doctor	= **Doctor**	= Dr.	**Period**
October	= **October**	= Oct.	
California	= **California**	= CA (postal abbreviation)	
Department of Motor Vehicles	= **Department Motor Vehicles**	= DMV	

* See the Unit 12 **Essential Word** list for more abbreviations.

Spelling Conventions

Spelling conventions are tips that help us remember how to spell English words.

Words ending with <u>v</u> or <u>s</u> + <u>e</u>

Almost no English words end in <u>v</u>. At the end of a word, <u>v</u> is almost always followed by <u>e</u>: have, give, live.

Often the <u>e</u> follows a single <u>s</u> at the end of the word. The <u>e</u> does not signal a long vowel.

promise	purchase

Double Consonants   (Unit 5)

Use double letters **-ss, -ff, -ll, -zz**:

- at the end of many words.
- in many one-syllable words.
- after one short vowel.

pass	stiff	will	jazz

Ways to Spell / k / (Unit 4)

The sound / k / is spelled three ways. The position of / k /
in the word signals how to spell it:

- Use **c** at the beginning of words before the vowel **a**: **c**at.

- Use **k** at the beginning of words before the vowel **i**: **k**id.

- Use **-ck** after one short vowel in one-syllable words: ba**ck**, si**ck**.

Adding -es (Unit 7)

Nouns and verbs ending in **s**, **z**, or **x** add **-es** to form plural
nouns or singular present tense verbs.

Plural Nouns: dresses fizzes boxes	
Singular Present Tense Verbs: presses buzzes waxes	

Using ch or -tch (Unit 8)

The sound / ch / is represented two ways. The position of
/ ch / in a word helps you spell it:

- Use **ch** at the beginnings of words.

ch	i	p

- Use **-tch** after a short vowel at the ends of one-syllable words.

m	a	tch

There are four exceptions: **much**, **such**, **rich**, and **which**.

Think of this sentence to remember these words: A **rich** person gave so **much**, **which** was **such** good news!

/ ŭ / Spelled o (Unit 9)

Some words keep an Old English spelling for the / ŭ / sound.

In these words, the vowel sound is spelled with the letter **o**:
front, shove, ton.

Final Silent e   (Unit 10)

The **e** at the end of the word is a signal to use the long vowel sound. The final **e** is silent. This is called the **final silent e** pattern.

The use of the final silent **e** can make a big difference in meaning.

$$m\breve{a}n + e = m\bar{a}n\cancel{e} \qquad p\breve{i}n + e = p\bar{i}n\cancel{e}$$

Spelling Rules

Spelling rules help us add endings to words.

Doubling Rule   (Unit 6)

When a

- 1-syllable word   hop
- with **1** vowel   hop
- ends in **1** consonant   hop

double the final consonant *before* adding a **suffix** that begins with a **vowel**.

$$\overset{v}{\text{hop} + \text{p} + \underbrace{\text{ing}}_{\text{suffix}}}$$

Do not **double** the consonant when the **suffix** begins with a consonant.

$$\text{cap} + \underbrace{\overset{c}{\text{ful}}}_{\text{suffix}} = \text{capful}$$

Advanced Doubling Rule   (Unit 22)

Double the final consonant in a word before adding a suffix
beginning with a vowel when:

- The word is more than one syllable.
- The final syllable is stressed.
- The final syllable has one vowel followed by one consonant.

Drop e Rule   (Units 10, 22)

When adding a suffix to a **final silent e** word:

If the suffix begins with a vowel, drop the **e** from the base word.

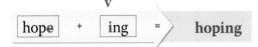

But, if the suffix begins with a consonant, **do not** drop the
e from the base word.

hope + ful = hopeful

When adding a suffix to a **final consonant + le** syllable:

If the suffix begins with a vowel, drop the **e** from the base word.

puzzle + ing = puzzling

If the suffix begins with a consonant, **do not** drop the **e**
from the base word.

Words Ending in o   (Unit 15)

When adding **-s** or **-es** to words ending in **o**:

If the words end in a **consonant + o**, add **-es** to form plural nouns and singular present tense verbs. The **-es** keeps the sound for **o** long.

| hero | + | es | = | heroes | | go | + | es | = | goes |

If the words end in a **vowel + o**, add **-s** to form noun plurals.

| video | + | s | = | videos |

The Change y Rule   (Unit 17)

When a base word ends in **y**:

If the word ends in **y** preceded by a consonant, change **y** to **i** before adding a suffix, except for **-ing**.

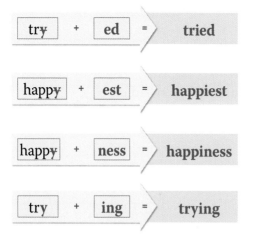

| try | + | ed | = | tried |

| happy | + | est | = | happiest |

| happy | + | ness | = | happiness |

| try | + | ing | = | trying |

STEP 3

Vocabulary and Morphology

Adding certain letters to words can add to or change their meanings.

Multiple Meanings

Sometimes the same word can mean different things.

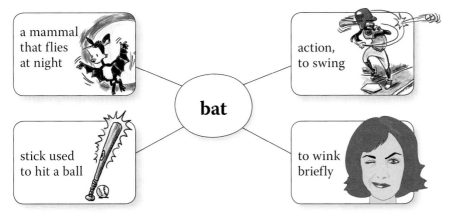

Meaning Parts • Noun Endings

See also
Noun Forms, Step 4,
page H34.

Adding **-s** or **-es** / Plural Nouns   (Units 1, 7)

Singular means "one of something." **Plural** means "more than one."

Adding -s changes a singular noun to a plural noun.

-s means more than one.

cat	cat**s**

Nouns ending in certain letters use **-es** to make them plural.

- Singular nouns ending in <u>s</u>, <u>z</u>, or <u>x</u>: **dresses, fizzes, boxes**
- Singular nouns ending in <u>ch</u>, <u>sh</u>, or <u>-tch</u>: **riches, dishes, matches**

Adding 's / Singular Possessive Nouns (Unit 2)

Adding 's (an apostrophe and an **s**) to a noun shows ownership, which means possession.

whale + 's

whale's tail

The tail belongs to the whale.

Adding s'/ Plural Possessive Nouns (Unit 11)

Adding s' signals plural possession. This means that more than one person or thing owns, has, or takes one or more things.

whale + s'

whales' tails

The tails belong to the whales.

Meaning Parts • Adjective Endings

Adding -er / Comparative Adjectives   (Unit 14)

Adding -er signals comparison between two nouns or pronouns.

Adding -est / Superlative Adjectives   (Unit 14)

Adding -est signals comparison among three or more nouns or pronouns.

Adjective	Comparative Adjective	Superlative Adjective
My little sister is **short**.	She is **shorter** than my older sister.	She is the **shortest** person in my family.

Before a multisyllabic adjective, we usually use **more** or **most** to make the comparative and superlative forms of the adjective.

Adjective	Comparative Adjective	Superlative Adjective
This is colorful art.	This art is **more** colorful than that one.	This is the **most** colorful art.

Meaning Parts • Verb Endings

See also
Verb Forms (Tense Timeline), Step 4, page H43.

Adding -s or -es / Singular Present Tense Verb   (Units 4, 8)

Adding -s or -es signals the number and tense (time) of a verb:

-s or -es means <u>singular</u> <u>present tense.</u>
one of something   happening now

> The ice **melts.**
>
> The runner **finishes** the race.

Adding -ed / Past Tense   (Unit 7)

Adding -ed signals past tense.

Adding -ing / Present and Past Progressive Forms   (Units 5, 9)

Adding -ing to a verb means an action is ongoing, or in progress.

The -ing ending signals the present progressive verb form when preceded by **am**, **are**, or **is**.

> am lock**ing**
>
> are lock**ing**
>
> is lock**ing**

The -ing ending signals the past progressive verb form when preceded by **was** or **were**.

> was push**ing**
>
> were push**ing**

Adding -ing / Present Participle (Unit 15)

When we add -ing to a verb, the new word can act as an adjective—a word that describes nouns.

The -ing form of a verb, which can be used to describe nouns, is called a **present participle**.

Present Progressive

The sun is shining.

Shining is a verb, with the action in progress.

Present Participle
Acting as an Adjective

The shining sun is hot.

Shining answers the question *What kind?* of sun.

Adding -ed or -en / Past Participle (Unit 16)

When we add -ed or -en to some verbs, the new word can also act as an adjective—a word that describes nouns. The -ed or -en form of a verb, when it describes a noun, is called a **past participle.**

Past Tense

The athlete injured his foot.

Injured is a verb, with the action in the past tense.

Past Participle
Acting as an Adjective

The injured athlete used crutches.

Injured is an adjective, answering the question *Which one?* about athlete.

Prefixes

What Is a Prefix? (Unit 13)

A prefix can add to or change the meanings of a word.

A prefix + a base word = a new word with a new meaning.

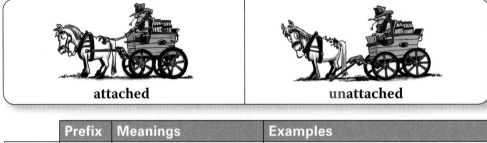

	attached		unattached

	Prefix	Meanings	Examples
Unit 19	fore-	before, in front of	forehand, foreman, foretell
	mid-	middle	midsummer, midterm, midyear
	mis-	wrongly, badly, not	misfile, misprint, misunderstand
	over-	beyond, above, too much	overdue, overpass, overslept
Unit 20	de-	from	decode, deduct, defrost
	ex-	out, from	excavate, expand, expel
Unit 21	con-	with, together	confident, conformist, contribute
	in-	not, into, toward	inactive, incomplete, independent income, ingrained, insider
Unit 22	dis-	not, absence of, apart	disgust, disinterest, discuss
	pro-	forward, in front of	progress, protect
Unit 23	per-	through, thoroughly, throughout	perfect, perform, permit

Assimilation (Unit 21)

A prefix often assimilates to the base word or root to which it is attached.

In **assimilation**, the last letter of the prefix changes or sounds similar to the first letter of the base or root. This change makes pronunciation easier. The meaning of the prefix does not change when it is assimilated.

in + legal = illegal	ex + mit = emit
con + bine = combine	ex + fect = effect
dis + fuse = diffuse	

Suffixes

What Is a Suffix? (Unit 17)

A suffix can add to or change the meaning of a word. It can also change the function of a word. Some suffixes can form participles. Some suffixes can form nouns, and some can form adjectives.

glad   gladly

	Suffix	Meanings	Examples
Unit 17	-ly	how something is done	quickly
Unit 19 (nouns)	-er	someone who, something that	entertainer, trainer, waiter
	-ist	someone who	artist, medalist, motorist
	-ment	the state, act, or process of	agreement, ailment, shipment
	-ness	the state, quality, condition, or degree of	lateness, sweetness, thickness
Unit 19 (verbs or adjectives)	-en	to become, made of, caused to be or have	deepen, stiffen, widen
	-ful	full of, characterized by	colorful, painful, skillful
	-less	without, lacking	helpless, spotless, useless
Unit 20 (adjectives)	-y	characterized by, consisting of, the quality or condition of	funny, stormy, tricky
Unit 21 (nouns)	-or	someone who, something that	director, donor, protector
Unit 20 (adjectives)	-able	capable of, can do	available, dependable, lovable
	-ous	full of, having, characterized by	humorous, rigorous, nervous
Unit 23 (verbs or adjectives)	-ate	cause to be, having the quality of	illustrate, operate, considerate

Inflectional Suffixes

These inflectional endings are used at the end of words to change number, possession, comparison, and tense.

For more about **Meaning Parts**, see pages H19–23.

Number	Possession	Comparison	Tense
-s	-'s	-er	-ing
-es	-s'	-est	-ed, -en

Roots (Unit 20)

- A root is the basic meaning part of a word. It carries the most important part of the word's meaning.

prefix	+	root	=	new word
ex	+	tract	=	extract
out	+	pull	=	to pull out

The word **extract** means *to pull out*.

- The root usually needs a prefix or suffix to make it into a word.

- Roots of English words often come from other languages, especially Latin.

	Root	Meanings	Examples
Unit 20	form	to take shape	inform, reform, transform
	port	to carry	deport, export, report
	tract	to pull	detract, extract, retract
Unit 21	duc/duct	to lead	conduct, educate, product
	scrib/script	to write	describe, inscribe, transcript
Unit 22	dic/dict	to say, tell	dedicate, indicate, predict
	spect	to look at, see, watch	inspect, spectator, expect
Unit 23	fac	to make, do	facsimile, faculty
	fact	to make, do	factory, benefactor, satisfactory
	fec	to make, do	affect, defector, disinfect
	fic	to make, do	difficult, significant, insignificantly
	ject	to throw	reject, object, projectile

Compound Words

For more about **Compound Words**, see Step 2, page H11.

Understanding the Meaning of Compound Words (Unit 3)

- Often the last part of a compound word provides information about the meaning of the word.

  A **sandbag** is a type of **bag**.

- Sometimes the first part and the last part combine to form an entirely new meaning. (Unit 4)

Both **hot** and **dog** are words, but **hotdog** is not a type of dog.

This is a **hot dog**, but not a **hotdog**.

Three Kinds of Compound Words (Unit 13)

Compound words are written in three ways.

Closed: written without a space between the words

downhill   The road to the school is all **downhill**.

laptop   She took a **laptop** to the park.

Open: written with a space between the words

jump shot   Trina sank a **jump shot** to win the basketball game.

base hit   He got a **base hit** in the ninth inning of the World Series game.

Hyphenated: written with a hyphen (-) between the words

plug-in   We need a **plug-in** air freshener for the laundry room.

left-hand   Make a **left-hand** turn at the intersection.

Expressions and Idioms

Expressions are a common way of saying something. They are similar to idioms. Expressions do not have a specific form.

Expression	Meaning	Sample Sentence
in the wind	likely to happen	The final vote is *in the wind*.

An **idiom** is a common phrase that cannot be understood by the meanings of its separate words. The idiom can only be understood by knowing the meaning of the entire phrase.

Idiom	Meaning	Sample Sentence
be up to speed (Unit 19)	perform at an acceptable level	After two weeks of intensive training, he felt he was *up to speed*, and could do the job well.
rock the boat (Unit 19)	make trouble; risk spoiling a plan	She did not want to *rock the boat* since she was new to the school.
let sleeping dogs lie (Unit 20)	leave a situation as is so that no more problems are created	When you've talked enough about a problem, sometimes it is best to *let sleeping dogs lie*.
play with fire (Unit 20)	take part in a dangerous or risky activity	Skiing without a helmet is *playing with fire*.
have a domino effect (Unit 21)	when one event sets off a chain of related events	The fog in Chicago's airport *had a domino effect* in delaying flights across the country.
run in the family (Unit 21)	common to many members of the same family	The ability to sing well *runs in the family*.
be on pins and needles (Unit 22)	be in a state of tense anticipation	The students *were on pins and needles* to find out their grades for the semester.
burn the candle at both ends (Unit 22)	work from early to late and not getting rest	He was *burning the candle at both ends* while studying for finals and working after school.
bring the house down (Unit 23)	get overwhelming audience applause	The school's rock band *brought the house down* at their first concert.
keep an ear to the ground (Unit 23)	pay attention to everything that's happening so you know what is going on	The police asked the neighbors to *keep an ear to the ground* for clues to the crime.
waste your breath (Unit 24)	tell or ask something that will have no effect	Don't *waste your breath* because he has made up his mind.
work like a dream (Unit 24)	work very well	The old clock *worked like a dream* after it has been repaired.

Word Relationships

One way to understand the meaning of a word is to compare it to other words.

Word Relationships	What Is It?	Examples
antonyms	Words that have opposite meanings	alike/different sweet/bitter
synonyms	Words that have the same or similar meaning	power/strength joy/happiness poisonous/toxic
attributes	Words that tell more about other words such as size, parts, color, and function	tiny/needle (size) apple/peel (part) grapes/purple (color)
homophones	Words that sound the same but have different meanings	road/rode weak/week break/brake

Degrees of Meaning   (Unit 19)

Antonyms are words with opposite meanings. Some antonyms are total opposites like **right** and **wrong**. There aren't any words between these opposites. Other antonyms have words between them along a scale of meaning. These words convey degrees of meaning between the two antonyms.

poor   **fair**   **good**   **excellent**

A word between the opposites can often convey a more precise meaning for a context. These two sentences mean almost the same thing. The slight difference in meaning gives us a more precise idea of what the weather is like.

> The weather was **poor** so we stayed home.
>
> The weather was **fair** so we went to the game.

Shades of Meaning

Synonyms are words with the same or similar meaning. Even though the meaning may be similar, there is often a shade of meaning, or connotation that makes one word a better choice to use in a specific context.

> **Fast** usually describes speed. A **fast** train
> (You wouldn't say a quick train.)
>
> **Quick** usually describes a length of time.
> A **quick** message
> (You wouldn't say a fast message.)

Words can tell about objects' **attributes**, such as size, parts, color, and function.

Categories and attributes help us define words.

Size
A windmill is **tall**.

Parts
A windmill has a **base and blades**.

Shape
Windmills are **narrow**.

Function
Windmills **catch wind energy to make electric energy**.

Definition
A windmill is a machine with a **base and blades** that **catches wind energy to make electric energy**.

Why? Word History

Speed—The Old English word *spēd* is the origin for our word **speed**. This word originally meant "prosperity, successful outcome, ability, or quickness." The corresponding verb, *spēdan*, or in Modern English, **speed**, meant "to succeed, prosper, or achieve a goal," and the Old English adjective, *spēdig*, the ancestor of our word **speedy**, meant "wealthy, powerful." Who knows at what point the idea of success became associated with being quick? Today, we use the word **speed** primarily to refer to the velocity of something and not as a synonym for success.

Tractor—Did you know that the word **tractor** comes from Latin? The Latin root *tract* means "to pull." As many as 60 percent of English words contain Latin roots. If we know the meaning of the Latin root, we can often work out the meaning of the English word. More than 130 English words have **tract** as their root.

Family—It may surprise you that in the 15th century, one definition of **family** was "the servants of a household." In fact, the word **family** originally comes from the Latin word for servant, *famulus*. Certainly, people today would not describe their family as servants. The meanings of **family** clearly have changed over the centuries.

Today, in informal speech, some people refer to their family as the *fam*. This shortened form of **family** came into use quite recently; however, shortened forms of English words for family members have been in use much longer. For example, *ma* and *pa*, shortened versions of *mama* and *papa*, have been in use for more than a century. So have *grandma* and *grandpa*.

Words such as *fam* are known as *clipped* words. Many clipped words are used in English. Some examples are: *limo* from *limousine*, *ref* from *referee*, *ad* from *advertisement*, and *sub* from *submarine*.

Why? Word History

The root *spect*—Did you know that gold diggers and football fans at games have something in common? Gold diggers are called **prospectors**. Fans at games are called **spectators**. Both of these words have the same root, **spect**. What does that root mean? "To look at, see, or watch."

Prospectors are people who look for natural deposits of valuable minerals such as gold, silver, or oil. Both prospectors and spectators are looking and waiting to see what will come next.

Perfume—**Per-** is a prefix that came into English from Latin. **Per-** means "through." And **fume**, from the Latin *fumus*, means "smoke." So how can we explain today's meaning of **perfume**? It surely doesn't mean "through the smoke." But centuries ago, in Italy, that's exactly what it meant: "to fill with smoke."

When English borrowed the word, it meant "fumes produced by burning a substance, such as incense." We know this from the work of early English writers. For example, in 1650, a writer wrote, "she dyed of the plage and they *perfumed* the house with the graines of juniper." Gradually, the ideas of burning and smoke were left behind and a perfume came to mean "a pleasant aroma."

Nightmare—We all dream when we sleep, but sometimes we experience nightmares. We're not sure what causes these scary dreams, but we do know the history of the word **nightmare**. The first syllable is obvious—most of us do most of our sleeping at night. But what about the second syllable, *mare*?

Speakers of Old English used the word *mare* to mean "goblin." In Middle English, *nightmare* meant "a scary creature that pesters sleeping people." Today, it means a dream that arouses fear, horror, or distress. We also use the word **nightmare** to describe an intensely distressing experience.

STEP

4

Grammar and Usage

When we understand words and their meanings, we can use them in sentences. Words have different jobs in sentences. Sometimes the same word can have different jobs depending on how it is used.

Nouns

Nouns can be singular or plural. See **Meaning Parts** in Step 3, page H19.

What Is a Noun?   (Units 1, 13)

A noun names a **person**, a **place**, a **thing,** or **idea**.

Common and Proper Nouns   (Unit 3)

Nouns may be common or proper.

- A **common noun** names a *general* person, place, or thing.

- A **proper noun** names a *specific* person, place, or thing.

Proper nouns begin with a capital letter.

Common Nouns	Proper Nouns
man	Mr. West
city	Boston
holiday	Independence Day
event	Olympics
historical period	Renaissance
days of the week	Saturday
months of the year	April

Concrete and Abstract Nouns   (Unit 3)

Nouns may be concrete or abstract.

- A **concrete noun** names a person, place, or thing that we *can see or touch.*

table	plate
car	teacher
pencil	

- An **abstract noun** names an idea or a thought that we *cannot see or touch.*

love	sports
Saturday	democracy

Noun Forms

See also
Meaning Parts
Step 3, page H19.

Singular noun   (Unit 1)

Singular means "one of something."

Plural noun   (Unit 1)

Adding **-s** changes a singular noun to a plural noun.

Adding the suffix **-s** to a singular noun . . . . makes a plural noun.	
■ lemon + s = lemons	■ **Lemons** taste good in tea.
Adding the suffix -es to nouns ending in s, z, x, ch, sh, or tch . . . makes a plural noun.	
■ dress + es = dresses	■ Rose bought three new **dresses**.
■ fizz + es = fizzes	■ They drank cherry **fizzes**.
■ box + es = boxes	■ The **boxes** were full of books.
■ rich + es = riches	■ The safe contains many **riches**.
■ dish + es = dishes	■ The **dishes** fell to the floor.
■ match + es = matches	■ The wet **matches** would not light.

Singular Possessive Noun (Unit 2)

Adding **'s** to a noun shows possession.

Adding the suffix **'s** to a singular noun . . . . makes a possessive singular noun.	
■ Stan + 's = Stan's	■ **Stan's** stamps are at camp.
■ van + 's = van's	■ The **van's** mat is flat.
■ man + 's = man's	■ The **man's** cap is black.

Plural Possessive Noun (Unit 11)

Plural nouns show possession through the use of **s'**.

Adding the suffix **-s'** to nouns . . . . makes a possessive plural noun.	
■ boy + s' = boys'	■ The **boys'** cards were missing.
■ girl + s' = girls'	■ The **girls'** snacks are on the table.
■ dog + s' = dogs'	■ The **dogs'** bowls are empty.

Noun Functions

Noun as a Subject (Unit 2)

Nouns can serve as the subjects of sentences. The **subject**:

- is one of two main parts of English sentences.
- names the person, place, or thing that the sentence is about.
- usually comes before the verb.
- answers "Who (what) did it?"

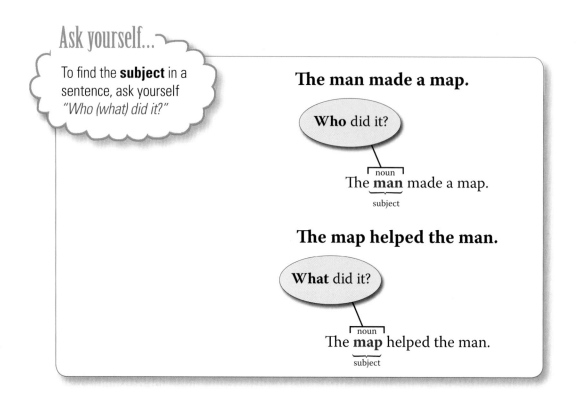

Ask yourself...

To find the **subject** in a sentence, ask yourself *"Who (what) did it?"*

The man made a map.

Who did it?

The **man** made a map.
subject

The map helped the man.

What did it?

The **map** helped the man.
subject

Simple Subject   (Unit 8)

The noun that the sentence is about is the **simple subject** of the sentence.

For **Compound Subjects**, go to Step 4, page H69.

The blue egg fell from the nest.
simple subject

Complete Subject

The simple subject and all of its modifiers are called the **complete subject**.

The blue egg fell from the nest.
complete subject

Noun as a Direct Object   (Unit 3)

A noun can be the direct object—the person, place, or thing that receives the action.

For **Compound Direct Objects**, go to Step 4, page H70.

The direct object:

- is in the predicate part of the sentence.

- answers "What did they (he, she, it) do it to?"

Ask yourself...

To find the **direct object**, ask yourself the following questions: *Who did it? What did it do?* Then ask: *Who did he do it to?*

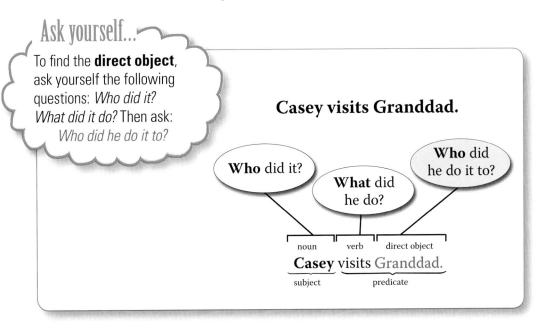

Casey visits Granddad.

Who did it?

What did he do?

Who did he do it to?

	noun	verb	direct object
	Casey	visits	Granddad.
	subject		predicate

Noun as an Indirect Object   (Unit 17)

Ask yourself...

To find the **indirect object**,
ask yourself the following questions:
Who did it? What did it do? Then ask:
To whom did he do it to?

Nikko gave Granddad a gift.

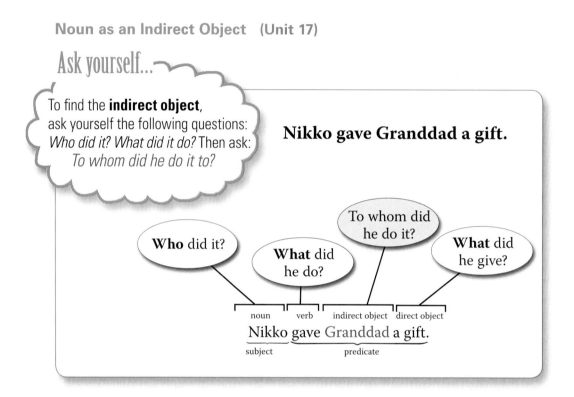

Who did it?

What did
he do?

To whom did
he do it?

What did
he give?

| noun | verb | indirect object | direct object |

Nikko gave Granddad a gift.

subject   predicate

Noun as Predicate Nominative   (Unit 19)

When a sentence has a form of **be** as the main verb,
the noun that follows is a **predicate nominative**.

See also
Linking Verbs,
page H51.

- The predicate nominative
  renames, or tells more about,
  the subject.

- The subject and the predicate
  nominative name the same person,
  place, thing, or idea.

The girl is a runner.
subject lv   predicate
                nominative

- Note: The verb **be** can never
  take a direct object.

Noun as an Object of the Preposition   (Unit 4)

A noun can be the **object of the preposition** in a prepositional phrase.

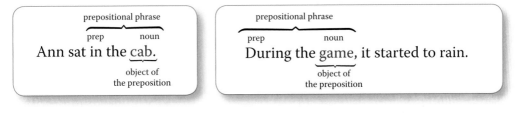

Noun as an Appositive   (Unit 17)

A noun or noun phrase can also serve as an **appositive**.

An appositive:

- follows another noun or pronoun and explains, renames, or identifies it.

- may have one or more modifiers.

- is usually set off from the rest of the sentence with commas.

> King Tut, an ancient **pharaoh**, was buried in a pyramid.
> noun   appositive

Noun as an Adjective   (Unit 21)

A noun can serve as an adjective.

> Anne Frank enjoyed a good **family** life.

In this sentence, **family** describes the noun *life*. It answers the question: *What kind?*

Verbs

Verbs describe actions. (Unit 1)

Every sentence has at least one verb or verb phrase.

We **can see** some actions:

jump   walk   clap

Some actions we **can't see**:

think   wish   dream

Verb Phrases (Unit 9)

A phrase is a group of words that does the same job as a single word.

A verb phrase:

- Does the job of a verb.
- Conveys tense.
- Has two parts: **helping verb** (HV) + **main verb** (MV).

verb phrase

The bus is stopping.

HV   MV

Helping verbs

am	were
is	will
was	

Phrasal Verbs (Unit 22)

A **phrasal verb** consists of a verb and a word whose form looks like a preposition. But the second word does not function as a preposition. Instead, it is part of the meaning of the phrasal verb. The meaning of the phrasal verb is usually different from the meanings of its individual words.

prepositional phrase

He ran into the store.

verb   prep.

He **ran into** the store with his car.

verbal phrase.

Phrasal Verb	Meaning	Phrasal Verb	Meaning
Unit 22			
catch on	learn, understand	pass down	teach or give something to the next generation
dream up	devise, invent	pick out	choose
eat out	dine in a restaurant	put off	postpone
fill out	complete	put out	extinguish
fill up	fill to capacity	puzzle out	identify
find out	discover	puzzle over	ponder
get by	survive	run across	find by chance
give back	return	run into	meet unexpectedly
go on	continue	show up	arrive
hand in	submit	take after	resemble
leave out	omit	take down	write, lower
look into	investigate	try on	test the fit
look up	search for	turn down	lower, reject
make up	invent	wake up	arise from sleep

Unit 23			
blow up	destroy by explosive	put on	put clothing on
do over	repeat, redo	set up	arrange
dust off	rush	switchoff	turn off
give away	give something for free	take down	write, lower
leave out	omit	throw away	discard
point out	show, indicate	turn down	lower, reject

Verb Forms

Verbs describe action. Verbs also signal time. (Unit 4)

Tense Timeline   (Unit 4)

A **tense timeline** shows three points in time—past, present, and future.

Yesterday	Today	Tomorrow
Past	Present	Future

Verb Forms • Present Tense   (Unit 4)

If something is happening right now, it is the **present tense**.

Yesterday	Today	Tomorrow
Past	Present	Future
	I sit.	
	He sits.	
	They sit.	

For third person singular, add **-s** to the verb to signal present tense.

Person	Singular	Plural
First Person	I sit.	We sit.
Second Person	You sit.	You sit.
Third Person	He (She, It) sits.	They sit.

Verb Forms • Past Tense

If something happened yesterday, it is usually past time, or **past tense**.

Yesterday	Today	Tomorrow
Past	Present	Future
They helped.		
They won.		

Regular Verb Forms

Most English verbs form the **past tense** by adding -ed.
These are called **regular verbs.**

Person	Singular	Plural
First Person	I pass**ed**.	We pass**ed**.
Second Person	You pass**ed**.	You pass**ed**.
Third Person	He (She, It) pass**ed**.	They pass**ed**.

Verb	Past Tense	Verb	Past Tense
Unit 13			
adapt	adapted	finish	finished
assist	assisted	punish	punished
attach	attached	select	selected
collect	collected	suspend	suspended
connect	connected	vanish	vanished
expand	expanded	visit	visited

Verb	Past Tense	Verb	Past Tense
Unit 16			
admire	admired	devote	devoted
complete	completed	erode	eroded

Irregular Past Tense Verbs (Units 1–18)

Some verbs signal past time through **irregular verb forms**.

Irregular verb forms:

- Do not use **-ed**.
- Have different endings or spellings.

Verb	Past Tense	Past Participle	Verb	Past Tense	Past Participle
Unit 19					
bleed	bled	bled	meet	met	met
breed	bred	bred	see	saw	seen
creep	crept	crept	seek	sought	sought
feed	fed	fed	sleep	slept	slept
feel	felt	felt	speed	sped	sped
flee	fled	fled	sweep	swept	swept
freeze	froze	frozen	weep	wept	wept
keep	kept	kept			
Unit 20					
beat	beat	beaten	leave	left	left
blow	blew	blown	lie (=recline)	lay	lain
break	broke	broken	pay	paid	paid
deal	dealt	dealt	read	read	read
eat	ate	eaten	say	said	said
grow	grew	grown	show	showed	shown
lay (=put)	laid	laid	speak	spoke	spoken
lead	led	led			
Unit 24					
buy	bought	bought	steal	stole	stolen
spread	spread	spread	teach	taught	taught
throw	threw	thrown	weave	wove/weaved	woven/weaved

Verb Forms • Future Tense

A verb phrase can convey future time. The verb **will** signals **future tense**.

Future verb phrase = **will** + **verb**

Yesterday	Today	Tomorrow
Past	Present	Future
		I will vote.
		They will ride.

Person	Singular	Plural
First Person	I will ride.	We will ride.
Second Person	You will ride.	You will ride.
Third Person	He (She, It) will ride.	They will ride.

Verb	Future Tense	Verb	Future Tense	Verb	Future Tense
Unit 13					
adapt	will adapt	connect	will connect	select	will select
assist	will assist	expand	will expand	suspend	will suspend
attach	will attach	finish	will finish	vanish	will vanish
collect	will collect	punish	will punish	visit	will visit

Verb Forms • Progressive

The **progressive form** of verbs means ongoing action.
The **-ing** ending on a main verb with a helping verb
signals the tense and ongoing action.

Yesterday	Today	Tomorrow
Past	Present	Future
was/were + verb + **-ing**	am/is/are + verb + **-ing**	will be + verb + **-ing**
I was sitting.	I am sitting.	I will be sitting.

Present Progressive   (Unit 15)

Present progressive word phrases mean that the action is
ongoing in present time.

Person	Singular	Plural
First Person	I am sitting.	We are sitting.
Second Person	You are sitting.	You are sitting.
Third Person	He (She, It) is sitting.	They are sitting.

Verb	Present Progressive	Verb	Present Progressive
Unit 15			
begin	am/is/are beginning	open	am/is/are opening
depress	am/is/are depressing	relax	am/is/are relaxing
evolve	am/is/are evolving	restrict	am/is/are restricting

Past Progressive (Unit 9)

Past progressive verb phrases mean that the action was ongoing in past time.

Person	Singular	Plural
First Person	I was passing.	We were passing.
Second Person	You were passing.	You were passing.
Third Person	He (She, It) was passing.	They were passing.

Verb	Past Progressive	Verb	Past Progressive
Unit 9			
brush	was/were brushing	hunt	was/were hunting
cut	was/were cutting	instruct	was/were instructing
duck	was/were ducking	rush	was/were rushing

Future Progressive   (Unit 11)

Future progressive verb phrases mean that the action will be ongoing in future time.

Person	Singular	Plural
First Person	I will be passing.	We will be passing.
Second Person	You will be passing.	You will be passing.
Third Person	He (She, It) will be passing.	They will be passing.

Verb	Future Progressive	Verb	Future Progressive
Unit 11			
act	will be acting	skate	will be skating
camp	will be camping	solve	will be solving
drive	will be driving	stand	will be standing
plant	will be planting	swim	will be swimming

Perfect Tense (Unit 21)

Verb phrases with forms of **have** signal time in special ways.

- **Present Perfect Tense** verbs always include the helping
  verb **has** or **have**. They tell about events that took place at
  some unspecified time in the past.

  > My sister **has planted** a big garden.

- **Past Perfect Tense** verbs always include the helping
  verb **had**. They tell about events that took place before
  another event happened in the past.

  > Before she planted this garden, she **had** only **grown** beans in a planter.
  >
  > event in the past   event further in the past

- **Future Perfect Tense** verbs always include the helping verb
  pair **will have**. They are used to tell about an action that
  will be completed before another action happens in the future.

  > By July she **will have harvested** her first crop of peas.

Verb Forms for *Be, Have,* and *Do*

For more about **Subject/Verb Agreement**, see Step 4, page H65.

- **Be**, **have**, and **do** can be main verbs or helping verbs.

- Different forms of **be, have,** and **do** are used with different personal pronouns to achieve **subject–verb agreement** in sentences.

Be	Past		Present		Future	
Person	**Singular**	**Plural**	**Singular**	**Plural**	**Singular**	**Plural**
First Person	I **was**	we **were**	I **am**	we **are**	I **will be**	we **will be**
Second Person	you **were**	you **were**	you **are**	you **are**	you **will be**	you **will be**
Third Person	he, she, it **was**	they **were**	he, she, it **is**	they **are**	he, she, it **will be**	they **will be**

Main Verb: He **is** an inventor.
MV

Helping Verb: He **is inventing** a car.
HV   MV

Have	Past		Present		Future	
Person	**Singular**	**Plural**	**Singular**	**Plural**	**Singular**	**Plural**
First Person	I **had**	we **had**	I **have**	we **have**	I **will have**	we **will have**
Second Person	you **had**	you **had**	you **have**	you **have**	you **will have**	you **will have**
Third Person	he, she, it **had**	they **had**	he, she, it **has**	they **have**	he, she, it **will have**	they **will have**

Main Verb: I **have** a secret.
MV

Helping Verb: I **have kept** the secret.
HV   MV

Do	Past		Present		Future	
Person	**Singular**	**Plural**	**Singular**	**Plural**	**Singular**	**Plural**
First Person	I **did**	we **did**	I **do**	we **do**	I will **do**	we will **do**
Second Person	you **did**	you **did**	you **do**	you **do**	you will **do**	you will **do**
Third Person	he, she, it **did**	they **did**	he, she, it **does**	they **do**	he, she, it will **do**	they will **do**

Main Verb: I **do** my homework.
        MV

Helping Verb: I **do rely** on my friends.
               HV   MV

Verb Forms: Linking Verbs (Unit 19)

For **Predicate Nominatives** and **Predicate Adjectives**, see pages H38 and H56.

Linking verbs connect, or link, the subject to a word in the predicate. They do not describe actions. They give us information about the subject. Forms of the verb **be** are often used as linking verbs.

Clas Thunberg **was** the king of speed skating.

The verb **was** links the information in the predicate to the subject.

When a noun follows a linking verb, it renames the subject and tells more about it. This noun is called a **predicate nominative**.

Lupe Medrano was the school's spelling bee champion.
     subject   predicate nominative

When an adjective follows a linking verb, it describes the subject. This adjective is called a **predicate adjective**.

Crossword puzzles are **fun**.
          subject   predicate
                         adjective

Predicate (Unit 2)

The **predicate** is the second of the two main parts of a sentence.

The **predicate:**

- contains the main verb of the sentence.
- describes the action.
- usually comes after the subject.
- answers "What did they (he, she, it) do?"

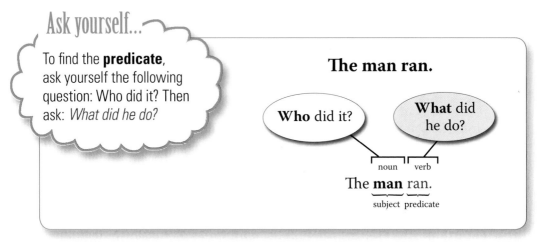

Ask yourself...

To find the **predicate**, ask yourself the following question: Who did it? Then ask: *What did he do?*

The man ran.

Who did it?

What did he do?

noun   verb

The **man** ran.

subject predicate

Simple Predicate   (Unit 8)

The verb that tells what the subject did is the **simple predicate**.

> The class <u>clapped</u> during the song.
>   simple predicate

For **Compound Predicates**, see Step 4, page H70.

Complete Predicate

The simple predicate and all its objects and modifiers are called the **complete predicate**.

> The class <u>clapped during the song.</u>
>   complete predicate

Adjectives describe nouns.

They answer:

- *how many?*
- *what kind?*
- *which one?*

Some prepositional phrases act like adjectives because they can also tell about attributes of a noun. These phrases begin with a preposition and end with a noun.

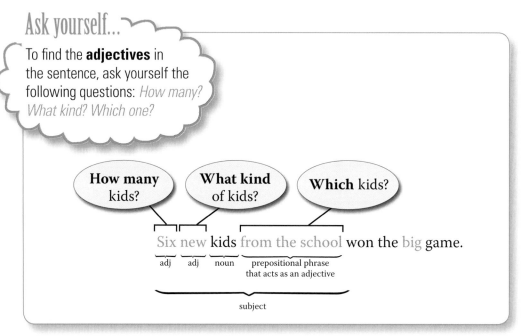

Ask yourself...

To find the **adjectives** in the sentence, ask yourself the following questions: *How many? What kind? Which one?*

How many kids?   What kind of kids?   Which kids?

Six new kids from the school won the big game.
adj   adj   noun   prepositional phrase
that acts as an adjective

subject

The subject of the sentence can have adjectives and prepositional phrases that act as adjectives describing the person, place, or thing that the sentence is about.

Adjectives can also describe other nouns in the sentence.

What kind of game? big

Adjectives for Comparison   (Unit 14)

Adjective endings signal a comparison between nouns or pronouns.

Comparative: Add **-er** to compare two nouns or pronouns
using the word **than.**

Superlative: Add **-est** to compare three or more nouns or pronouns.

Adjective: He was **short.**

Comparative: He was **shorter** than his brother.

Superlative: He was the **shortest** member of the band.

Adjectives with Conjunctions   (Unit 16)

Two adjectives of the same kind that modify the same noun
are joined by a conjunction: **and, or,** or **but.**

---

and: The **dark** and **stormy** night frightened me.

or: **Hot** or **cold** meals were choices on the menu.

but: The **tired** but **determined** athlete finished the game.

Types of Adjectives   (Unit 16)

- Single words   The **red** apples fell from the tree.
- Prepositional phrases   The truck, **with the metallic finish,** was cool.
- Present participles   The **eroding** hillside put the homes in danger.
- Past participles   The **injured** athlete limped.

Participial Phrases Acting as Adjectives   (Unit 16)

A participle can introduce a **participial phrase**.

- The entire phrase acts as an adjective to modify a noun.
- A participial phrase can come before or after the noun it modifies.
- In a participial phrase, the first word is the participle.
- Commas are used to set off a participial phrase.

Answers the question *Which* one?

The athlete, **injured** by his fall, used crutches.

participial phrase

Predicate Adjective   (Unit 20)

When a form of the verb **be** is used as the main verb, it is a linking verb. It links what comes after the verb to the subject.

When an adjective follows the linking verb and describes the subject, it is called a **predicate adjective**.

Kokopelli's music **is** beautiful.

Beautiful is an adjective describing *music*. It is part of the predicate.

Adverbs (Unit 6)

Adverbs are words that describe verbs.

For more about **Prepositions**, see Step 4, page H58.

Adverbs and prepositional phrases that act as adverbs tell:

- *when?*
- *where?*
- *how?*

Some prepositional phrases act like adverbs. Prepositional phrases begin with a preposition and end with a noun. **On Monday**, **in the house**, **with a bang**, and **to the class** are prepositional phrases.

Ask yourself...

To find the **adverb** in each sentence, ask yourself *"when, where,* or *how?"*

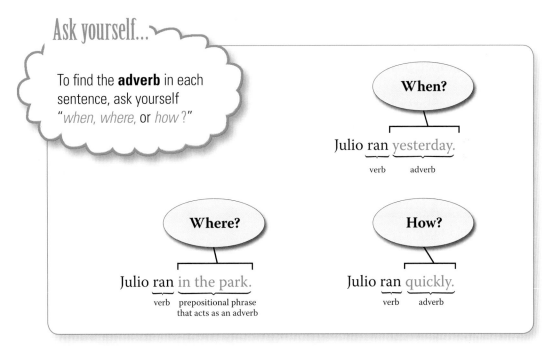

When?

Julio ran yesterday.
verb adverb

Where?

Julio ran in the park.
verb prepositional phrase
that acts as an adverb

How?

Julio ran quickly.
verb adverb

A **preposition** is a function word that begins a prepositional phrase.

A **prepositional phrase** is a group of words that begins with a preposition and ends with a noun or pronoun that is the **object of the preposition**.

Prepositions show the position or relationship between the noun or pronoun and some other word in the sentence.

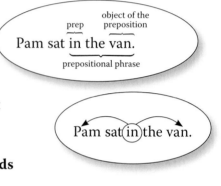

In this sentence, **in** (the preposition) shows a relationship between **van** (the object of the preposition) and **Pam** (the subject of the sentence).

Some of the **Unit Words** and **Essential Words** in Units 1–12 are prepositions:
in, as, at, from, of, past, to, into, for.

Prepositions Show Relationship (Unit 6)

Most prepositions show a position in

- space (inside, over, under)
- time (during, since, until)
- space and time (after, from, through)

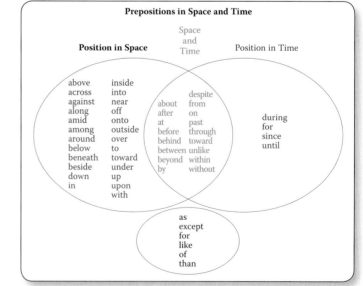

Pronouns

Pronouns are function words that are used in place of nouns. Different groups of pronouns have different functions.

Subject (Nominative) Pronouns   (Unit 4)

Nominative pronouns take the place of the subject in a sentence.

> **I, you, he, she, it, we, you,** and **they** are nominative pronouns.

> **Jack** sat in a cab.
>
> **He** sat in a **cab**.
>
> (**He** replaces **Jack** in the sentence.)

Subject Pronouns		
Person	**Singular**	**Plural**
First Person	I	we
Second Person	you	you
Third Person	he, she, it	they

Antecedents   (Unit 23)

Most pronouns have **antecedents**—nouns to which they refer.

> *Ken* is on the football team. **He** plays fullback.
>
> (**He** refers to *Ken. Ken* is the antecedent.)

Object Pronouns (Unit 6)

Some pronouns take the place of **objects**. They are called **object pronouns**.

Me, you, him, her, it, us, and **them** are object pronouns.

Carla is handing the plant to **Sally**.

Carla is handing the plant to **her**.

(**Her** replaces **Sally** in the sentence.)

Person	Singular	Plural
First Person	me	us
Second Person	you	you
Third Person	him, her, it	them

Possessive Pronouns (Unit 7)

These pronouns show ownership (possession). They are called **possessive pronouns**.

my	mine	your	yours	our	ours
his	her	hers	its	their	theirs

Sometimes a possessive pronoun functions as an adjective.

My desk is a mess.

Or, sometimes the possessive pronoun replaces the noun.

Mine is a mess.

Indefinite Pronouns   (Unit 23)

Indefinite pronouns do not refer to definite people or things. They refer to unspecified or unknown people or things. Indefinite pronouns do not have antecedents.

> Ramdas believes that **someone** with an injury should not play.
>
> (**Someone** is an **indefinite** pronoun. It does not refer to a **specific person** or **thing**.)

all	both	few	no one	several
another	each	many	nothing	some
any	either	most	one	somebody
anybody	everybody	neither	ones	someone
anyone	everyone	nobody	other	something
anything	everything	none	others	

Conjunctions

See also
Compound Subjects, page H69, and
Compound Predicates, page H70.

Conjunctions join words, phrases, or clauses in a sentence. They also join sentences.

Coordinating Conjunctions   (Unit 7)

Coordinating conjunctions are the most common type of conjunction. They connect words that have the same function. Two common coordinating conjunctions are **and** and **but**.

- The conjunction **and** relates two similar ideas.

> Ellen rested. Her friends rested.
>
> Ellen **and** her friends rested.
>
> compound subject

- The conjunction **but** signals contrasting ideas.

> The hurricane hit land. The people escaped.
>
> The hurricane hit land, **but** the people escaped.
>
> <u>compound sentence</u>

- The conjunction **or** signals an alternative or choice.

> An artist can sculpt stone. An artist can carve stone.
>
> An artist can carve **or** sculpt stone.
>
> <u>compound predicate</u>

The predicates, *sculpt* and *carve*, are joined by the conjunction **or** to build a compound predicate.

Multiple Functions of Words

Words in Context

In English, words have different functions (jobs). Sometimes the same word can have multiple functions. The context helps determine the function of the word.

Noun	Verb	Adjective
The **dig** was a success in Africa.	Scientists **dig** to find bones.	The scientists went to the **dig** site.

Syllable Stress   (Unit 13)

Sometimes words can look the same but be pronounced two different ways by shifting the syllable stress. Shifting the stress changes the meaning and function of the word.

Noun	Verb
pro´ duce	pro duce´

Adding a Suffix   (Unit 19)

Adding a suffix can change a word's function. The suffixes **-less**, **-ful**, **-y**, **-ous**, **-ing**, and **-ed** can change nouns into adjectives.

For more about **Suffixes**, see Step 3, page H25.

help**less**	humor**ous**
color**ful**	drain**ing**
storm**y**	beach**ed**

Present and past participles, which have suffixes **-ing** and **-ed**, can also function as adjectives.

sail**ing** ship	seal**ed** letter

Sentences

What Is a Sentence? (Unit 1)

A **sentence** conveys a complete thought by answering two questions:

- Who (What) did it?
- What did they (he, she, it) do?

We put nouns and verbs together to make **sentences**.

Simple Sentences (Unit 2)

A **simple sentence** has one subject and one predicate.

- The subject answers: "Who (What) did it?"
- The verb in the predicate answers: "What did they (he, she, it) do?"

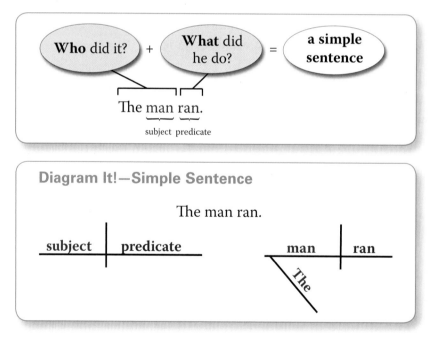

Subject/Verb Agreement   (Unit 7)

The sentence subject and predicate verb must agree in number.

Singular verbs are used with singular subjects, and plural verbs are used with plural subjects.

My sister chats online with her friends.
singular   singular
subject   verb

My brothers play games on the Internet.
plural subject   plural verb

Don't be confused by the -s.

A singular subject (without adding -s) agrees with a singular verb (with an -s).

My brother chats.
singular   singular
subject   verb

A plural subject with an -s agrees with a plural verb (without an -s).

My brothers chat.
plural subject   plural verb

Sentence Expansion

For more about **Noun as a Direct Object**, see Step 4, page H37.

Predicate Expansion with Direct Object   (Unit 3)

You can expand the predicate in a sentence by adding a direct object.

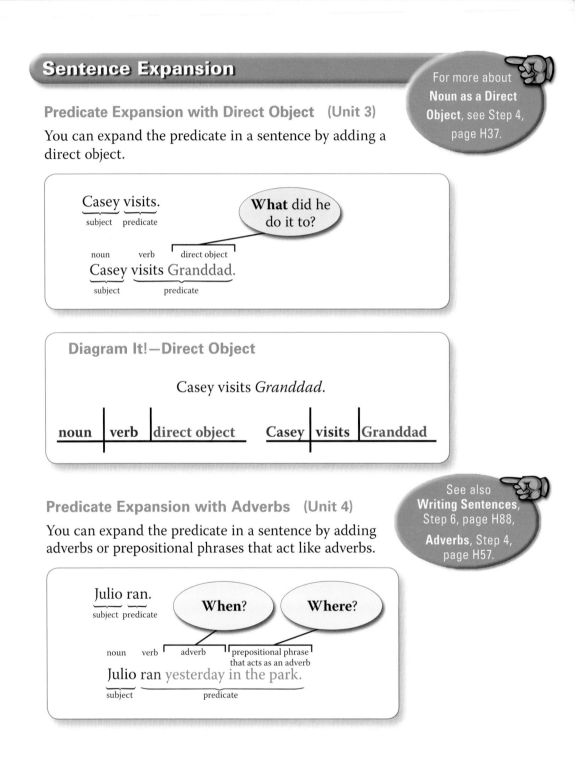

Casey visits.

subject   predicate

What did he do it to?

noun   verb   direct object

Casey visits Granddad.

subject   predicate

Diagram It!—Direct Object

Casey visits *Granddad.*

| **noun** | **verb** | **direct object** | **Casey** | **visits** | **Granddad** |

See also **Writing Sentences**, Step 6, page H88, **Adverbs**, Step 4, page H57.

Predicate Expansion with Adverbs   (Unit 4)

You can expand the predicate in a sentence by adding adverbs or prepositional phrases that act like adverbs.

Julio ran.

subject predicate

When?   **Where?**

noun   verb   adverb   prepositional phrase that acts as an adverb

Julio ran yesterday in the park.

subject   predicate

Moving Adverbs in a Sentence   (Unit 5)

Words or phrases that answer the questions "when, where, or how" can be moved within the sentence.

Diagram It!—Adverbs

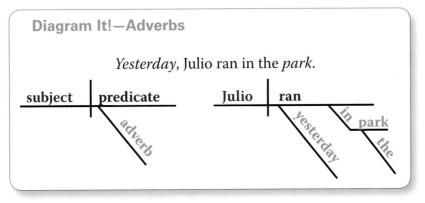

Subject Expansion with Adjectives   (Unit 6)

You can expand the subject of a sentence by adding adjectives.

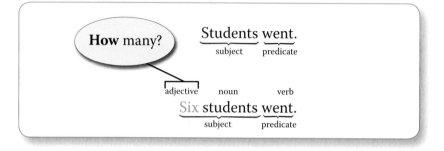

Diagram It!—Adjectives

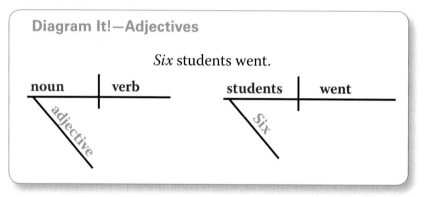

Compound Sentence Parts

For more about **Coordinating Conjunctions**, see Step 4, page H61.

Compound Subject   (Unit 7)

A **compound subject** is two subjects joined by a **conjunction**.

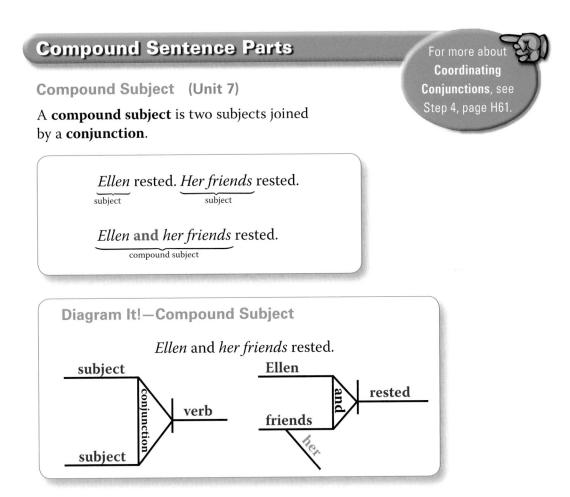

Ellen rested. *Her friends* rested.
subject   subject

Ellen **and** *her friends* rested.
compound subject

Diagram It!—Compound Subject

Ellen and *her friends* rested.

Compound subjects require plural verbs.

Compound subjects joined by **and** are plural subjects, since they name more than one person, place, or thing.

Ezra and Fred send emails.
compound subject   plural verb

Compound Predicate   (Unit 8)

A **compound predicate** is two simple predicates joined by a **conjunction**.

> The class *sang*. The class *clapped*.
>   predicate   predicate
>
> The class *sang* **and** *clapped*.
>   compound predicate

For more about
**Coordinating
Conjunctions**, see
Step 4, page H61.

Diagram It!—Compound Predicate

The class *sang* and *clapped*.

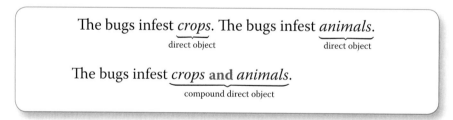

Compound Direct Object   (Unit 9)

A **compound direct object** is two direct objects joined by a **conjunction**.

> The bugs infest *crops*. The bugs infest *animals*.
>   direct object   direct object
>
> The bugs infest *crops* **and** *animals*.
>   compound direct object

Diagram It!—Direct Objects

The bugs infest *crops* and *animals*.

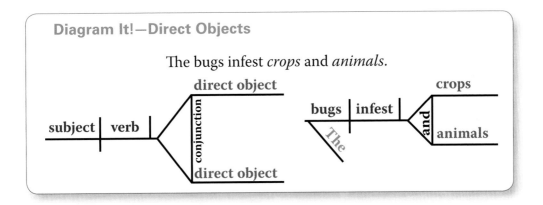

Compound Predicate Nominative / Predicate Adjective   (Unit 22)

Predicate nominatives and **predicate adjectives** can be compounded with the conjunctions **and, or,** and **but.**

Diagram It!—Compound Predicate Nominative

The exits were the *fire escape* **and** the *stairs*.

Diagram It!—Compound Predicate Adjective

The detective's work was *dangerous* **and** *challenging*.

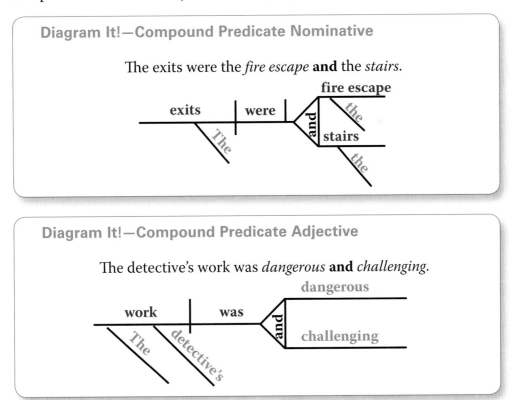

Compound Sentence   (Unit 10)

A **compound sentence** is two sentences joined by a conjunction.

- The **conjunction** *and*

    The word **and** is a conjunction that relates two similar ideas.

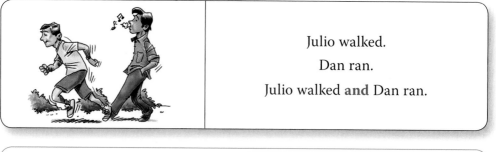

Julio walked.

Dan ran.

Julio walked **and** Dan ran.

Diagram It!—Compound Sentence

Julio walked and *Dan ran.*

subject	verb		Julio	walked
	conjunction			and
subject	verb		Dan	ran

Mechanics • Punctuation

End Punctuation	
Punctuation marks—**periods, question marks,** and **exclamation points**—can be used to end a sentence. (Unit 1))	The cat sat.
	Where did it sit?
	It sat on my lap!
Apostrophes	
An apostrophe is used with the letter <u>s</u> to show possession. (Unit 2)	Tyrone's map
	the whales' fins
An apostrophe shows where letters are left out in a contraction. (Unit 7)	I am I'm
Commas	
Phrases: Commas can be used to set off phrases at the beginning of sentences. (Unit 5)	At the end of the song, Juan clapped.
Adjectives of the same kind: A comma can be used to separate adjectives of the same kind. (Unit 16)	The big, black cat sat.
Appositives: Commas are usually used to separate the appositive and its modifiers from the rest of the sentence. (Unit 17)	Sam, my pet cat, is black.
In dates: A comma separates the day from the year in a date. (Unit 16) If a date is in a sentence, a comma follows the year. (Unit 20)	December 1, 2009 On December 1, 2008, the store opened.
In addresses: A comma separates the city from the state in an address. (Unit 16) If the address is in a sentence, a comma follows the state. Also in a sentence, a comma separates the street name from the city. (Unit 20)	Denver, CO 80020 We are moving to 300 New Street, Denver, Colorado, in June.
In letters: A comma is often used after the greeting and the closing.	Dear Uncle Tran, Thank you,
In a series: When three or more words or word groups are listed together in a sentence, a comma separates the items in the series. The last item is usually connected to the others in the series by **and** or **or.**	*Skating, swimming,* and *running* are speed sports.

Colons and Semicolons	
Colons in business letters: One use for the colon is after the greeting in a business letter.	Dear Coach Conner:
Semicolons: One use of the semicolon is to combine two related sentences.	The gym will be closed on Monday; we will practice on the outside courts instead.
Quotation Marks	
Direct quotations: Use quotation marks in text to record the exact words a person has spoken. They are placed before the first word and after the last word spoken. Usually there are words before or after the quotation that indicate who is speaking. Note that commas and periods always go inside the quotation marks.	"Try to get the tape off," Jack said.
Titles: Quotation marks are used around titles of magazine articles, newspaper articles, and songs. Italics are used for titles of magazines, newspapers, works of art, and musicals.	I read the article "Basketball and You."

Mechanics • Capitalization

Capitalize the following:	
Proper nouns.	Alberto, Canada, Grand Canyon, Congress
The first word in a sentence.	Many puzzling tales were told.
The first word of a direct quotation.	He said, "Wait for me." "We'll be late," she said.
The first word of a greeting or closing.	Dear Aunt Kim, Sincerely,
Titles of magazines, newspapers, works of art, musical compositions, and organizations.	*Newsweek*; *Chicago Tribune*; *Mona Lisa*; *The Lion King*; United Nations

Listening and Reading Comprehension

Vocabulary Strategies   (Unit 7)

The context provides clues to figure out the meaning of vocabulary words you don't know. Here are five **Use the Clues** vocabulary strategies:

❶ Meaning Cues:

Look for meaning cue words. They provide cues to the definition of a word in context. Meaning cue words include *is/are, it means, which stands for, can be defined as,* and more.

The <u>Internet</u> (is) a network of computers.

Punctuation marks, including commas and dashes, can also set off the meaning of a word.

The <u>Internet</u>, a network of computers, transmits information quickly.

❷ Substitutions:

Look for words or phrases that rename nouns. Substitutions are often synonyms or distinctive features of the noun.

The Internet <u>links</u>, or <u>connects</u>, computers around the world.

The word **connects** renames the word **links**.

❸ Pronoun Referents:

Use pronouns to identify meaning clues to define unknown vocabulary words in context.

Oliver Zompro is an <u>entomologist</u>.

(He) is <u>a scientist who studies insects.</u>

❹ Context Cues:

Look for cues to the meaning of an unfamiliar word. Add up the cues to define the word.

It is a movie <u>review</u>. The writer <u>gives an opinion</u> about a new movie.

❺ Visual Information:

Use pictures, charts, and other visual information that accompanies the text to understand the meaning of new vocabulary words.

Also, the Web is organized in a special way. It is made up of home pages. A <u>home page</u> is usually the <u>first page</u> you see <u>on a Web site.</u>

This first page on the NASA Web site is its home page.

Types of Text (Unit 15)

Reading selections, also called text, come in different types. There are two main categories of text: **expository** and **narrative**. All types of writing have a purpose. Some text may have more than one purpose.

Type of Text	Author's Purpose	Media (print or online)	
expository text informational nonfiction	to inform, to describe, to persuade, to entertain	textbooks encyclopedias newspapers	magazines Web sites
narrative text tells a story	to describe an event or experience; to teach us something about our lives; to entertain	novels anthologies	magazines Web sites

Types of Imaginative Literature

There are different types of narrative text called imaginative literature. Each type is defined by its characters, setting, and purpose.

Type	Characters	Setting	Purpose
fable	animals or inanimate objects	imagined place and time	to teach a moral lesson
science fiction	fantastic or futuristic people or other things	fantastic or futuristic place and time	comments on current society; describes future science and technology
folktale	fictional, everyday people	imagined place and time, often associated with a group of people or culture	makes sense of the world and human existence through stories passed down from one generation to another
legend	a particular person	a particular time and place in history, often based on real events	explains, often using exaggeration, how something came about in history
myth	supernatural beings, superheroes	a time before recorded history	describes how the world, people, and creatures came to be the way they are

Text Features   (Unit 1)

Writers of **informational text**—also called **nonfiction**—use **text features** to provide clues to the topic and other important information.

Title–indicates the topic of the informational text

Heading–names the topics of each subsection of the informational text

Pictures and Captions–provide visual and textual information that supports or adds to the information in the text

Margin Information–defines vocabulary or offers short explanations or illustrations of some part of the text

Text Features of a Newspaper

Every newspaper, whether published in print or online, is divided into **sections**.

Print Newspaper

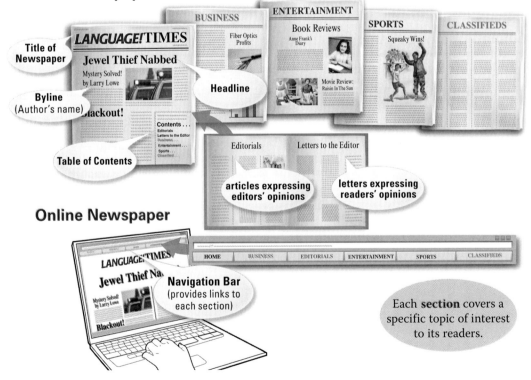

Online Newspaper

Each **section** covers a specific topic of interest to its readers.

Text Features of a Play (Unit 15)

Writers of plays use specific text features to guide the people
who direct and act in the play.

❶ **Preface:** sets up the theme of the play

❷ **List of characters:** names who is in the play

❸ **Set:** tells how the stage will look for each section of the play

❹ **Props:** tell what furniture or other items are needed on the sets

❺ **Costumes:** tell what the actors will wear

❻ **Bold names:** tell who performs the dialog or
actions following each name

❼ **Parenthetical references:**

- are not read aloud

- tell what happens before
the actors speak, or
tell about a change
in the stage set

- tell the actors what
to do, how to do it,
or how to say the
words

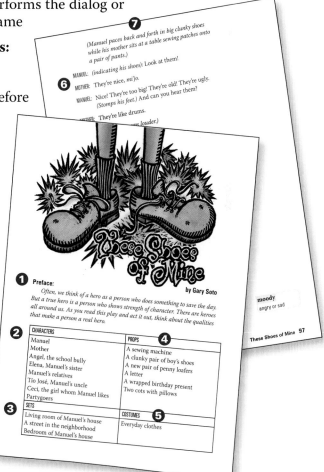

❼

(*Manuel paces back and forth in big clunky shoes
while his mother sits at a table sewing patches onto
a pair of pants.*)

MANUEL: (*indicating his shoes*): Look at them!

❻ MOTHER: They're nice, mi'jo.

MANUEL: Nice! They're too big! They're old! They're ugly.
(*Stomps his feet.*) And can you hear them?

MOTHER: They're like drums.
                      ns louder.)

❶ Preface:
Often, we think of a hero as a person who does something to save the day.
But a true hero is a person who shows strength of character. There are heroes
all around us. As you read this play and act it out, think about the qualities
that make a person a real hero.

by Gary Soto

moody
angry or sad

These Shoes of Mine 97

❷ | CHARACTERS | | PROPS ❹ |
|---|---|---|
| Manuel | | |
| Mother | | A sewing machine |
| Angel, the school bully | | A clunky pair of boy's shoes |
| Elena, Manuel's sister | | A new pair of penny loafers |
| Manuel's relatives | | A letter |
| Tío José, Manuel's uncle | | A wrapped birthday present |
| Ceci, the girl whom Manuel likes | | Two cots with pillows |
| Partygoers | | |

❸ | SETS | COSTUMES ❺ |
|---|---|
| Living room of Manuel's house | Everyday clothes |
| A street in the neighborhood | |
| Bedroom of Manuel's house | |

Comprehension Questions

For more about **Writing Sentences,** see Step 6, page H88.

How to Answer Open-Ended Questions (Unit 1)

Use these steps to answer a short-answer question with a complete sentence:

❶ Look for a signal word to know what the question is asking.

❷ Find information in the text to answer the question.

❸ Plan and write the answer.

❹ Check the answer.

Example question:

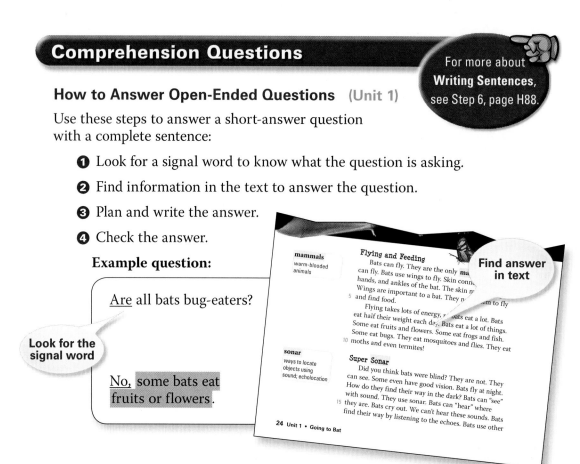

Find answer in text

mammals
warm-blooded animals

Flying and Feeding
Bats can fly. They are the only ma___
can fly. Bats use wings to fly. Skin conn___
hands, and ankles of the bat. The skin ___
Wings are important to a bat. They n___ ___m to fly
5 and find food.
Flying takes lots of energy, s___ ___ats eat a lot. Bats
eat half their weight each da___. Bats eat a lot of things.
Some eat fruits and flowers. Some eat frogs and fish.
Some eat bugs. They eat mosquitoes and flies. They eat
10 moths and even termites!

sonar
ways to locate objects using sound; echolocation

Super Sonar
Did you think bats were blind? They are not. They
can see. Some even have good vision. Bats fly at night.
How do they find their way in the dark? Bats can "see"
with sound. They use sonar. Bats can "hear" where
15 they are. Bats cry out. We can't hear these sounds. Bats
find their way by listening to the echoes. Bats use other

24 Unit 1 • Going to Bat

Are all bats bug-eaters?

Look for the signal word

No, some bats eat fruits or flowers.

Signal words help you know how to answer the question.

See page H82 for more **Signal Words**.

Signal words	How to answer
If the question asks...	Your answer must include...
Is/are	A "yes" or a "no"
Who	Information about a person or group
Do/does	A "yes" or a "no"
What	An action or name of a thing
When	A specific time, date, or event
Why	A reason or explanation
Where	A general location or specific place
How	The way something is done

How to Answer Multiple-Choice Questions (Unit 3)

Use these steps to answer multiple-choice questions:

❶ Read carefully for signal words.

❷ Look back in the text for information.

❸ Try to eliminate distracter items.

Example question:

The Touareg are

Ⓐ a tribe of people who live in Niger.

Ⓑ special dinosaurs in Africa.

Ⓒ big animals that live in Africa.

Ⓓ scientists who work in Niger.

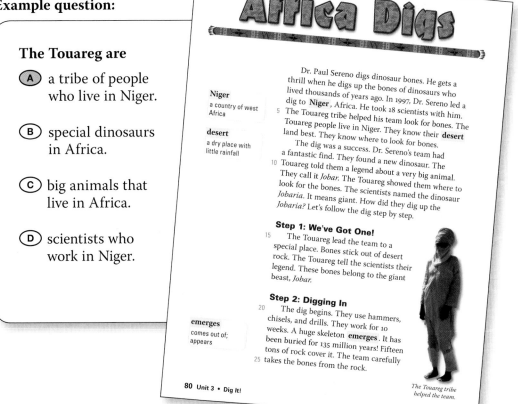

Africa Digs

Dr. Paul Sereno digs dinosaur bones. He gets a thrill when he digs up the bones of dinosaurs who lived thousands of years ago. In 1997, Dr. Sereno led a dig to **Niger**, Africa. He took 18 scientists with him.
5 The Touareg tribe helped his team look for bones. The Touareg people live in Niger. They know their **desert** land best. They know where to look for bones.

The dig was a success. Dr. Sereno's team had a fantastic find. They found a new dinosaur. The
10 Touareg told them a legend about a very big animal. They call it *Jobar*. The Touareg showed them where to look for the bones. The scientists named the dinosaur *Jobaria*. It means giant. How did they dig up the *Jobaria*? Let's follow the dig step by step.

Step 1: We've Got One!
15   The Touareg lead the team to a special place. Bones stick out of desert rock. The Touareg tell the scientists their legend. These bones belong to the giant beast, *Jobar*.

Step 2: Digging In
20   The dig begins. They use hammers, chisels, and drills. They work for 10 weeks. A huge skeleton **emerges**. It has been buried for 135 million years! Fifteen tons of rock cover it. The team carefully
25 takes the bones from the rock.

Niger
a country of west Africa

desert
a dry place with little rainfall

emerges
comes out of; appears

The Touareg tribe helped the team.

80 Unit 3 • Dig It!

Signal Words

Signal words	How to answer
If the question asks...	Your answer must include...
state	say or write specific information
recognize	use information you have learned
name	label specific information
locate	find specific information or show the position of something
list	state a series of names, ideas, or events
choose	make choices from specific information
describe	state detailed information about an idea or concept
tell	say or write specific information
define	tell the meaning
predict	use known information to say what might happen in the future
conclude	put information together to reach an understanding about something
illustrate	present an example or explanation in pictures or words
identify	give the name of something or select information from the text
explain	express understanding of an idea or concept
tell when	state a specific time or a period of time
discuss	present detailed information or examine a subject
paraphrase	restate information in different words to clarify meaning
contrast	state the differences between two or more ideas or concepts
categorize	create groups and place information into those groups based on certain shared characteristics
compare	state the similarities between two or more ideas or concepts
sort	place or separate into groups
match	put together or connect things that are alike or similar
classify	arrange or organize information into groups with similar characteristics

Remember (Units 7–8)

Understand (Units 9–12)

Signal words	How to answer
If the question asks...	Your answer must include...
infer	provide a logical conclusion using information or evidence
generalize	draw a conclusion based on presented information
show	demonstrate an understanding of information
use	apply a procedure
select	choose from among alternatives
distinguish	find differences that set one thing apart from another
organize	arrange in a systematic pattern
outline	arrange information into a systematic pattern of main ideas and supporting details
assess	determine value or significance
justify	prove or give reasons that something is right or valid
critique	examine positive and negative features to form a judgement
judge	form an opinion or estimation after careful consideration
compose	make or create by putting parts or elements together
design	devise a procedure to do a task
plan	devise a solution to solve a problem
hypothesize	formulate a possible explanation; speculate
revise	modify or change a plan or product

Apply (Units 13–15)

Analyze (Units 16–18)

Evaluate (Units 19–21)

Create (Units 22–24)

Listening Tips

- Demonstrate active listening by:
  - Asking thoughtful questions and responding to relevant questions
  - Identifying main ideas of an informational presentation
  - Retelling the plot of a story
  - Taking notes
- Distinguish between fact and opinion (from a presentation of a media source).
- Evaluate the accuracy of information (from a presentation or a media source).
- Determine the purpose for listening (to obtain information, to solve problems, for enjoyment).

Well-written text has organization. Informational text is organized using main ideas and supporting details.

The main idea tells what the paragraph is about.

The supporting details give more specific information about the main idea.

Ask yourself...

Which sentence tells what all of the sentences are about?

Ask yourself...

Which sentences support the main idea?

The bat can fly. It is the only mammal that can fly. Bats use wings to fly. Skin connects parts of the bat. It joins its hands, arms, and ankles. The skin makes wings. Bats fly to look for food. They fly at night. They need their wings to eat.

Bats eat a lot. Bats eat half their weight each day! Food makes energy. Flying takes energy. Bats eat a lot of things. Some eat fruits. Some eat flowers. Some eat frogs and fish. Some eat lizards. Some eat bugs. They eat mosquitoes. They eat flies. They eat moths. They even eat termites!

6 Speaking and Writing

Structure of Writing

Graphic organizers can show the structure of text.

An **Informal Outline** shows the relationship between the main ideas (walls) and supporting details.

Topic: Batty About Bats	
☆ Bats can fly.	—only mammals that can fly
	—use wings to fly
	—fly to look for food
☆ Bats eat a lot.	—eat half their weight each day
	—eat a lot of things
☆ Bats "see" with sound.	—use sonar
	—"hear" where they are
	—Use other sound clues

Summary Writing

Simple Summary (Unit 1)

Topic: Batty About Bats	
☆ Bats can fly.	—only mammals that can fly
	—use wings to fly
	—fly to look for food
☆ Bats eat a lot.	—eat half their weight each day
	—eat a lot of things
☆ Bats "see" with sound.	—use sonar
	—"hear" where they are
	—Use other

A summary tells the most important ideas from a text selection. A **simple summary** uses only the main ideas.

"Batty About Bats!" explains facts about bats. Bats can fly. They eat a lot. Bats "see" with sound.

Expanded Summary (Unit 1)

Sometimes a summary has more detail. An **expanded summary** uses main ideas and some supporting details.

Topic: Batty About Bats	
☆ Bats can fly.	—only mammals that can fly
	—use wings to fly
	—fly to look for food
☆ Bats eat a lot.	—eat half their weight each day
	—eat a lot of things
☆ Bats "see" with sound.	—use sonar
	—"hear" where they are
	—Use other sound clues

"Batty About Bats!" explains facts about bats. Bats can fly. They are the only mammals that fly. Bats eat a lot of things each day. Bats "see" with sonar and other sound clues.

Speaking Tips

Organization and Content

- Stay on topic.
- Organize content in a logical sequence.
- Provide a beginning, middle and end.
- Emphasize important points and details that support ideas.
- Use examples to clarify meaning.
- Use specific vocabulary.

Delivery

- Speak clearly and at an appropriate pace.
- Use volume, pitch, and phrasing to enhance meaning.
- Make eye contact with listener.
- Use correct grammar.
- Use props, visuals, or media to make points.

Sentences are pictures in words. To write a **Masterpiece Sentence** follow these steps:

Stage 1: Prepare Your Canvas (Unit 1)

Write the base sentence. Answer these questions:

Who (what) did it?	What did they (he, she, it) do?
the man	ran

Stage 2: Paint Your Predicate (Unit 3)

Expand the predicate. Use these questions:

When?	Where?	How?
during the race	on the track	fast

the **man ran** fast on the track during the race

Stage 3: Move the Predicate Painters (Unit 5)

Vary the sentence. Move the predicate painters. Notice the picture *doesn't* change!

during the race the **man ran** fast on the track

Stage 4: Paint Your Subject   (Unit 6)

Expand the subject. Use these questions:

How many?	**Which are?**	**What kind?**
	in the red	
	shirt	

during the race **the man** in the red
shirt **ran** fast on the track

....

Stage 5: Paint Your Words

Improve your words. Be descriptive.

During the race the man in the
red shirt ran fast on the track.

During the last lap of the race the
track star wearing his team's red
shirt sprinted around the track as fans cheered.

....

Stage 6: Finishing Touches

Check spelling and punctuation.

During the last lap of the race, the track star,
wearing his team's red shirt, sprinted around the track
as fans cheered.

Writing Paragraphs

Parts of a Paragraph

A paragraph is a group of sentences. Each sentence in the paragraph has a specific job.

The Benefits of Exercise

Indent paragraphs

Regular exercise benefits people's health in two important ways. One benefit is that exercise improves people's physical health. It makes the heart, lungs, bones, and muscles stronger and keeps people at a healthy weight. Exercise is also good for the mind. It makes people feel better about themselves and calms them down when they are angry or stressed. When people regularly do physical activities they enjoy, their bodies and minds stay fit, happy, and healthy.

The **Topic Sentence** tells what the paragraph is about.

Supporting Details give facts or reasons about the topic.

Transition words link one supporting detail to the next.

E's add interest for the reader. E's are:
- explanations
- examples
- evidence

The **conclusion** ties the parts together. Often it restates the topic.

Topic Sentence

The **topic sentence** in a paragraph states the topic of the paragraph. It is often the first sentence.

There are many types of topic sentences. Here are three of them:

IVF Topic Sentence (Unit 1)

An **IVF topic sentence** has three parts. It is a good type of topic sentence for a summary paragraph.

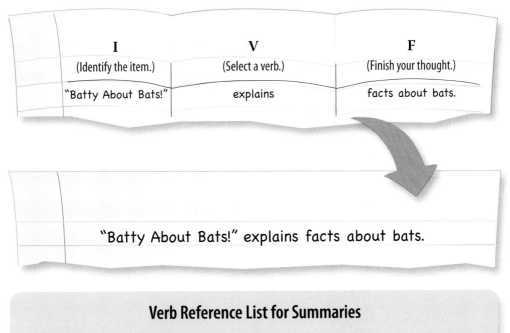

I	V	F
(Identify the item.)	(Select a verb.)	(Finish your thought.)
"Batty About Bats!"	explains	facts about bats.

"Batty About Bats!" explains facts about bats.

Verb Reference List for Summaries

explains	compares	tells	provides	presents
describes	gives	shows	lists	teaches

Number Topic Sentence   (Unit 3)

A **Number topic sentence** includes the topic and a number word. The **topic** tells what the whole paragraph will be about. The **number** tells how many supporting details to include about the topic.

Three problems led to the Big Dig project in Boston.

Boston leaders identified **several** traffic problems.

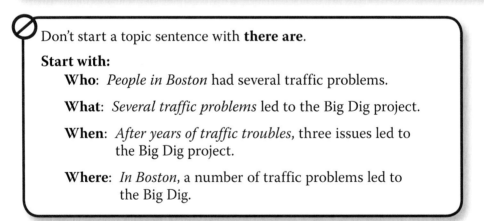

Number Words

two	three	four	several	some
a number of	a few	a couple	many	

Don't start a topic sentence with **there are**.

Start with:

Who: *People in Boston* had several traffic problems.

What: *Several traffic problems* led to the Big Dig project.

When: *After years of traffic troubles,* three issues led to the Big Dig project.

Where: *In Boston,* a number of traffic problems led to the Big Dig.

Turn Prompt Topic Sentence   (Unit 4)

A **Turn Prompt topic sentence** works well to answer a specific question. Part of the prompt becomes part of the topic sentence. Direction words, such as **explains**, tell you what you need to do.

Prompt:
   Write a paragraph that <u>explains</u> how maps are made.

Topic sentence:
   Maps are made in several layers.

Supporting Details

Supporting Details   (Unit 3)

Supporting details are sentences that provide **facts** or **reasons** to support a topic sentence.

Transition words link supporting details within a paragraph. Transition words and phrases also link ideas between paragraphs.

Transition Sets		
First of all ▶	The next ▶	Another
One ▶	Also	
One ▶	Another ▶	Finally
One example ▶	Another example	
The first ▶	The second ▶	Last
To begin ▶	However	

E's Are Elaborations

The E's (Unit 5)

The E's are sentences that support the topic and supporting details in a paragraph.

Here are three kinds of E's. There are more!

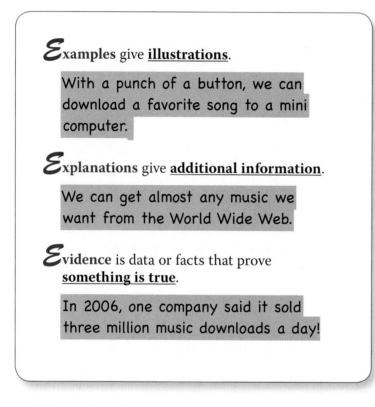

*E*xamples give **illustrations**.

> With a punch of a button, we can download a favorite song to a mini computer.

*E*xplanations give **additional information**.

> We can get almost any music we want from the World Wide Web.

*E*vidence is data or facts that prove **something is true**.

> In 2006, one company said it sold three million music downloads a day!

Find these E's in "Computer Music" on the next page. Look for the supporting details on which they elaborate.

Conclusion

Concluding Sentence   (Unit 5)

The concluding sentence in a paragraph often restates the topic sentence.

Computer Music

Computers are changing the way we make and listen to music. For one thing, the computer has changed how we create songs. For example, composers can write concert music on laptops. Musicians can even make their computers "sing" like a huge choir. And DJs can use computer "drum machines" to lay down beats for their next hip hop show. Computers are also changing the way we listen to tunes. We can get almost any music we want from the World Wide Web. With a punch of a button, we can download a favorite song to a mini computer. These mini computers are called MP3 players. They let us take music almost anywhere. In 2006, one company said it sold three million music downloads a day! According to a computer magazine, the number of downloads will keep growing. New technology offers new ways to make and hear beautiful music.

Topic Sentence

Conclusion

Writing a Report

A paragraph can be stretched to become a report.
Each part of a paragraph can expand to write a report.

The Benefits of Exercise

Regular exercise benefits people's health in two important ways. One benefit is that exercise improves people's physical health. It makes the heart, lungs, bones, and muscles stronger and keeps people at a healthy weight. Exercise is also good for the mind. It makes people feel better about themselves and calms them down when they are angry or stressed. When people regularly do physical activities they enjoy, their bodies and minds stay fit, happy, and healthy.

Parts of a Report

The **Introductory Paragraph** states the topic of the entire report.

Body Paragraphs tell more about the topic.

The **Concluding Paragraph** links to the introductory paragraph and ties the whole report together.

The Benefits of Exercise

Regular exercise can benefit your health in two important ways. It improves your physical health and is good for your mind.

First exercise improves people's physical health. It makes the heart, lungs, bones, and muscles stronger. The heart and lungs work together day and night to keep the body alive. Exercise strengthens them. It improves blood flow. Blood carries food and oxygen to the rest of the body. Exercise also helps to keep calcium in the body. Calcium is needed to build strong bones and muscles. Since bones grow the most during childhood, exercise is very important for young people. Exercise also helps people maintain a healthy weight. This lowers the risk of developing diseases such as diabetes.

Exercise is also good for the mind. It makes people feel better about themselves. It calms them down. When people exercise, their brains produce chemicals. These chemicals make people feel happier! They also provide natural pain relief, and help people to relax. A workout or even a brisk walk can greatly reduce feelings of anger and stress. Exercise helps people's minds in another way, too. When people are fit, they feel more positive about themselves.

It is clear that exercise is great for both the body and the mind. The benefits of exercise are just too important to ignore.

Parts of a Report

A report is made up of a group of paragraphs. Each paragraph
in the report has a specific job.

Introductory Paragraph

An **introductory paragraph** states the topic for the entire report.
There are different ways to write an introductory paragraph.
One way is a **Two-Sentence Introductory paragraph**.

State the Topic: The first sentence tells the *topic* of the report.

> Exercise can benefit your health in two ways.

State the Plan: The second sentence tells how the report will
address the topic. It usually tells the *ideas* that will be covered
in the body paragraphs.

> Regular exercise improves your physical health
> and is good for your mind.

Combine these two sentences to write an introductory paragraph.

> Exercise can benefit your health in two ways.
> Regular exercise improves your physical health
> and is good for your mind.

Body Paragraphs

Body paragraphs tell more about the topic. Often a body paragraph begins with a transition topic sentence . It also includes E's (elaborations)— explanations, examples, and evidence — that support the topic sentence. Transition words are important to link ideas between paragraphs.

Find the transition topic sentences and E's in "The Benefits of Exercise" report on page H97.

Concluding Paragraph

A **concluding paragraph** links to the introductory paragraph and ties the whole report together.

Look at this concluding paragraph and see how it restates the introductory paragraph on page H97.

> It is clear that exercise is great for both the body and the mind. The benefits of exercise are just too important to ignore.

The concluding paragraph for an Opinion Essay should **reinforce the opinion or position taken** in the essay. This paragraph should also sum up the reasons in the body paragraphs.

Another strategy for writing a concluding paragraph is to provide **food for thought**; that is, to leave readers with a question or an idea that keeps them thinking about the topic or helps them understand what makes the topic so interesting.

Attributes of Different Types of Writing

How are Reports and Personal Narratives Alike?   (Unit 9)

- A report focuses on one topic and a personal narrative describes one experience.

- Both have an introductory paragraph, body paragraphs, and a concluding paragraph.

How are Reports and Personal Narratives Different?

Report	Personal Narrative
■ The body paragraphs of a report tell different points about the topic. Each point is stated in a transition topic sentence. ■ A report gives information about a topic; it does not include any personal details.	■ The body paragraphs of a personal narrative tell a story. The story has a beginning, middle, and end. ■ A personal narrative shares a true story that happened to the writer. The writer uses "I" to tell the story. ■ A personal narrative includes a message. The message may be a lesson that the writer learned from the experience he or she is writing about.

Transitions for Stories

while	the following day	later	that night
when	some time later	next	hours went by
after	the next morning	suddenly	at first I saw
during	after that		

Look for the transitions in the personal narrative on page H103.

Personal Narratives Let the Writer...

Describe events in a clear, interesting way	■ Show rather than tell the events of the story. ■ Include details to show what people, places, or things looked like. ■ Write sentences to entertain readers. ■ Choose words that express your feelings.
Use your own personal voice	■ Use "I" to write your story. ■ Tell your story as you would tell it to a friend or family member. ■ Include your personal opinions and feelings about events.
Share your feelings	■ Use language to express how you felt: "I was so **happy** that...!" "I was **worried** about..." "It made me **proud** that..." "I was **disappointed** that..." "Wow! It was so **exciting** that..."
Tell readers a message	■ Share a lesson about life. ■ Tell what you learned about yourself or someone else. ■ Tell what you gained from the experience.

Opinion Essays Let the Writer...

- ■ Share an opinion or position about a question or issue; that is, agree (pro) or disagree (con) with an issue or question.
- ■ Use words that signal to the reader the position the writer is taking.

Pro	Con
I am in favor	I do not think
I agree	I don't favor
I support	I disagree

Personal Narrative Planner

Personal Narrative Planner

Title: One Sport I Like

Introduction: I never thought I was good at sports because I can't throw a ball or run very fast.

Story

Beginning
- moved to a new neighborhood
- I was bored
- Carlos invited me to go running

Middle
- I ran around the block, I got really tired
- Carlos gave me lots of encouragement
- I became a stronger runner

End
- can run twenty times around my block
- I tried out for the cross-country team
- running practice every afternoon
- have met lots of other kids on the team

Conclusion: You've got to find the sport that is right for you.

One Sport I Like

Title

I never thought I was good at sports because I can't throw a ball or run very fast. Then last summer I found a sport I like.

Introduction

Last June my family moved to a new neighborhood. I didn't know anybody, and I was bored, bored, bored. One day I saw a boy across the street. He was wearing jogging shorts. I saw him stretch out and then take off down the street. In about five minutes he came around the block. He kept on running. As I sat on my lawn, I counted him circle the block ten times. When he finished, he came over and introduced himself. His name was Carlos. He invited me to go running the next day.

Beginning of the Story

The next morning I put on a pair of shorts and tennis shoes and met Carlos out in front of my house. I wasn't sure about running, but I figured I had nothing better to do. The first time I ran around the block, I got really tired. I was huffing and puffing. My sides hurt. Carlos gave me lots of encouragement, and he told me funny stories while we were running. He took my mind off how tired I was. I met Carlos every morning for the next few weeks. Little by little, I became a stronger runner.

Middle of the Story

Now I can run twenty times around my block! This fall I tried out for the cross-country team with Carlos. I made the team! I was so surprised. We have running practice every afternoon. It has been really great. I have met lots of other kids on the team. Now I have new friends as well as a sport I like.

End of the Story

What I learned was that not everybody is good at every sport. You've got to find the sport that is right for you.

Conclusion (with message)

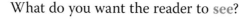

Sensory word choice is the key to descriptive writing. Word choice and the use of comparisons help the reader or listener create an image of what is being described. When writing descriptive compositions, ask the following questions:

What do you want the reader to see?

Hints: colors, shapes, weather, expressions on faces, gestures, people doing things alone or with others, objects, natural features

What do you want the reader to **hear**?

Hints: volume, tone, and expression of people's voices, music, rain, wind, trains, airplanes, traffic, animal sounds

What do you want the reader to smell?

Hints: flowers and trees, perfume, food, smoke, exhaust, rain

What do you want the reader to **taste**?

Hints: food or drink that is sweet, sour, salty, or bitter

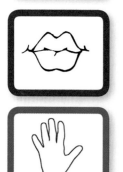

What do you want the reader to **touch**?

Hints: surfaces of different temperatures and textures; liquids of different types and forms

Draft Paragraph

During the next few weeks, Ali, my sister, and I grew closer. I showed her how to apply makeup. I gave her some of my clothes—a sweater and boots that were all right for a twelve year old to wear. One day, we even walked to the mall together. At the cosmetic counter, we sprayed ourselves with some perfume. Later, at the food court, we shared our favorite snack—a big plate of French fries. We talked every night to each other. I was starting to feel glad that I had a sister as great as Ali. I said to her, "You're ok, you know that?" She would just shrug.

Revised Paragraph with Description

During the next few weeks, Ali, my sister, and I grew closer. I showed her how to apply makeup, especially the dark gray and peach colors that would go with her dark brown eyes. I gave her some of my clothes—a fuzzy, blue sweater and some soft, black leather boots that were all right for a twelve year old to wear. One day, we even walked in a cold, pouring rain to the mall together. At the cosmetic counter, we laughed out loud as we sprayed ourselves with some stinky perfume. Later, at the food court, we shared our favorite snack—a big plate of hot, salty French fries. We talked every night to each other, and sometimes we would fall asleep on the bedroom floor listening to some of our favorite CDs. I was starting to feel glad that I had a sister as great as Ali. I said to her, "You're ok, you know that?" She would just shrug, giggle, and blush a little.

Parts of a Story

This graphic organizer shows how the parts of a story relate to each other in a sequence.

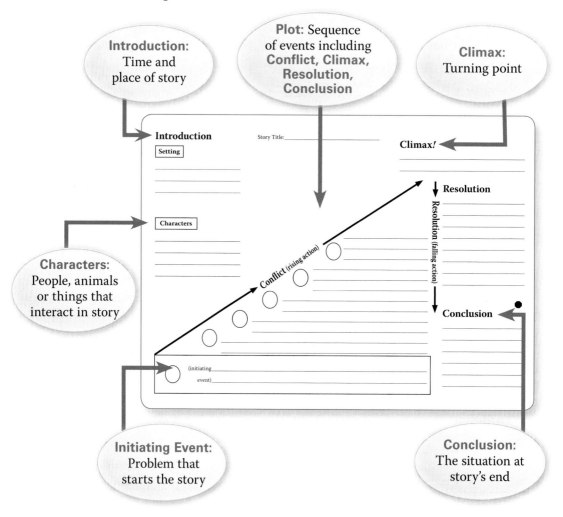

Introduction:
Time and place of story

Plot: Sequence of events including Conflict, Climax, Resolution, Conclusion

Climax:
Turning point

Characters:
People, animals or things that interact in story

Initiating Event:
Problem that starts the story

Conclusion:
The situation at story's end

Introduction
Setting

Story Title:

Characters

Conflict (rising action)

Climax!

Resolution

Resolution (falling action)

Conclusion

(initiating event)

Types of Conflicts

A conflict drives the plot of a story. Many stories are based on these basic conflicts:

Character with a personal problem or goal—A character may solve a problem, reach his goal, or change his attitude or feelings.

"A Game of Catch" (Book D)
"Satyagraha: Power for Change" (Book D)

Boy meets girl—A boy and a girl encounter problems that they need to handle and resolve.

Romeo and Juliet (movie, 1996)
"The End of Ali" (Book D)

Character vs. Nature—A character confronts and battles an aspect of nature.

Call of the Wild (Book E; movie, 1975)

Good Guys vs. Bad Guys—Good guys fight to defeat the bad guys and usually win.

The Treasure of the Sierra Madre (Book F; movie, 1948)

Mystery and solution—Characters solve mysteries or crimes, and the bad guys are punished.

"The Disappearing Man" (Book D)
"Tell-Tale Heart" (Book F)

Ways to Start a Story

Provide a Where—Let your readers know where the story takes place. When you do this, you set the scene.

> *I was sitting at my desk in my bedroom practicing my signature when my brother came in...*
>
> ("My Side of the Story," Book D)

Provide a When—Give your reader an idea of when the story takes place.

> *One hot and muggy summer afternoon, the Hare was boasting to a huge crowd of animals...*
>
> ("The Tortoise and the Hare: A Fable," Book D)

Provide an Action—Write a sentence that describes an action. These sentences have strong, active verbs.

> *Maitn shimmied up the branches of the pear tree, her feet feeling for a firm hold.*
>
> ("Zaaaaaaaap!," Book D)

Introduce a Character—Tell your reader about a character(s) in your story.

> *Monk and Glennie were playing catch on the side lawn of the firehouse when Scho caught sight of them.*
>
> ("A Game of Catch," Book D)

Make a Simple But Interesting Comment—Make an interesting comment to get the attention of your reader, and give a hint about your story.

> *I'm not often on the spot when Dad's on one of his cases, but I couldn't help it this time.*
>
> ("The Disappearing Man," Book D)

Start a Dialogue—Use dialogue.

> *Ramdas Bahave met me at the sidelines. "In what part of the body are you wounded, Kenneth?" he asked.*
>
> ("Satyagraha: Power for Change," Book D)

Ways to End a Story

Finish a story with a strong sentence(s) that will help your reader:

Feel a Feeling—Make an emotional connection.

Joshua took a huge bite from his prize pear, and offered one to Maitn, his way of thanking her for his rescue. She took the bite willingly, and tucked her smaller pear into his pocket for later. Energized by the power of hope, the two headed home.

("Zaaaaaaaap!," Book D)

Remember a Character—Focus on the impact of a character in the story.

I looked at him, saw his eyes shining and something that might have been laughter or maybe joy I didn't understand but thought I recognized from the old black-and-white pictures of Ghandi and his followers.

("Satyagraha: Power for Change," Book D)

Get Your Point Across—Understand the message of the story.

All animals cheered gleefully. It was clear that speed alone was not enough to make the Hare finish first.

("The Tortoise and the Hare: A Fable," Book D)

Think About the Story—Reflect on the message of the story.

We stand there with this big smile of respect between us. It's about a real smile as girls can do for each other, considering we don't practice real smiling every day you know, cause maybe we too busy being flowers or fairies or strawberries instead of something honest and worthy of respect...you know...like being people.

("Raymond's Run," Book D)

Writing Compare and Contrast Paragraphs

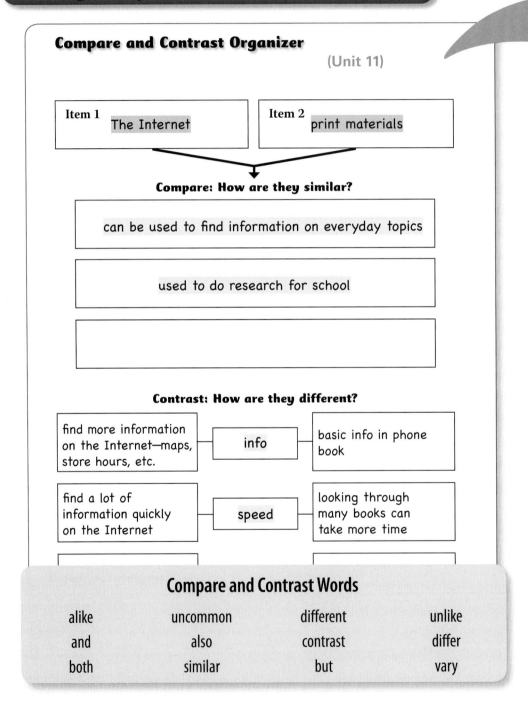

Compare and Contrast Organizer
(Unit 11)

Item 1	Item 2
The Internet	print materials

Compare: How are they similar?

can be used to find information on everyday topics

used to do research for school

Contrast: How are they different?

find more information on the Internet—maps, store hours, etc.	info	basic info in phone book

find a lot of information quickly on the Internet	speed	looking through many books can take more time

Compare and Contrast Words

alike	uncommon	different	unlike
and	also	contrast	differ
both	similar	but	vary

Internet or Print

When people need information, they can look in print materials such as books, or they can look on the Internet. The Internet and print materials share a lot in common, but they have many differences as well.

Introductory Paragraph

The Internet and print materials are alike in some ways. First, both the Internet and print media can be used to find information on everyday topics. People who want a telephone number for a business can look for it on the Internet. They can use a phone book, which is print material, too. If you want the schedule for the movies for Saturday night, you can look up the times in the newspaper and on the Internet. What if you are looking for directions to get someplace? You can buy a map to see how to get there. You can also find a map on the Internet. Second, both the Internet and print media can be used to do research for school. For example, students can read magazines, newspapers, or even books on the Internet just as they can in print. Students can find encyclopedias and dictionaries online, too. If they want information on a person or a place or need to know the meaning of a word, people have a choice of using a computer or looking up the information in a book.

Note the compare and contrast words circled in the paragraph.

The Internet and print materials also have many differences. First, people can often find more information on the Internet than they can in print media. For example, in a phone book, you can find some basic information about a place to order pizza, but on the Internet, you can find a lot more information. The Internet provides the telephone number of the restaurant, as well as the address and the hours it is open. You may also be able to read the pizza menu and look at a map to see how to get to the restaurant. Second, students can often find information they need for school faster on the Internet. It can take them a long time to find information for a report by looking through books. In contrast, they can usually find a lot of information quickly on the Internet. Although students still have to read the information, they can search for it much faster. That's because the Internet provides information from so many different sources.

The Internet and print media share a lot in common. However, they are really more different than they are similar.

Concluding Paragraph

An **informal letter** is written to someone the writer knows well, such as a friend or relative. It is also called a friendly or personal letter.

Informal letters can be handwritten or typed.

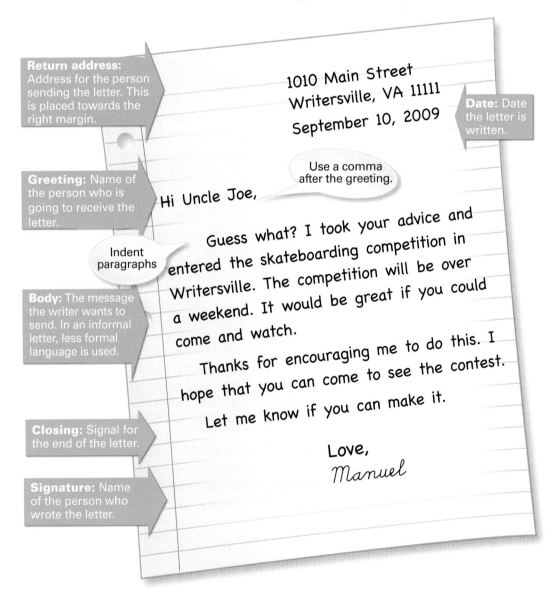

Return address: Address for the person sending the letter. This is placed towards the right margin.

1010 Main Street
Writersville, VA 11111
September 10, 2009

Date: Date the letter is written.

Use a comma after the greeting.

Greeting: Name of the person who is going to receive the letter.

Hi Uncle Joe,

Indent paragraphs

Guess what? I took your advice and entered the skateboarding competition in Writersville. The competition will be over a weekend. It would be great if you could come and watch.

Body: The message the writer wants to send. In an informal letter, less formal language is used.

Thanks for encouraging me to do this. I hope that you can come to see the contest. Let me know if you can make it.

Closing: Signal for the end of the letter.

Love,
Manuel

Signature: Name of the person who wrote the letter.

Business Letters   (Unit 16)

A **business letter** is written to someone the writer does not know or who is in a position of authority, such as a government agency, teacher, minister, or other person of authority. It is also called a formal letter.

Business letters are usually typed.

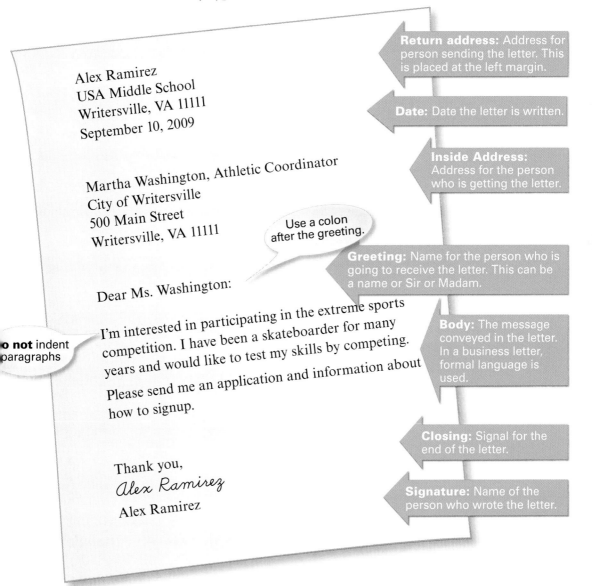

Alex Ramirez
USA Middle School
Writersville, VA 11111
September 10, 2009

Martha Washington, Athletic Coordinator
City of Writersville
500 Main Street
Writersville, VA 11111

Dear Ms. Washington:

I'm interested in participating in the extreme sports competition. I have been a skateboarder for many years and would like to test my skills by competing. Please send me an application and information about how to signup.

Thank you,
Alex Ramirez
Alex Ramirez

Return address: Address for person sending the letter. This is placed at the left margin.

Date: Date the letter is written.

Inside Address: Address for the person who is getting the letter.

Use a colon after the greeting.

Greeting: Name for the person who is going to receive the letter. This can be a name or Sir or Madam.

Do **not** indent paragraphs

Body: The message conveyed in the letter. In a business letter, formal language is used.

Closing: Signal for the end of the letter.

Signature: Name of the person who wrote the letter.

Trait		What does this mean?
	Ideas and Content	Focus on the main ideas or story line. Supporting details (expository) or images/events (narrative) build understanding.
	Organization	Order of ideas and supporting details (expository) or clear beginning, middle, and end (narrative) make sense. Introduction, transitions, and conclusion help keep the reader hooked on the writing.
	Voice and Audience Awareness	Style suits both the audience and purpose of the writing.
	Word Choice	"Just right" words for the topic and audience.
	Sentence Fluency	Varied sentence use; no run-on sentences and sentence fragments.
Editor's Marks ∧ add or change text ℓ delete text ⌒→ move text ¶ new paragraph ≡ capitalize / lowercase ⊙ insert period ◯ check spelling or spell out word	**Conventions**	Spelling, punctuation, grammar and usage, capitalization, and indenting paragraphs.

Writer's Checklist for Book D

Key: Blue=expository only   Red=narrative only   Black=expository and narrative

Trait	Did I...?	Unit
Ideas and Content	Expository Writing: ❑ Clearly state the topic of my composition ❑ Focus each paragraph on the topic ❑ Include examples, evidence, and/or explanations to develop each paragraph Literary Analysis: ❑ Analyze and evaluate one element in a work of literature ❑ Write a clear thesis statement that is a "map" for my essay ❑ Include support for my thesis, e.g., details, examples, explanations, and quotations from the story Personal Narrative: ❑ Tell a single true story ❑ Include enough description and detail to develop the message/lesson learned Fictional Narrative: ❑ Include characters, setting, plot ❑ Create an opening that grabs reader's attention ❑ Include enough description so that the reader can picture the characters and setting	 7 7 7 20 20 20 9 9 22 22 23
Organization	Paragraphs: ❑ Tell things in an order that makes sense ❑ Include all elements of a paragraph Expository essay: ❑ Write an introductory paragraph that states the topic and the plan ❑ Use transition sentences to connect paragraphs ❑ Write a concluding paragraph that restates the introduction, summarizes the ideas, or gives the reader something to think about Literary analysis: In addition to the essay requirements listed above— ❑ Include the title of the work and the name of the author in my introductory paragraph ❑ Write a conclusion that ties the analysis together and offers my evaluation of the element about which I am writing Personal narrative: ❑ Write an introductory paragraph that hints at the message/lesson learned ❑ Write middle paragraphs that communicate the beginning, middle, and end of the story ❑ Use story transitions to connect anecdotes/events ❑ Write a concluding paragraph that explains the message/lesson learned	 1 6 7 8,14,17 20 20 9 9 9 9

continued

Trait	Did I...?	Unit
Organization *(continued)*	Fictional narrative:	
	❏ Create an initiating event, conflict (or rising action), and climax	22
	❏ Include a resolution and a conclusion that ties everything up	22
	❏ Create a clear sequence of events	22
Voice and Audience Awareness	❏ Think about my audience and purpose for writing	6
	❏ Write in a clear and engaging way that makes my audience want to read my work; can my reader "hear" me speaking	6
	❏ Use the word *I* to write about myself	9
Word Choice	❏ Try to find my own way to say things	2
	❏ Use words that are lively and specific to the content	2
Sentence Fluency	❏ Write complete sentences	1
	❏ Expand some of my sentences by painting the subject and/or predicate	3–18
	❏ Write a compound sentence part or a compound sentence	7–18
	❏ Write a sentence with a direct object	3–18
Conventions	Capitalize words correctly:	
	❏ Capitalize the first word of each sentence	1
	❏ Capitalize proper nouns, including people's names	3
	Punctuate correctly:	
	❏ Put a period or question mark at the end of each sentence	1
	❏ Put an apostrophe before the **s** for a singular possessive noun	2
	❏ Put an apostrophe after the **s** for a plural possessive noun	11
	❏ Use an apostrophe with contractions	7
	❏ Use a comma after a long adverb phrase at the beginning of a sentence	5
	❏ Use a comma to separate the appositive and its modifiers from the rest of the sentence	10–12
	Use grammar correctly:	
	❏ Use the correct verb tense	4
	❏ Make sure the verb agrees with the subject in number	4
	Spell correctly:	
	❏ Spell all **Essential Words** correctly	1–18
	Apply spelling rules	
	❏ The doubling rule (1-1-1)	6
	❏ The drop **e** rule	10, 16
	❏ The words ending in **o** preceded by a consonant rule	15
	❏ The change **y** rule	17

Using the Six Traits to Revise a Paragraph (Unit 12)

Draft Paragraph

Editor's Marks

∧	add or change text
ℒ	delete text
⟳→	move text
¶	new paragraph
≡	capitalize
/	lowercase
⊙	insert period
◯	check spelling or spell out word

Maria is the main character in "The End of Ali." Her main trait is cruelty. She is not very nice and she is really mean to her little sister Ali. She mostly hurts Ali's feelings and doesn't pay attention to her, but sometimes she yells at her for just about anything. When Maria has a boyfriend, she is nice and even shares her things with her sister and gives Ali advice such as how to put on make-up and things like that. But when her boyfriend Alex brakes up with Maria, she is miserable and boy, does she ever take it out on Ali! She does mean things again. She tries to be mean when she says "you're getting on my nerves" and calls Ali a loser. She tells her no one will ever like her, especially her. By the end of the story, Maria's cruelty causes her to lose the love and friendship of her little sister, maybe forever.

Draft Paragraph with Edits

Maria is the main character in "The End of Ali." Her main trait
a   person.   especially
is cruelty. She is not very nice and she is really mean to her little
          often   by not paying
sister Ali. She mostly hurts Ali's feelings and doesn't pay attention to
                                                        and never
                                                        apologizes for it.
her, but sometimes she yells at her for just about anything.
          gentler and kinder   clothes
When Maria has a boyfriend, she is nice and even shares her things
                    advises her
with her sister and gives Ali advice such as how to put on make-up.
          However,   breaks
and things like that. But when her boyfriend Alex brakes up with
                    once again is nasty to her sister.
Maria, she is miserable and boy, does she ever take it out on Ali! She
                    hurts Ali's feelings   Can't you see that
does mean things again. She tries to be mean when she says "you're
              Finally, she   and says,
getting on my nerves" and calls Ali a loser. She tells her no one will
          you   me
ever like her, especially her. By the end of the story, Maria's cruelty

causes her to lose the love and friendship of her little sister, maybe

forever.

Revised Paragraph

Maria, the main character in "The End of Ali," is a cruel person. She is especially mean to her little sister Ali. She often hurts Ali's feelings by not paying attention to her, but when Maria is in a bad mood she yells "at her for just about anything" and never apologizes for it. When Maria has a boyfriend, she is gentler and kinder to Ali. She even shares her clothes with her sister and advises her on make-up. [Deleted "boy, does she ever take it out on Ali!" because it is not in a proper voice.] However, when her boyfriend Alex breaks up with Maria, Maria is miserable and once again is nasty to her sister. She hurts Ali's feelings by saying, "Can't you see that you're getting on my nerves?" Finally, she calls Ali a loser and says, "No one will ever like you, especially me." By the end of the story, Maria's cruelty causes her to lose the love and friendship of her little sister, maybe forever.

Six Traits	Problem	Revision
Ideas and Content	(line 4) The writer did not provide detailed information about Maria's cruelty and its impact on Ali. (line 9) Writer needs direct quote from story to emphasize Maria's cruelty.	(line 5) Details about never apologizing were added. (lines 11–13) Add direct quotations from the story.
Organization	No transition to indicate a change has happened in story. No transition to final piece of evidence.	Add "however" to the beginning of the sentence. Add "finally" to the beginning of the sentence.
Voice	The language is too informal for literary analysis.	The language of the sentence was made more formal and more specific.
Word Choice	The writer uses *nice, really,* and *things* instead of more specific words.	More precise words were used to replace *nice, really, mostly,* and *things.*
Sentence Fluency	Too many simple sentences in a row.	Sentences were combined using an appositive.
Conventions	*Brakes* was misspelled for this context.	Spelling corrected.

Pronunciation Key

Consonants

p	pup, rapped, pie		zh	vision, treasure, azure
b	bob, ebb, brother		h	hat, here, hope
t	tire, jumped, hurt		ch	church, match, beach
d	deed, mad, filed		j	judge, enjoy, jell
k	cat, kick, cut		m	mop
g	get, gill, magazine		n	not
f	fluff, rough, photo		ng	sing
v	valve, every, eleven		l	land
th	thin, three, math		w	with, wagon, west
th	this, there, mother		r	ramp
s	sod, city, list		y	yard, yes, yellow
z	zebra, has, bees		sh	ship, sugar, machine

Vowels

ē	beet	(bēt)		ō	boat	(bōt)
ĭ	bit	(bĭt)		o͝o	put	(po͝ot)
ā	bait	(bāt)		o͞o	boot	(bo͞ot)
ĕ	bet	(bĕt)		oi	boil	(boil)
ă	bat	(băt)		ou	pout	(pout)
ī	bite	(bīt)		î	peer	(pîr)
ŏ	pot	(pŏt)		â	bear	(bâr)
ô	bought	(bôt)		ä	par	(pär)
ŭ	but	(bŭt)		ô	bore	(bôr)
ə	rabbit	(ră′ bət)		û	pearl	(pûrl)

Unit 19

Word List

Essential Words

abroad, against, captain, curtain, language, nuisance

Unit Words

ai	maintain	vain	feet	seen	wheel
afraid	nail	waist	fifteen	sheep	**oa**
aid	obtain	wait	free	sheet	approach
aim	pain	**ee**	freeze	sleep	boat
bait	paint	agree	green	speech	coal
brain	praise	asleep	greet	speed	coast
chain	rail	bee	heel	squeeze	coat
complain	rain	beef	jeep	steel	float
contain	raise	between	keep	steep	goal
daily	remain	breeze	meet	street	goat
entertain	retain	cheese	need	sweep	load
explain	sail	coffee	queen	sweet	loan
faint	snail	creep	screen	teeth	oak
faith	tail	deep	see	three	road
grain	tailor	fee	seed	tree	roast
jail	trail	feed	seek	weed	soap
mail	train	feel	seem	week	throat

Spelling Lists

Lessons 1–5			Lessons 6–10	
abroad	entertain	rain check	agreement	explained
against	freestyle	speeding	aimlessly	foresee
captain	keeping	training	appraiser	midweek
coaching	language		artist	miscalculated
curtain	nuisance		boastful	mistake
download	railroad		colorful	sailor
			darkness	waiter
			details	

Word List

Essential Words

course, friend, guarantee, guard, guess, guest

Unit Words

ay for / ā /	stay	deal	leave	factories	own
away	tray	decrease	meal	field	shadow
bay	way	disease	mean	priest	shallow
clay		each	meanwhile	shield	show
day	**ea for / ā /**	eager			slow
decay	break	ease	**ey for / ē /**	**ie for / ī /**	snow
delay	great	east	chimney	lie	sow
hay		easy	donkey	tie	window
lay	**ea for / ē /**	eat	key		yellow
may	beam	feast	money	**ow for / ō /**	
maybe	beast	grease	monkey	blow	**oe for / ō /**
pay	beat	increase	valley	borrow	hoe
play	beneath	lead		bowl	toe
pray	cheap	leaf	**ie for / ē /**	grow	
ray	clean	lean	believe	hollow	
say	cream	least	chief	low	

Spelling Lists

Lessons 1–5			**Lessons 6–10**		
chimney	friend	guest	contract	informal	supported
course	great	hollow	decay	payment	tractor
decrease	guarantee	meanwhile	exporter	pretest	tricky
delay	guard	relieve	extracted	squeaky	unblocked
feast	guess	shallow	formula	subtracted	uninformed

Word List

Essential Words

beautiful, beauty, business, busy, leopard, women

Unit Words

Begin or end with a

alike	amuse	ashamed	astonish	extra
among	apart	aside	camera	

Unaccented syllable in two-syllable words

accuse	combine	frequent	merchant	refresh	trial
admire	compete	grammar	model	regret	wicked
afford	confuse	instant	modest	retire	witness
arrest	cruel	kitchen	moral	rival	
attend	custom	lessen	neglect	sacred	
attract	dollars	lesson	offend	seldom	
canal	formal	level	prefer	travel	

Unaccented syllable in multisyllable words

accustom	different	holiday	multiply	probably	similar
animal	difficult	horizon	mystery	recommend	sympathy
consider	family	hospital	numeral	regular	theater
consonant	favorite	imitate	opposite	remedy	umbrella
cultivate	finally	immediate	particular	restaurant	universe
delicate	funeral	important	permanent	salary	violent
determine	hesitate	industry	practical	separate	
diamond	history	melody	president	several	

Spelling Lists

Lessons 1–5

accuse	extra	melody
among	formal	opposite
beautiful	history	women
beauty	industry	
business	leopard	
busy	level	

Lessons 6–10

compressor	inability	recommend
confident	income	salary
correct	incomplete	senator
director	merchants	several
dollars	products	transcripts

Word List

Essential Words

colleague, extraordinary, iron, journal, journey, peculiar

Unit Words

Final consonant + le

able	bundle	giggle	needle	settle	title
angle	candle	handle	nibble	simple	tremble
ankle	cattle	hobble	pimple	single	triangle
apple	cripple	humble	puddle	stable	uncle
article	eagle	idle	purple	steeple	vehicle
assemble	enable	jungle	puzzle	syllable	whistle
battle	example	kettle	rattle	table	
bottle	fiddle	little	riddle	tangle	
bubble	freckle	marble	saddle	tattle	
buckle	gargle	middle	sample	tickle	

ea for / ĕ /

ahead	deaf	heaven	pleasant	thread	weather
bread	death	heavy	ready	threaten	widespread
breakfast	feather	instead	spread	wealth	
breath	head	lead	steady	weapon	
dead	health	leather	sweat		

ou for / ŭ /

country	cousin	southern	trouble
couple	double	touch	young

ui for / ĭ /

build	built	guild	guilty

Spelling Lists

Lessons 1–5

apple	iron	table
build	journal	touch
colleague	journey	weather
cousin	peculiar	
extraordinary	puzzle	
guilty	ready	

Lessons 6–10

distracted	regrettable	unanimous
inspector	ridiculous	vehicle
nervous	saddled	verdict
predictable	spectator	
predicted	suspect	
professor	trouble	

Word List

Essential Words

courage, debt, herb, honest, honor, hour

Unit Words

oi	boy	cloud	mouth	trout	drown
avoid	destroy	compound	noun	underground	drowsy
boil	enjoy	couch	outcome	without	eyebrow
coin	joy	counselor	output		flower
disappoint	loyal	count	outside	ow	growl
exploit	oyster	encounter	playground	allow	however
join	royal	farmhouse	pouch	anyhow	howl
joint	soy	flour	pound	bow	meow
moist	toy	found	profound	brown	owl
noise		fountain	proud	browse	plow
point	ou	ground	round	clown	powder
poison	account	hound	scout	cow	power
soil	aloud	house	shout	coward	shower
spoil	amount	loud	sour	crowd	towel
toilet	around	mound	south	crown	tower
	blouse	mount	stout	download	town
oy	bound	mountain	thousand	downtown	vowel
annoy	boundary	mouse	trousers		

Spelling Lists

Lessons 1–5

courage	honest	noise	aloud	downtown	perfectly
debt	honor	point	approximate	escaped	perform
drowned	hour	pounds	defects	estimate	rejected
enjoy	however	power	difficult	factories	thousand
herb	loyal	without	disappointed	memorize	underground

Lessons 6–10

Word List

Essential Words

half, limousine, listen, pour, tambourine, villain

Unit Words

adequate	correspond	expense	intermediate	raised	subtitle
administrator	counterpoint	fabulous	joined	razor	supper
aggregate	cried	female	liquid	reached	syllables
agony	curl	flowers	meteoroid	ruler	temper
ambiguous	curse	friends	midst	satisfactory	thorn
anthropoid	curve	hinder	mischief	scorn	tidy
bible	cuticle	hours	nuclear	sediment	tied
bitter	details	hypothesis	orchard	semiprivate	upper
callous	died	immense	perform	seventeen	utilize
capitol	dinner	immigrate	plains	shelter	waste
classify	dream	implicate	poet	shouted	wheels
clever	elder	indicate	pounds	shown	whisper
compromise	enclose	inform	preamble	skirt	
consequent	entitle	inquire	preserve	slowly	
coordinate	entity	instruments	professorial	spontaneous	
copper	exasperate	integrate	propagandize	stir	
corporate	excuse	integrity	qualitative	subsequent	

Spelling Lists

Lessons 1–5

cuticle	limousine
details	listen
dream	pour
flowers	preamble
friends	slowly
half	tambourine
hours	villain
joined	

Lessons 6–10

actor	flammable
antsy	forgivable
beagle	ineffective
building	midmorning
conduct	misbehaved
departed	perfectly
disposable	winterize
famous	

Unit 19

ai	lain	**ee**	indeed	sneeze	goad
ail	mailbox	beech	keel	streetcar	groan
attain	mainland	bleed	keen	tee	inroad
avail	mainstay	cheek	meek	teen	lifeboat
await	maize	creek	nineteen	thirteen	loaf
braid	railroad	decree	peek	upkeep	moan
braille	raincoat	deed	peel	weekend	oat
constrain	raindrop	degree	peep	weep	oath
daisy	remainder	discreet	peeve	**oa**	overcoat
detail	restrain	eel	redeem	boast	reproach
domain	sailboat	esteem	reed	charcoal	roadside
drain	sailor	feedback	reef	cloak	roadway
gain	saint	flee	referee	coach	soak
gait	sprain	fleet	screech	coastal	toad
hail	stain	freehand	seedling	coax	toast
ingrain	sustain	glee	sheepskin	cocoa	towboat
laid		greed	sixteen	croak	

Unit 20

ay for / ā /	**ea** for / ē /	peacock	teach	relief	minnow
birthday	appeal	peanut	underneath	relieve	owe
crayon	beach	preach	weave	thief	pillow
daytime	beak	reach			row
display	bean	real	**ey** for / ē /	**ie** for / ī /	rowboat
driveway	beaver	really	alley	die	sorrow
gray	breathe	release	barley	pie	throw
jay	cheat	retreat	hockey		widow
layer	defeat	reveal	honey	**ow** for / ō /	
okay	heal	scream	turkey	below	**oe** for / ō /
relay	heap	sea		bow	doe
spray	heat	seal	**ie** for / ē /	crow	foe
subway	jeans	season	achieve	elbow	oboe
	leak	squeak	belief	fellow	
	leap	squeal	brief	flow	
ea for / ā /	pea	steal	diesel	follow	
steak	peach	tea	handkerchief	glow	

Bonus Words

Unit 21

Begin or end with <u>a</u>
abandon
address
adjust
alarm
atomic
banana
panda

Unaccented syllable in two-syllable words
bacon
bias
camel
carbon
collapse
comfort
confer
confine
conform
converse

dial
effort
label
lizard
mustard
oven

Unaccented syllable in multisyllable words
accurate
advocate
allocate
analyze
annual
benefit
buffalo
calendar
carpenter
colony
compensate
component
concurrent

contradict
critical
definite
delivery
democrat
demonstrate
deposit
domestic
dominant
dominate
eleven
enemy
estimate
evident
external
factory
federal
festival
forthcoming
illustrate
innovate
internal

interval
isolate
justify
liberal
lullaby
manual
maximize
medical
memory
mercury
microscope
minimize
minimum
modify
molecule
museum
occupy
octopus
organize
potato
protocol
radical

realize
recognize
regulate
relevant
republican
senator
statistic
stimulate
telegram
terminate
thermometer
typical
ultimate
uniform
valentine
vertical
vitamin

Bonus Words

Unit 22

final consonant +le

ample
axle
babble
barnacle
battlefield
beetle
boggle
bridle
bristle
brittle
bugle
cable
chuckle
coddle
crackle
cradle

dangle
dazzle
dimple
disgruntle
dribble
fable
frizzle
gable
gaggle
gamble
gobble
grapple
grumble
hassle
huddle
jumble
ladle
maple

mingle
multiple
muzzle
noble
nobleman
nozzle
paddle
pebble
pickle
pineapple
ramshackle
rattlesnake
rectangle
rifle
ripple
rubble
ruffle
sable

scribble
scuffle
shingle
shuffle
shuttle
spectacle
sprinkle
staple
startle
stifle
struggle
stumble
supple
tackle
temple
throttle
timetable
topple

trample
trifle
tumble
ventricle
wiggle
wobble

ea for / ĕ /
breastbone
dealt
dread
endeavor
headquarters
heather
homestead
peasant
realm

sweater
tread

ou for / ŭ /
countryside
couplet
troublemaker
troublesome

ui for / ĭ /
buildup
guilt
rebuild

Unit 23

oi
adjoin
adroit
android
anoint
appoint
asteroid
broil

charbroil
checkpoint
conjoin
despoil
devoid
doily
embroider
enjoin

flashpoint
foible
foil
foist
groin
hoist
loiter
midpoint

ointment
pinpoint
poise
recoil
rejoinder
sirloin
spoilsport
tabloid

tenderloin
thyroid
trapezoid
void

oy
boycott
convoy
corduroy

coy
decoy
employ
envoy
loyalist
ploy

(continued)

Bonus Words

Unit 23 (continued)

ou			**ow**		
arouse	devour	groundhog	bow-wow	flowerpot	uptown
astound	doghouse	loudspeaker	brow	frown	vow
battleground	dour	outfield	chow	glower	wow
birdhouse	douse	pout	chowder	gown	
bout	flounder	roundup	cower	prowl	
countdown	foul	scour	downsize	sow	
county	greenhouse	spouse	downstream	sunflower	
	grouch	spout		touchdown	

Unit 24

abound	card	entertainment	impound	predispose	spreadsheet
administer	carpetbagger	escrow	impulse	prominent	sprout
arch	clout	establish	indisposed	repeated	standpoint
beagle	coil	faculty	jiggle	reserved	stretch
bedspread	cows	feeble	jingle	reside	sweatshirt
beginning	crumble	feeling	juggle	retouch	transfuse
bittersweet	deploy	fickle	magazine	rubbish	treadmill
bounty	developed	fifteenth	misinterpret	satellite	unplanned
brownout	diary	forgetting	mucous	satire	unsteady
bruise	disloyal	fowl	muffle	seeds	usher
building	drizzle	grader	myrtle	settled	valedictorian
campground	effect	griddle	nursery	shimmer	zenith
candlestick	elements	haste	pity	slouch	
cape	empower	holy	popular	snuggle	
capsule		illegal	porous	spleen	

Text Selections

"*You must be the change you wish to see in the world.*"
—Mohandas Gandhi (1869–1948)

Unit 19

Go With Speed

3

Early Olympic Speeders

Betty Robinson (center) winning the 100-meter dash in the 1928 Olympics.

As every fan knows, speed counts when it comes to most sports. At the Olympic level, runners, swimmers, and speed skaters move at amazing speeds. Here's a look at three speed champions from an earlier time.

Early Sprinting: Betty Robinson, Gold Medalist

5 In 1928, an unknown 16-year-old girl won Olympic gold. This high school junior raced to first place in the 100-meter dash. The event itself was a first that year. One could say that women's track and field was born. The sport had entered the Olympic Games.

10 Betty Robinson was that young woman. Growing up, Robinson had never dreamed of becoming a champion sprinter. One afternoon, she was running to catch a train. She was spotted by a track coach. A few weeks later, she placed second in a district championship. Next, she won

15 the Chicago-area Olympic trials and then finished second at the national Olympic trials. After that, she sped to victory in the 100-meter dash at the Amsterdam Olympics. Her time of 12.2 seconds set an Olympic record.

In 1931, Robinson barely survived a plane crash. Doctors
20   thought she would never walk again, but she recovered and
returned to training. She ran again in the 1936 Olympics
in Berlin. There, she won another gold medal as part of the
U.S. women's relay team.

Early Swimming: Ethelda Bleibtrey, Gold Medalist

As a child, Ethelda Bleibtrey started swimming
25   to recover from polio, a crippling disease. Later, her
swimming ability turned her into an Olympic champion.

Belgium hosted the 1920 Games. The Games had added
women's swimming, and there were three events. Bleibtrey,
a member of the U.S. team, raced in all three. She won three
30   gold medals! She is the only woman to have won all the
swimming events at any Olympics games. In the 100-meter
freestyle, she finished in 1:13.6. That time set a new record.

Over the next two years, Bleibtrey won every race she
entered. These included freestyle and backstroke events.
35   She won short- and long-distance races. She became a
celebrated athlete.

Bleibtrey was a winner in and out of the water. She
worked to get more swimming pools built
for the public. To make her point, she

*Clas Thunberg, the
"king of speed skating."*

40   once swam in a New York City lake where
swimming was not allowed. The police
arrested her. In response, people protested
in support of her goal. In the end, the city
built its first large public swimming pool.

Early Ice Speed Skating: Clas Thunberg, Gold Medalist

45   They called Finland's Clas Thunberg
the "king of speed skating." He worked
as a master bricklayer, but he found fame
on the ice. He won three gold medals in the 1924 Winter
Olympics. He also took home a silver and a bronze. Four
50   years later, he continued his Olympic success. He captured
two more gold medals. Thunberg set the 1,500-meter
record that year with a time of 2:20.8.

Thunberg won his last Olympic gold at age 34. This made him the oldest champion in Olympic speed skating
55　history. He continued skating competitively until he was 42.

The speeds of Olympic athletes have always been fast. Their times have only grown faster over the years. What are the reasons? Better equipment is a big factor. Better training has resulted in faster speeds, as well. Timekeeping has also
60　improved. What else could make athletes speed up?

Look at this chart of recent Olympic results. It shows the winning times from the 2004 and 2006 Olympics. Compare these winning times with the winning times cited in the article to see how times have changed.

Recent Olympic Results

Sport	Year	Event	Winner	Nation	Winning Time
Sprinting	2004	100m	Yuliya Nesterenko	BLR	10.93
Swimming	2004	100m freestyle	Jodie Henry	AUS	53.84
Speed Skating	2006	1500m	Enrico Fabris	ITA	1:46.22

Fiber Optics:

High-Speed Highways for LIGHT

Faster than a bolt of lightning, able to carry billions of light pulses a second, yet thinner than a human hair, it's . . . optical fiber!

What happens when you download research from the Internet? What carries your messages when you chat online with a friend? You may be using fiber **optics**. Fiber optic **cables** hide under the streets of many of our cities and towns. These cables carry all kinds of information.

Fiber optic technology is being used more and more. It has been around since the 1930s. Today, though, as much as 2,000 miles of fiber optic cable are being laid every hour. Why is the use of fiber optics increasing?

One reason to use fiber optics is the material. It's better than materials currently in use. Electric **signals** use wires that carry electrical **pulses**. The electricity moves through the wires quickly. What is the problem? The metal in the wire slows down the signal along the way. Fiber optics is different. It uses long, thin tubes. Instead of wire, these tubes are made from glass. They carry pulses of light instead of electricity. They deliver light signals.

A second reason for using fiber optics is speed. Glass carries the light signals fast. Glass allows light signals to travel at the speed of light. That's millions of times faster

optics
instruments that use, modify, or enhance light

cables
heavy, braided ropes, usually made of metal or plastic

signals
basic messages

pulses
regular or rhythmic surges

than any racing car! The glass tubes can even be bent. Light
25 moves at such quickness that some bending doesn't bother
the signal.

A final reason for using fiber optics is space. It uses less
space. Glass fibers are thin. They are thinner than metal
wires, and that means more fibers can fit into a cable. The
30 more optical fibers there are, the more signals can be sent.

The use of fiber optics has improved **communications**.
Light signals can send huge amounts of information. Cable
TV is faster because of fiber optics. Thanks to fiber optics,
we have high-speed Internet. Phone lines could never carry
35 this much information this fast.

Fiber optics has changed the way some people do their
work. Doctors can now see into a person's body without
doing major surgery. How do they do it? Doctors place
special scopes inside a person's body. Fiber optics is used
40 to send a picture for the doctor to see. Astronomers use
fiber optics to learn more about space. Special optic fibers
receive and **interpret** signals that come from telescopes.
The system lets scientists measure changes in the light and
temperature of stars and planets. Fiber optics is also used
45 by engineers to light homes and offices by feeding sunlight
into buildings.

The fiber optic age has just begun. As it develops, how
will it affect your life?

Adapted with permission from "High-Speed Highways for Light"
by Nancy Day

communications

ways of sharing
information

interpret

to explain the
meaning of

Answer It

1. Justify using fiber optics rather than electric wires.

2. Medical costs are rising. Justify a doctor's request for using fiber optics.

3. Imagine you are building a new school. Assess its needs for communication
   (television, phone lines, etc.).

4. Summarize ways that fiber optics has changed the way some people work.

5. Do you use fiber optics at school or at home? Predict how fiber optics will
   affect your life in the future.

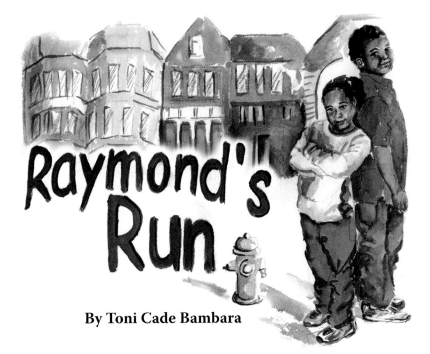

Raymond's Run

By Toni Cade Bambara

I don't have much work to do around the house like some girls. My mother does that. And I don't have to earn my pocket money by hustling; George runs errands for the big boys and sells Christmas cards. And anything else that's
5 got to get done, my father does. All I have to do in life is **mind** my brother Raymond, which is enough.

Sometimes I slip and say my little brother Raymond. But as any fool can see he's much bigger and he's older too. But a lot of people call him my little brother cause he
10 needs looking after cause he's not quite right. And a lot of smart mouths got lots to say about that too, especially when George was minding him. But now, if anybody has anything to say to Raymond, anything to say about his big head, they have to come by me. And I don't play the
15 dozens or believe in standing around with somebody in my face doing a lot of talking. I much rather just knock you down and take my chances even if I am a little girl with skinny arms and a squeaky voice, which is how I got the name Squeaky. And if things get too rough, I run. And as
20 anybody can tell you, I'm the fastest thing on two feet.

There is no track meet that I don't win the first place medal. I use to win the twenty-yard dash when I was a little kid in kindergarten. Nowadays it's the fifty-yard dash.

mind
to take care of; watch closely

subject

likely to;
expected to

subject

prone; having a
tendency toward

And tomorrow I'm **subject** to run the quarter-mile relay
25　all by myself and come in first, second, and third. The big
kids call me Mercury cause I'm the swiftest thing in the
neighborhood. Everybody knows that—except two people
who know better, my father and me.

　　He can beat me to Amsterdam Avenue with me having
30　a two fire-hydrant headstart and him running with his
hands in his pockets and whistling. But that's private
information. Cause can you imagine some thirty-five-year-
old man stuffing himself into PAL shorts to race little kids?
So as far as everyone's concerned, I'm the fastest and that
35　goes for Gretchen, too, who has put out the tale that she
is going to win the first place medal this year. Ridiculous.
In the second place, she's got short legs. In the third place,
she's got freckles. In the first place, no one can beat me and
that's all there is to it.

40　　I'm standing on the corner admiring the weather and
about to take a stroll down Broadway so I can practice
my breathing exercises, and I've got Raymond walking on
the inside close to the buildings, cause he's **subject** to
fits of fantasy and starts thinking he's a circus performer
45　and that the curb is a tightrope strung high in the air.
And sometimes after a rain, he likes to step down off his
tightrope right into the gutter and slosh around getting
his shoes and cuffs wet. Then I get hit when I get home.
Or sometimes if you don't watch him, he'll dash across
50　traffic to the island in the middle of Broadway and give the
pigeons a fit. Then I have to go behind him apologizing to
all the old people sitting around trying to get some sun and
getting all upset with the pigeons fluttering around them,
scattering their newspapers and upsetting the waxpaper
55　lunches in their laps. So I keep Raymond on the inside of
me, and he plays like he's driving a stage coach which is
O.K. by me so long as he doesn't run me over or interrupt
my breathing exercises, which I have to do on account of
I'm serious about my running and don't care who knows it.

60　　Now some people like to act like things come easy
to them, won't let on that they practice. Not me. I'll high
prance down 34th Street like a rodeo pony to keep my

knees strong even if it does get my mother uptight so that she walks ahead like she's not with me, don't know me, is
65 all by herself on a shopping trip, and I am somebody else's crazy child.

Now you take Cynthia Procter for instance. She's just the opposite. If there's a test tomorrow, she'll say something like, "Oh I guess I'll play handball this afternoon and watch
70 television tonight," just to let you know she ain't thinking about the test. Or like last week when she won the spelling bee for the millionth time, "A good thing you got 'receive,' Squeaky, cause I would have got it wrong. I completely forgot about the spelling bee." And she'll clutch the lace on
75 her blouse like it was a narrow escape. Oh, brother.

But of course when I pass her house on my early morning trots around the block, she is practicing the scales on the piano over and over and over and over. Then in music class, she always lets herself get bumped around so
80 she falls accidentally on purpose onto the piano stool and is so surprised to find herself sitting there, and so decides just for fun to try out the ole keys and what do you know— Chopin's waltzes just spring out of her fingertips and she's the most surprised thing in the world. A regular **prodigy**.
85 I could kill people like that.

I stay up all night studying the words for the spelling bee. And you can see me anytime of day practicing running. I never walk if I can trot and shame on Raymond if he can't keep up. But of course he does, cause if he hangs
90 back someone's liable to walk up to him and get smart, or take his allowance from him, or ask him where he got that great big pumpkin head. People are so stupid sometimes.

So I'm strolling down Broadway breathing out and breathing in on counts of seven, which is my lucky number,
95 and here comes Gretchen and her sidekicks—Mary Louise who used to be a friend of mine when she first moved to Harlem from Baltimore and got beat up by everybody till I took up for her on account of her mother and my mother used to sing in the same choir when they were young girls,
100 but people ain't grateful, so now she hangs out with the new girl Gretchen and talks about me like a dog; and Rosie

> **prodigy**
> an exceptionally talented child or youth

who is as fat as I am skinny and has a big mouth where Raymond is concerned and is too stupid to know that there is not a big deal of difference between herself and Raymond
105 and that she can't afford to throw stones. So they are steady coming up Broadway and I see right away that it's going to be one of those Dodge City scenes cause the street ain't that big and they're close to the buildings just as we are. First I think I'll step into the candy store and look over the new
110 comics and let them pass. But that's chicken and I've got a reputation to consider. So then I think I'll just walk straight on through them or over them if necessary. But as they get to me, they slow down. I'm ready to fight, cause like I said I don't feature a whole lot of chitchat, I much prefer to just
115 knock you down right from the jump and save everybody a lotta precious time.

"You signing up for the May Day races?" smiles Mary Louise, only it's not a smile at all.

A dumb question like that doesn't deserve an answer.
120 Besides, there's just me and Gretchen standing there really, so no use wasting my breath talking to shadows.

"I don't think you're going to win this time," says Rosie, trying to **signify** with her hands on her hips all salty, completely forgetting that I have whupped her behind
125 many times for less salt than that.

signify

to indicate; show

"I always win cause I'm the best," I say straight at
Gretchen who is, as far as I'm concerned, the only one
talking in this ventriloquist-dummy routine.

Gretchen smiles but it's not a smile and I'm thinking
130   that girls never really smile at each other because they
don't know how and don't want to know how and there's
probably no one to teach us how cause grown-up girls don't
know either. Then they all look at Raymond who has just
brought his mule team to a standstill. And they're about to
135   see what trouble they can get into through him.

"What grade you in now, Raymond?"

"You got anything to say to my brother, you say it to
me, Mary Louise Williams of Raggedy Town, Baltimore."

"What are you, his mother?" sasses Rosie.
140   "That's right, Fatso. And the next word out of anybody
and I'll be their mother too." So they just stand there and
Gretchen shifts from one leg to the other and so do they.
Then Gretchen puts her hands on her hips and is about to
say something with her freckle-face self but doesn't. Then
145   she walks around me looking me up and down but keeps
walking up Broadway, and her sidekicks follow her. So me
and Raymond smile at each other and he says, "Gidyap"
to his team and I continue with my breathing exercises,
strolling down Broadway toward the icey man on 145th with
150   not a care in the world cause I am Miss Quicksilver herself.

I take my time getting to the park on May Day because
the track meet is the last thing on the program. The biggest
thing on the program is the May Pole dancing which I
can do without, thank you, even if my mother thinks it's
155   a shame I don't take part and act like a girl for a change.
You'd think my mother'd be grateful not to have to make
me a white organdy dress with a big satin sash and buy me
new white baby-doll shoes that can't be taken out of the
box till the big day. You'd think she'd be glad her daughter
160   ain't out there prancing around a May Pole getting the new
clothes all dirty and sweaty and trying to act like a fairy
or a flower or whatever you're supposed to be when you
should be trying to be yourself, whatever that is, which is,
as far as I am concerned, a poor Black girl who really can't

165 afford to buy shoes and a new dress you only wear once a
lifetime cause it won't fit next year.

I was once a strawberry in a Hansel and Gretel pageant
when I was in nursery school and didn't have no better
sense than to dance on tiptoe with my arms in a circle over
170 my head doing umbrella steps and being a perfect fool just
so my mother and father could come dressed up and clap.
You'd think they'd know better than to encourage that
kind of nonsense. I am not a strawberry. I do not dance
on my toes. I run. That is what I am all about. So I always
175 come late to the May Day program, just in time to get my
number pinned on and lay in the grass till they announce
the fifty-yard dash.

I put Raymond in the little swings, which is a tight
squeeze this year and will be impossible next year. Then I
180 look around for Mr. Pearson who pins the numbers on. I'm
really looking for Gretchen if you want to know the truth,
but she's not around. The park is jam-packed. Parents in
hats and corsages and breast-pocket handkerchiefs peeking
up. Kids in white dresses and light blue suits. The parkees
185 unfolding chairs and chasing the rowdy kids from Lenox
as if they had no right to be there. The big guys with their
caps on backwards, leaning against the fence swirling
the basketballs on the tips of their fingers waiting for all
these crazy people to clear out the park so they can play.
190 Most of the kids in my class are carrying bass drums and
glockenspiels and flutes. You'd think they'd put in a few
bongos or something for real like that.

Then here comes Mr. Pearson with his clipboard and
his cards and pencils and whistles and safety pins and fifty
195 million other things he's always dropping all over the place
with his clumsy self. He sticks out in a crowd because he's
on stilts. We used to call him Jack and the Beanstalk to get
him mad. But I'm the only one that can outrun him and get
away, and I'm too grown for that silliness now.
200   "Well, Squeaky," he says checking my name off the
list and handing me number seven and two pins. And I'm
thinking he's got no right to call me Squeaky, if I can't call
him Beanstalk.

"Hazel Elizabeth Deborah Parker," I correct
205 him and tell him to write it down on his board.
"Well, Hazel Elizabeth Deborah Parker,
going to give someone else a break this
year?" I squint at him real hard to see
if he is seriously thinking I should
210 lose the race on purpose just to give
someone else a break.
"Only six girls running this time,"
he continues, shaking his head sadly like
it's my fault all of New York didn't turn
215 out in sneakers. "That new girl should give
you a run for your money." He looks around
the park for Gretchen like a periscope in
a submarine movie. "Wouldn't it be a nice
gesture if you were . . . to ahhh . . ."
220   I give him such a look he couldn't
finish putting that idea into words.
Grownups got a lot of nerve
sometimes. I pin number seven to
myself and stomp away—I'm so
225 burnt. And I go straight for the track
and stretch out on the grass while the
band winds up with "Oh the Monkey
Wrapped His Tail Around the Flag Pole," which my teacher
calls by some other name. The man on the loudspeaker
230 is calling everyone over to the track and I'm on my back
looking at the sky trying to pretend I'm in the country, but
I can't, because even grass in the city feels hard as sidewalk
and there's just no pretending you are anywhere but in a
"concrete jungle" as my grandfather says.
235   The twenty-yard dash takes all of the two minutes
cause most of the little kids don't know no better than to
run off the track or run the wrong way or run smack into
the fence and fall down and cry. One little kid though has
got the good sense to run straight for the white ribbon
240 up ahead so he wins. Then the second graders line up for
the thirty-yard dash and I don't even bother to turn my
head to watch cause Raphael Perez always wins. He wins

gesture
an act meant to
convey meaning

before he even begins by psyching the runners, telling them
they're going to trip on their shoelaces and fall on their
245 faces or lose their shorts or something, which he doesn't
really have to do since he is very fast, almost as fast as I am.
After that is the forty-yard dash which I use to run when
I was in first grade. Raymond is hollering from the swings
cause he knows I'm about to do my thing cause the man
250 on the loudspeaker has just announced the fifty-yard dash,
although he might just as well be giving a recipe for angel
food cake cause you can hardly make out what he's saying
for the static. I get up and slip off my sweat pants and then
I see Gretchen standing at the starting line kicking her
255 legs out like a pro. Then as I get into place I see that ole
Raymond is in line on the other side of the fence, bending
down with his fingers on the ground just like he knew what
he was doing. I was going to yell at him but then I didn't. It
burns up your energy to holler.
260   Every time, just before I take off in a race, I always feel
like I'm in a dream, the kind of dream you have when you're
sick with fever and feel all hot and weightless. I dream I'm
flying over a sandy beach in the early morning sun, kissing
the leaves of the trees as I fly by. And there's always the
265 smell of apples, just like in the country when I was little
and use to think I was a choo-choo train, running through
the fields of corn and chugging up the hill to the orchard.
And all the time I'm dreaming this, I get lighter and lighter
until I'm flying over the beach again, getting blown through
270 the sky like a feather that weighs nothing at all. But once I
spread my fingers in the dirt and crouch over for the Get
on Your Mark, the dream goes and I am solid again and
am telling myself, Squeaky you must win, you must win,
you are the fastest thing in the world, you can even beat
275 your father up Amsterdam if you really try. And then I feel
my weight coming back just behind my knees then down
to my feet then into the earth and the pistol shot explodes
in my blood and I am off and weightless again, flying past
the other runners, my arms pumping up and down and the
280 whole world is quiet except for the crunch as I zoom over
the gravel in the track. I glance to my left and there is no

one. To the right a **blurred** Gretchen who's got her chin
jutting out as if it would win the race all by itself. And on
the other side of the fence is Raymond with his arms down
285 to his side and the palms tucked up behind him, running
in his very own style and it's the first time I ever saw that
and I almost stop to watch my brother Raymond on his
first run. But the white ribbon is bouncing toward me and I
tear past it racing into the distance till my feet with a mind
290 of their own start digging up footfuls of dirt and brake me
short. Then all the kids standing on the side pile on me,
banging me on the back and slapping my head with their
May Day programs, for I have won again and everybody on
151st Street can walk tall for another year.
295   "In first place . . ." the man on the loudspeaker is clear
as a bell now. But then he pauses and the loudspeaker starts
to whine. Then static. And I lean down to catch my breath
and here comes Gretchen walking back for she's overshot
the finish line too, huffing and puffing with her hands on
300 her hips taking it slow, breathing in steady time like a real
pro and I sort of like her a little for the first time. "In first
place . . ." and then three or four voices get all mixed up on
the loudspeaker and I dig my sneaker into the grass and

blurred

unclear; hazy

stare at Gretchen who's staring back, we both wondering
305 just who did win. I can hear old Beanstalk arguing with
the man on the loudspeaker and then a few others running
their mouths about what the stop watches say.

Then I hear Raymond yanking at the fence to call me
and I wave to shush him, but he keeps rattling the fence,
310 but then like a dancer or something he starts climbing up
nice and easy but very fast. And it occurs to me, watching
how smoothly he climbs hand over hand and remembering
how he looked running with his arms down to his side
and with the wind pulling his mouth back and his teeth
315 showing and all, it occurred to me that Raymond would
make a very fine runner. Doesn't he always keep up with
me on my trots? And he surely knows how to breathe in
counts of seven cause he's always doing it at the dinner
table, which drives my brother George up the wall. And
320 I'm smiling to beat the band cause if I've lost this race, or
if me and Gretchen tied, or even if I've won, I can always
retire as a runner and begin a whole new career as a coach
with Raymond as my champion. After all, with a little more
study I can beat Cynthia and her phony self at the spelling
325 bee. And if I bugged my mother, I could get piano lessons
and become a star. And I have a big rep as the baddest
thing around. And I've got a roomful of ribbons and medals
and awards. But what has Raymond got to call his own?

So I stand there with my new plans, laughing out
330 loud by this time as Raymond jumps down from the fence
and runs over with his teeth showing and his arms down
to the side which no one before him has quite mastered
as a running style. And by the time he comes over I'm
jumping up and down so glad to see him—my brother
335 Raymond, a great runner in the family tradition. But of
course everyone thinks I'm jumping up and down because
the men on the loudspeaker have finally gotten themselves
together and compared notes and are announcing "In first
place—Miss Hazel Elizabeth Deborah Parker." (Dig that.)
340 "In second place—Miss Gretchen P. Lewis." And I look
over at Gretchen wondering what the P stands for. And I
smile. Cause she's good, no doubt about it. Maybe she'd

like to help me coach Raymond; she obviously is serious about running, as any fool can see. And she nods to
345 congratulate me and then she smiles. And I smile. We stand there with this big smile of respect between us. It's about as real a smile as girls can do for each other, considering
350 we don't practice real smiling every day you know, cause maybe we too busy being flowers or fairies or strawberries instead of something honest and worthy of respect . . . you
355 know . . . like being people.

Used by permission of Random House, Inc.

Answer It

1. Assess what it means when people mistake Raymond for Squeaky's little brother.

2. Assess the encounter Squeaky and Raymond had with Gretchen and her sidekicks, Mary Louise and Rosie.

3. State reasons the author titled this selection "**Raymond's Run.**"

4. Explain how the relationship between Squeaky and Raymond developed from the beginning to the end of the story.

5. Describe the meaning of the smile between Gretchen and Squeaky at the end of the story.

A SLOW TAKE ON FAST FOOD

Food at Different Speeds

Is it always better to be fast than slow? You would certainly think so if you trained a team of sprinters for the Olympics. But what if you trained a team of doctors for brain surgery? You definitely would *not* want them to rush
5 through an operation, especially if you were the one being operated on!

The point is that faster is not always better. It all depends on the situation. And one situation is the speed at which we eat. That is, not only what we eat, but how fast we eat.
10 For thousands of years, people have eaten in the same basic way all around the world. First, they spend hours, days, weeks, or months just to hunt, gather, fish, or farm for their food. If they are successful in their efforts, they spend hours or days to prepare the food, start a fire, then slowly
15 cook their meal. Given all of the time and effort spent on the whole process, it is easy to imagine that they enjoy every last morsel.

Today, eating for some of us is changing. We can prepare, cook, and eat meals more quickly. However, some
20 people think things have become too fast for our own good. They **promote** *slow food* meals that are carefully planned and slowly prepared, cooked, enjoyed, and shared.

promote

to support;
encourage

Early Fast Food

Let's first look at how our eating habits have sped up over time. For thousands of years, people have been drying,
25 salting, and pickling food so that they could eat it later. About two hundred years ago, people figured out how to store products in jars and cans. Preparing food ahead of time made mealtimes quicker.

After the invention of canned food, you could reach for
30 a jar of fruit prepared years ago, open it, and eat right then. It was a revolution in food history, matched only by the later invention of iceboxes, which kept food cold in airtight boxes full of blocks of ice.

Transportation also had a huge impact on our eating
35 habits. It's one thing to store food and another to move it from one place to another. The invention of the steam engine allowed trains and ships to quickly transport food from faraway places. These inventions took place before the twentieth century. So, it's interesting to note that *your*
40 great-grandparents' food already was much faster than that of *their* great-grandparents.

Faster Food

Meanwhile, new events further improved methods for preparing, packaging, and storing food. For example, electric refrigerators were a big improvement on
45 iceboxes. World War II alone saw many advances in food production, storage, and **distribution** . After all, it's hard to win a war on an empty stomach. It's also no easy task to feed millions of soldiers and keep them moving fast across deserts and jungles. Canned meals called C rations fed
50 American soldiers.

distribution

the act of supplying products to stores and customers

After the war, new and faster foods made their way from grocery stores into the home. Refrigerated items, known as "frozen foods," became popular. This included fully prepared meals called "TV dinners," which you
55 could eat while watching TV. There also were frozen concentrates, frozen pizzas, boxes of cereal, and all sorts of foods that were ready to eat after adding water or heating them up.

Faster foods were a great help to mothers, who did
60 most of the cooking. More moms than ever were working
full-time jobs, and fast foods saved them precious time. So
did other new, fast, and **convenient** appliances, such as
dishwashers.

convenient

easy to use; useful

Fast Food Goes into Business
The whole world seemed to be speeding up. And the
65 most famous newcomer in fast food never could have
occurred without these developments. It was the fast food
restaurant.

The 1950s saw an explosion in this type of business,
usually in the form of "hamburger joints." Most of these
70 were individual- or family-owned, but all relied on "pre-
processed" foods. This simply refers to items that are ready
to cook or serve with minimum preparation.

Some of these restaurants were extremely popular. It
wasn't long before their owners realized that they could
75 repeat their successes in more than one location. So, they
decided to open one restaurant after another across the
country, like links on a chain. In fact, that's exactly what
they were called—"restaurant chains."

Before long, Americans were eating out at these
80 restaurants on a regular basis. The practice has become
so common that now nearly every community in the
United States includes at least one fast food restaurant,
and often many.

No longer do fast food restaurants offer only
85 hamburgers, and no longer do they operate only in the
United States. Today's fast food restaurants provide many
types of **cuisine** and operate in nearly every country on
the globe. Some of these businesses are now the world's
largest companies.

cuisine

food; French for
"food" and
"kitchen"

The Faults of Fast Food
90 According to supporters of the Slow Food movement,
all of this speed and convenience has come at a great cost.
Carlo Petrini, an Italian food critic, founded the Slow

Food movement in Paris in 1989. Basically, this movement believes that fast food means bad food.

95   For starters, they believe the taste of fast food is inferior to slow-cooked meals that use fresh ingredients. Just as important, they criticize fast food for using unhealthy ingredients. Of course, everyone may have his or her own tastes, but health experts agree that fast food often includes
100 too much fat and salt and too many calories.

     In addition, members of the Slow Food movement believe that fast food encourages us to eat too quickly. Most medical professionals agree that we should not eat too fast, because it is bad for our digestion.

105   Slow Food promoters also believe that fast food is bad for our mental health. That's because it encourages people to rush through their meals, and, all too often, to eat alone, on the run, in the car, or in unattractive settings.

Slow Is Good

     The slow food alternative values healthy whole grains,
110 fruits, and vegetables bought from farmers' markets or local grocers. It prizes planning and cooking meals that are **savored** and shared with good company, like a special occasion dinner. The point isn't to take time or waste time, but to make the most of it with a
115 quality eating experience.

savored

tasted or smelled with pleasure

     As an added benefit, slow food may reduce **caloric intake**. The reason has to do with how our bodies handle what we eat. As the stomach digests
120 food, it sends chemicals to the brain

caloric intake

the amount of calories eaten

letting us know when we're full. However, it takes a while for these signals to reach the brain.

Unfortunately, when we quickly gobble down large portions of food, our brain may not get the message that
125 we've eaten too much until the meal is already over! Eating slowly gives the brain time to get the message that the stomach has had enough.

Almost everybody agrees that it is a good thing to slow down our lives once in a while, including our eating. This
130 probably explains why there are now tens of thousands of members of the Slow Food movement throughout roughly fifty countries.

However, is slow food simply too slow and impractical for most people's fast-paced lives? Fast food may give you
135 extra time, but what if one of the best things you can do with your free time is to cook and share a meal? Then again, what if there are other things that you enjoy doing even more with your time, such as visiting friends, reading books, or playing sports? One thing is for sure, whether
140 you think fast food or slow food is better, it's time to think about what's at the end of your fork and what's the best choice for you.

Think About It

1. List two inventions that changed the way food was stored or transported.

2. Explain how fast food helps working mothers.

3. Who invented the Slow Food movement? What year? Describe the Slow Food movement.

4. Explain how eating alone, on the run, in the car, or in unattractive settings may be bad for your mental health.

5. Justify the need to quickly prepare meals. How does this help in your life?

6. Assess the author's point of view regarding fast food and the Slow Food movement.

The Tortoise and the Hare: A Fable

One hot and muggy summer afternoon, the Hare was boasting to a huge crowd of animals who had gathered in a **verdant** forest clearing: "I'm the fastest animal in the forest, and no one can beat me, even on my slowest day!"

5   "Why is it so important to be the fastest?" asked the Tortoise.

"Because faster is superior!" replied the Hare. "My speed is unbeatable, and I can do anything faster than any other animal, so I am the most superior animal in the forest."

10   "Speed, perhaps, can be a good thing, but it doesn't automatically make one animal more superior or important than any other animal," responded the Tortoise **indignantly**.

"If you really don't think my speed makes me superior, why don't you prove it? Suppose the two of us run a race to 15 see who's right?" exclaimed the Hare. "We can race down the four-mile path along the edge of the forest. You're so slow and sluggish that I'll probably finish the race before you get a third of the way." The Hare began to laugh at the thought of the Tortoise racing, and he fell to the ground in 20 a fit of laughter, snorting and spitting great guffaws.

Although the Tortoise had **disdain** for the Hare's display of insensitive behavior and preferred not to enter into a race with such an **egocentric** fool, he accepted the Hare's challenge because he wanted to confront the 25 Hare's taunting. He stashed a bottle of water in his shell in anticipation of the sweltering race ahead.

verdant
green; covered with green plants

indignantly
angrily

disdain
a feeling of contempt

egocentric
selfish; self-centered

Without doing anything to prepare for the hot and humid weather, the Hare lined up at the starting line next to the Tortoise. The other animals, hoping for the 30 impossible—that the Hare would get his just rewards— shouted, "Go!" and the Hare took off with unbelievable speed, darted up the first hill, and soon disappeared from sight. The Tortoise set off with a gradual and methodical pace, and steadily climbed up the hill after the Hare. Seeing 35 this, most of the animals calculated that the Tortoise's chances of winning were slim to nil.

The Hare seemed unstoppable as he passed the three-mile mark on the path. However, because he did not prepare for the hot day, he began languishing in the heat and 40 decided to stop at one of the rest stops along the path for a little refreshment. "I'm so far ahead of that laboriously slow Tortoise that I have lots of time," he concluded. With great confidence in his anticipated victory, he strolled into his favorite fast food restaurant and demanded a jumbo-sized 45 carrot juice and an extra-large salad.

After he had finished his repast, he noticed a nearby skateboarding course across the meadow. "I'm so far ahead of that pitiful Tortoise that I still have time for some amusement," considered the Hare. "The Tortoise probably 50 hasn't even reached a mile yet." Chuckling at the Tortoise, and with great confidence in himself, the Hare rented a skateboard, kneepads, and a helmet, and hit the course. He skateboarded at such great speed that he literally "hit" the course and landed on his own tail! The Hare did not 55 hurt himself badly, but his great **audacity** left him with a bruised ego. He arose sheepishly and limped off the course.

Following his skateboarding accident, the Hare tried to start sprinting. Because of his bruises and full stomach, he was unable to run as swiftly as before. "Even though I can't 60 run as fast, I'll still beat that tedious Tortoise," proclaimed the Hare. However, the broiling temperature made running difficult, and the Hare soon felt totally exhausted. After running for only a half mile, the Hare decided to take another short rest, and he sat down near a gurgling brook. 65 "I'll just rest here for a few minutes, and then I'll have more

audacity

overconfidence; fearless daring

energy for racing." Although he would eventually regret it, the Hare nestled in a bed of leaves, immediately fell asleep, and began snoring very loudly.

70 Meanwhile, the Tortoise continued to trudge along the path at the edge of the forest; he knew that he could not afford to stop, and more importantly, he knew that the overconfident Hare would stop many times. "Even though it's hot, I have plenty of water, so there's no need to stop until I finish the race," the Tortoise told himself. "Plus, it's
75 never a good idea to eat and run."

Soon, the Tortoise was passing the brook where the Hare napped comfortably. The Tortoise heard the Hare's loud snoring, which gave the Tortoise an added degree of confidence. He calculated that if he were able to keep up
80 his steady pace, he had a good chance of finishing first. The Tortoise thanked the Hare for being true to his foolish character, and he continued to plod steadily toward the finish line.

As the Tortoise slowly approached the end of the
85 path, the Hare suddenly awoke and bolted upright from his leaf-nest. Realizing that he could potentially lose the race, the Hare jumped up and raced back onto the path. Unfortunately, his pace was even slower than before because he wasn't yet fully awake and still felt groggy.
90 As the Hare moved along the path as fast as he could, he noticed that the Tortoise was just a few yards away from the finish line. He knew that his only chance of winning was to trick the Tortoise. He called to the Tortoise, "Tortoise, I'm hurt. Can you help me?"
95 The Tortoise stopped and looked back, "How do I know that you're telling the truth?"

"My tail hurts. Please help me," begged the Hare, as he pretended to be in great pain.

Fortunately, the Tortoise had heard the Hare's loud
100 snoring, so he knew that the Hare was trying to deceive him.

"What can I do to help you?" asked the Tortoise.

"Please help me get to the clearing," pleaded the Hare.

"Did you enjoy your sleep?" questioned the Tortoise, immune to the Hare's antics.

105 "Yes . . . err. No, wait!" shouted the harebrained Hare.

"I knew you were sleeping after I heard your loud snoring," declared the Tortoise. "I'll see you on the other side of the finish line."

lethargy

a lack of energy; inactivity

Despite his **lethargy**, the Hare made a mad dash 110 to catch the Tortoise. But he was too late. The Tortoise crossed the finish line just ahead of the Hare. The Hare crossed the line and collapsed on the ground.

"You boast too much, you're arrogant, and you rarely consider others' feelings, so I'm not surprised that you tried 115 to deceive me," the Tortoise said calmly.

All the animals cheered gleefully. It was clear that speed alone was not enough to make the Hare finish first.

The Moral: Slow and steady wins the race.

Adapted from "The Hare and the Tortoise," *Aesop's Fables*

Think About It

1. Explain why the Tortoise accepted the Hare's challenge. Do you think that the Tortoise believed he had a chance of winning?

2. Tell what the Tortoise did to prepare for the race in hot weather.

3. Find the idioms **slim to nil** in line 36 and **made a mad dash** in line 109. Use the context to figure out the meanings. Write an explanation of one of the idioms.

4. Explain the meaning of the Tortoise's statement to the Hare, "I'm not surprised that you tried to deceive me." What does this statement reveal about the Hare's character?

5. Assess the moral of the fable. What is another way to express "Slow and steady wins the race"?

Unit 20

Play On

29

Nash's Bashes

Word Play

Some folks use words to get attention.
Most folks use words to get things done.
Bad folks say words we shouldn't mention.
But Ogden Nash used words for fun.

5   Ogden Nash was known for playing, and his kind of playfulness was unique. He was a 20th-century poet who delighted readers with word play. He became famous for creating poems that brought smiles and chuckles to people's lives.

10   When Nash's career began, Americans were in need of a little laughter. The year was 1930, and times were bleak. The Great Depression had begun. The year before, the stock market had crashed, and many banks and businesses closed. Investors lost vast sums of money, and unemployment hit families hard.

15 By 1930, one person in five was out of work. People suffered, and life offered few opportunities for fun or play.

Nash knew his talents could help people. He understood words and how they work. He was gifted at fooling around with language and using it to entertain. He knew something

20 else—humor could relieve despair and decrease hopelessness.

In his poems, it's Nash's word play that grabs our attention. It is funny, yet makes us think and even see the world around us in new ways. It's humor for people who like having fun with words.

25   Often, Nash played with word sounds. He knew what word repetition could do, and rhythm, too. He played with rhyme and even made up ridiculous words. His skills helped him celebrate language. A celebration is a bash. Nash had a bash with words, and we can have fun with

30 him. A few of Nash's bashes follow.

The Eel

I don't mind eels,
except as meals.

The Rhinoceros

The rhino is a homely beast,
For human eyes he's not a feast.
Farewell, farewell, you old rhinoceros,
I'll stare at something less prepoceros.

The Cow

The cow is of the bovine ilk;
One end is moo, the other, milk.

The Termite

Some primal termite knocked on wood
And tasted it, and found it good,
And that is why your Cousin May
Fell through the parlor floor today.

The Wasp

The wasp and all his numerous family
I look upon as a major calamily.
He throws open his nest with prodigality,
But I distrust his waspitality.

The Lama

The one-l lama,
He's a priest.
The two-l llama,
He's a beast.

And I will bet
A silk pajama
There isn't any
Three-l lllama.

The Ostrich

The ostrich roams the great Sahara.
Its mouth is wide, its neck is narra.
It has such long and lofty legs.
I'm glad it sits to lay its eggs.

Reprinted by permission of Curtis Brown, Ltd.

The Marble Champ
by Gary Soto

Lupe Medrano, a shy girl who spoke in whispers, was the school's spelling bee champion, winner of the reading contest at the public library three summers in a row, blue ribbon awardee in the science fair, the top student at her
5 piano recital, and the playground grand champion in chess. She was a straight-A student and—not counting kindergarten, when she had been stung by a wasp—never missed one day of elementary school. She had received a small trophy for this honor and had been congratulated by
10 the mayor.

But though Lupe had a razor-sharp mind, she could not make her body, no matter how much she tried, run as fast as the other girls'. She begged her body to move faster, but could never best anyone in the fifty-yard dash.
15 The truth was that Lupe was no good in sports. She could not catch a pop-up or figure out in which direction to kick the soccer ball. One time she kicked the ball at her own goal and scored a point for the other team. She was no good at baseball or basketball either, and even had a hard
20 time making a hula-hoop stay on her hips.

It wasn't until last year, when she was eleven years old, that she learned how to ride a bike. And even then she had to use training wheels. She could walk in the swimming pool but couldn't swim, and chanced roller-skating only when her father held her hand.

"I'll never be good at sports," she fumed one rainy day as she lay on her bed gazing at the shelf her father had made to hold her awards. "I wish I could win something, anything, even marbles."

At the word "marbles," she sat up. "That's it. Maybe I could be good at playing marbles." She hopped out of bed and **rummaged** through the closet until she found a can full of her brother's marbles. She poured the rich glass treasure on her bed and picked five of the most beautiful marbles.

rummaged
searched by sorting through things

She smoothed her bedspread and practiced shooting, softly at first so that her aim would be **accurate** . The marble rolled from her thumb and clicked against the targeted marble. But the target wouldn't budge. She tried again and again. Her aim became accurate, but the power from her thumb made the marble move only an inch or two. Then she realized that the bedspread was slowing the marbles. She also had to admit that her thumb was weaker than the neck of a newborn chick.

accurate
precise; without error

She looked out the window. The rain was letting up, but the ground was too muddy to play. She sat cross-legged on the bed, rolling her five marbles between her palms. Yes, she thought, I could play marbles, and marbles is a sport. At that moment she realized that she had only two weeks to practice. The playground championship, the same one her brother had entered the previous year, was coming up. She had a lot to do.

To strengthen her wrists, she decided to do twenty push-ups on her fingertips, five at a time. "One, two, three . . ." she groaned. By the end of the first set she was breathing hard, and her muscles burned from exhaustion. She did one more set and decided that was enough push-ups for the first day.

She squeezed a rubber eraser one hundred times, hoping it would strengthen her thumb. This seemed to work because the next day her thumb was sore. She could

hardly hold a marble in her hand, let alone send it flying
with power. So Lupe rested that day and listened to her
brother, who gave her tips on how to shoot: get low, aim
65 with one eye, and place one knuckle on the ground.

"Think 'eye and thumb'—and let it rip!" he said.

After school the next day she left her homework in her
backpack and practiced three hours straight, taking time
only to eat a candy bar for energy. With a popsicle stick,
70 she drew an odd-shaped circle and tossed in four marbles.
She used her shooter, a milky agate with hypnotic swirls, to
blast them. Her thumb had become stronger.

After practice, she squeezed the eraser for an hour.
She ate dinner with her left hand to spare her shooting
75 hand and said nothing to her parents about her dreams of
athletic glory.

Practice, practice, practice. Squeeze, squeeze, squeeze.
Lupe got better and beat her brother and Alfonso, a
neighbor kid who was supposed to be a champ.

80   "Man, she's bad!" Alfonso said. "She can beat the other
girls for sure, I think."

The weeks passed quickly. Lupe worked so hard that
one day, while she was drying dishes, her mother asked why
her thumb was swollen.

85   "It's muscle," Lupe explained. "I've been practicing for
the marbles championship."

"You, honey?" Her mother knew Lupe was no good at sports.

"Yeah. I beat Alfonso, and he's pretty good."

90 That night, over dinner, Mrs. Medrano said, "Honey, you should see Lupe's thumb."

"Huh?" Mr. Medrano said, wiping his mouth and looking at his daughter.

"Show your father."

95 "Do I have to?" an embarrassed Lupe asked.

"Go on, show your father."

Reluctantly, Lupe raised her hand and flexed her thumb. You could see the muscle.

The father put down his fork and asked, "What 100 happened?"

"Dad, I've been working out. I've been squeezing an eraser."

"Why?"

"I'm going to enter the marbles championship."

105 Her father looked at her mother and then back at his daughter. "When is it, honey?"

"This Saturday. Can you come?"

The father had been planning to play racquetball with a friend Saturday, but he said he would be there. He knew 110 his daughter thought she was no good at sports and he wanted to encourage her. He even rigged some lights in the backyard so she could practice after dark. He squatted with one knee on the ground, **entranced** by the sight of his daughter easily beating her brother.

115 The day of the championship began with a cold blustery sky. The sun was a silvery light behind slate clouds.

"I hope it clears up," her father said, rubbing his hands together as he returned from getting the newspaper. They ate breakfast, paced nervously around the house waiting 120 for 10:00 to arrive, and walked the two blocks to the playground (though Mr. Medrano wanted to drive so Lupe wouldn't get tired). She signed up and was assigned her first match on baseball diamond number three.

reluctantly
unwillingly; hesitantly

entranced
fascinated; enchanted

Lupe, walking between her brother and her father,
125 shook from the cold, not nerves. She took off her mittens,
and everyone stared at her thumb. Someone asked, "How
can you play with a broken thumb?" Lupe smiled and said
nothing.

She beat her first **opponent** easily, and felt sorry for
130 the girl because she didn't have anyone to cheer for her.
Except for her sack of marbles, she was all alone. Lupe
invited the girl, whose name was Rachel, to stay with them.
She smiled and said, "OK." The four of them walked to a
card table in the middle of the outfield, where Lupe was
135 assigned another opponent.

She also beat this girl, a fifth-grader named Yolanda,
and asked her to join their group. They proceeded to more
matches and more wins, and soon there was a crowd
of people following Lupe to the finals to play a girl in a
140 baseball cap. This girl seemed dead serious. She never even
looked at Lupe.

"I don't know, Dad, she looks tough."

Rachel hugged Lupe and said, "Go get her."

"You can do it," her father encouraged. "Just think of
145 the marbles, not the girl, and let your thumb do the work."

The other girl broke first and earned one marble. She
missed her next shot, and Lupe, one eye closed, her thumb
quivering with energy, blasted two marbles out of the circle
but missed her next shot. Her opponent earned two more
150 before missing. She stamped her foot and said, "Shoot!"
The score was three to two in favor of Miss Baseball Cap.

The referee stopped the game. "Back up, please, give
them room," he shouted. Onlookers had gathered too
tightly around the players.

155 Lupe then earned three marbles and was set to get her
fourth when a gust of wind blew dust in her eyes and she
missed badly. Her opponent quickly scored two marbles,
tying the game, and moved ahead six to five on a lucky
shot. Then she missed, and Lupe, whose eyes felt scratchy
160 when she blinked, relied on instinct and thumb muscle to
score the tying point. It was now six to six, with only three
marbles left. Lupe blew her nose and studied the angles.

She dropped to one knee, steadied her hand, and shot so
hard she cracked two marbles from the circle. She was the
165 winner!

"I did it!" Lupe said under her breath. She rose from her
knees, which hurt from bending all day, and hugged her
father. He hugged her back and smiled.

Everyone clapped, except Miss Baseball Cap, who
170 made a face and stared at the ground. Lupe told her she
was a great player, and they shook hands. A newspaper
photographer took pictures of the two girls standing
shoulder-to-shoulder, with Lupe holding the bigger trophy.

Lupe then played the winner of the boys' division, and
175 after a poor start beat him eleven to four. She blasted the
marbles, shattering one into sparkling slivers of glass. Her
opponent looked on **glumly** as Lupe did what she did
best—win!

The head referee and the President of the Fresno
180 Marble Association stood with Lupe as she displayed her
trophies for the newspaper photographer. Lupe shook
hands with everyone, including a dog who had come over
to see what the commotion was all about.

glumly
sadly; unhappily

That night, the family went out for pizza and set the
185 two trophies on the table for everyone in the restaurant
to see. People came up to congratulate Lupe, and she
felt a little embarrassed, but her father said the trophies
belonged there.

Back home, in the privacy of her bedroom, she
190 placed the trophies on her shelf and was happy. She had
always earned honors because of her brains, but winning
in sports was a new experience. She thanked her tired
thumb. "You did it, thumb. You made me champion."
As its reward, Lupe went to the bathroom, filled the
195 bathroom sink with warm water, and let her thumb swim
and splash as it pleased. Then she climbed into bed and
drifted into a hard-won sleep.

Reprinted by permission of Harcourt, Inc.

Answer It

1. Wanting to win at something, Lupe made a decision to participate in the sport of marbles. Judge Lupe's decision to compete in the sport of marbles.

2. Explain why Lupe was reluctant to show her thumb to her father.

3. Identify evidence that Lupe's father supported her decision to compete in marbles.

4. Compare the personality traits of Lupe, in **"The Marble Champ,"** and Squeaky, in **"Raymond's Run."** Include examples from each story.

5. Pretend you review books and movies for the local newspaper. Critique **"The Marble Champ."** Be sure to include your opinion about whether this story should appear on the newspaper's recommended reading list.

A Game of Catch

by Richard Wilbur

How could something as innocent as a game of catch result in such painful consequences?

Monk and Glennie were playing catch on the side lawn of the firehouse when Scho caught sight of them. They were
5 good at it, for seventh-graders, as anyone could see right away. Monk, wearing a catcher's mitt, would lean easily sidewise and back, with one leg lifted and his throwing hand almost down to the grass, and then lob the white ball straight up into the sunlight. Glennie would shield his eyes
10 with his left hand and, just as the ball fell past him, snag it with a little dart of his glove. Then he would burn the ball straight toward Monk, and it would spank into the round mitt and sit, like a still-life apple on a plate, until Monk flipped it over into his right hand and, with a negligent flick
15 of his hanging arm, gave Glennie a fast grounder.

They were going on and on like that, in a kind of slow, mannered, **luxurious** dance in the sun, their faces perfectly blank and entranced, when Glennie noticed Scho dawdling along the other side of the street and called hello
20 to him. Scho crossed over and stood at the front edge of the lawn, near an apple tree, watching.

"Got your glove?" asked Glennie after a time. Scho obviously hadn't.

luxurious

extremely enjoyable; self-indulgent

"You could give me some easy grounders," said Scho. "But don't burn 'em."

"All right," Glennie said. He moved off a little, so the three of them formed a triangle, and they passed the ball around for about five minutes, Monk tossing easy grounders to Scho, Scho throwing to Glennie, and Glennie burning them in to Monk. After a while, Monk began to throw them back to Glennie once or twice before he let Scho have his grounder, and finally Monk gave Scho a fast, bumpy grounder that hopped over his shoulder and went into the brake on the other side of the street.

"Not so hard," called Scho as he ran across to get it.

"You should've had it," Monk shouted.

It took Scho a little while to find the ball among the ferns and dead leaves, and when he saw it, he grabbed it up and threw it toward Glennie. It struck the trunk of the apple tree, bounced back at an angle, and rolled steadily and stupidly onto the cement apron in front of the firehouse, where one of the trucks was parked. Scho ran hard and stopped it just before it rolled under the truck, and this time he carried it back to his former position on the lawn and threw it carefully to Glennie.

"I got an idea," said Glennie. "Why don't Monk and I catch for five minutes more, and then you can borrow one of our gloves?"

"That's all right with me," said Monk. He socked his fist into his mitt, and Glennie burned one in.

"All right," Scho said, and went over and sat under the tree. There in the shade he watched them resume their skillful play. They threw lazily fast or lazily slow—high, low, or wide—and always handsomely, their expressions **serene**, changeless, and forgetful. When Monk missed a low backhand catch, he walked **indolently** after the ball and, hardly even looking, flung it sidearm for an imaginary put-out. After a good while of this, Scho said, "Isn't it five minutes yet?"

"One minute to go," said Monk, with a fraction of a grin.

serene
calm; peaceful

indolently
lazily

Scho stood up and watched the ball slap back and forth for several minutes more, and then he turned and pulled himself up into the crotch of the tree.

65 "Where you going?" Monk asked.

"Just up the tree," Scho said.

"I guess he doesn't want to catch," said Monk.

Scho went up and up through the fat light-
70 gray branches until they grew slender and bright and gave under him. He found a place where several supple branches were knit to make a dangerous chair, and sat there with his head coming out of the
75 leaves into the sunlight. He could see the two other boys down below, the ball going back and forth between them as if they were bowling on the grass, and Glennie's crew-cut head looking like a sea urchin.

80 "I found a wonderful seat up here," Scho said loudly. "If I don't fall out." Monk and Glennie didn't look up or comment, and so he began **jouncing** gently in his chair of branches and singing "Yo-ho, heave ho" in an exaggerated way.

jouncing
moving with bumps and jolts

85 "Do you know what, Monk?" he announced in a few moments. "I can make you two guys do anything I want. Catch that ball, Monk! Now you catch it, Glennie!"

"I was going to catch it anyway," Monk suddenly said. "You're not making anybody do anything when they're
90 already going to do it anyway."

"I made you say what you just said," Scho replied joyfully.

"No, you didn't," said Monk, still throwing and catching but now less serenely absorbed in the game.

95 "That's what I wanted you to say," Scho said.

The ball bounded off the rim of Monk's mitt and plowed into a gladiolus bed beside the firehouse, and Monk ran to get it while Scho jounced in his treetop and sang, "I wanted you to miss that. Anything you do is what I wanted
100 you to do."

"Let's quit for a minute," Glennie suggested.

"We might as well, until the peanut gallery shuts up," Monk said.

They went over and sat cross-legged in the shade of
105 the tree. Scho looked down between his legs and saw them on the dim, spotty ground, saying nothing to one another. Glennie soon began abstractedly spinning his glove between his palms; Monk pulled his nose and stared out across the lawn.

110 "I want you to mess around with your nose, Monk," said Scho, giggling. Monk withdrew his hand from his face.

"Do that with your glove, Glennie," Scho persisted. "Monk, I want you to pull up hunks of grass and chew on it."

115 Glennie looked up and saw a self-delighted, intense face staring down at him through the leaves. "Stop being a dope and come down and we'll catch for a few minutes," he said.

tentatively

cautiously;
hesitantly

Scho hesitated, and then said, in a **tentatively** mocking voice, "That's what I wanted you to say."

120 "All right, then, nuts to you," said Glennie.

"Why don't you keep quiet and stop bothering people?" Monk asked.

"I made you say that," Scho replied, softly.

"Shut up," Monk said.

125 "I made you say that, and I want you to be standing there looking sore. And I want you to climb up the tree. I'm making you do it!"

Monk was scrambling up through the branches, awkward in his haste, and getting snagged on twigs. His
130 face was furious and foolish, and he kept telling Scho to shut up, shut up, shut up, while the other's **exuberant** and

exuberant

enthusiastic; joyful

panicky voice poured down upon his head.

"Now you shut up or you'll be sorry," Monk said, breathing hard as he reached up and threatened to shake
135 the cradle of slight branches in which Scho was sitting.

"I want—" Scho screamed as he fell. Two lower branches broke his rustling, crackling fall, but he landed on his back with a deep thud and lay still, with a strangled look on his face and his eyes clenched. Glennie knelt down

140 and asked breathlessly, "Are you O.K., Scho? Are you O.K.?"
while Monk swung down through the leaves crying that
honestly he hadn't even touched him, the crazy guy just let
go. Scho doubled up and turned over on his right side, and
now both the other boys knelt beside him, pawing at his
145 shoulder and begging to know how he was.

Then Scho rolled away from them and sat partly up,
still struggling to get his wind but forcing a species of smile
onto his face.

"I'm sorry, Scho," Monk said. "I didn't mean to make
150 you fall."

Scho's voice came out weak and gravelly, in gasps.
"I meant—you to do it. You—had to. You can't do—
anything—unless I want—you to."

Glennie and Monk looked helplessly at him as he sat
155 there, breathing a bit more easily and smiling fixedly, with
tears in his eyes. Then they picked up their gloves and the
ball, walked over to the street, and went slowly away down
the sidewalk, Monk punching his fist into the mitt, Glennie
juggling the ball between glove and hand.

160   From under the apple tree, Scho, still bent over a little for lack of breath, croaked after them in triumph and misery, "I want you to do whatever you're going to do for the whole rest of your life!"

Reprinted by permission of Harcourt, Inc.

Answer It

1. Monk threw a fast, bumpy grounder to Scho. Explain why Monk might have behaved in this manner.

2. Glennie and Monk continued to play catch longer than the agreed upon five minutes, when Scho was supposed to be able to play with them again. Explain how Scho responded as the other boys continued to play on and on without him.

3. Pretend you are a judge. Decide which boy is responsible for Scho being left alone at the end of the story: Glennie, Monk, or Scho. Explain your answer.

4. List ways to help a person feel included, rather than excluded.

5. Select one of the characters in the story: Glennie, Monk, or Scho. Describe how that character could have handled the situation differently.

Yo-Yo Ma Plays the World

"It is so easy to be cynical. It's an accurate reflection of reality. It's much harder; it takes a philosophical point of view, to be optimistic. You have to work at it every day. One of the joys of working with children is that they are still unspoiled by cynicism."   Yo-Yo Ma

Yo-Yo Ma, famous cellist.

Who Is He?

Who is Yo-Yo Ma? Is he a great philosopher? Is he a great humanist? Is he a great counselor? Is he a great philanthropist? Is he a cultural ambassador to the world? Yo-Yo Ma is all of these, and more.

5   Yo-Yo Ma has created a global music community. One of the finest **cellists** of all time, he is one of the world's best-selling solo artists. He has recorded more than 75 albums and has won 15 Grammy awards. His intense, passionate, and joyful concerts are legendary.

cellists
musicians who play the cello

10   Ma's colossal **stamina** has led to comparisons with great athletes. Conductor David Zinman, a frequent collaborator, says, "I see Tiger Woods as the Yo-Yo Ma of golf." (Others have called Michael Jordan the Yo-Yo Ma of basketball, Yo-Yo Ma the Peyton Manning of music, and so

stamina
endurance

15 forth.) "On our last tour," says Zinman, "Ma said, 'You have to expend energy in order to produce energy. If you empty

yourself, you're going to fill yourself even more.' Sometimes
he sleeps; sometimes he doesn't. He's one of those people
who can sleep on a dime. If he has 10 minutes before a
20 concert, he can just zzzzzzz out, then throw some water on
his face and be radiant."

An Extraordinary Life

Yo-Yo Ma was born in Paris in 1955 to a talented
Chinese family. At four, he began cello lessons; at five,
he gave his first **recital**. But his life hasn't followed a
25 typical classical music path. Yes, he plays million-dollar
instruments, including a 1733 Montagnana cello from
Venice and a 1712 Davidoff Stradivarius cello, but Yo-Yo
Ma doesn't play classical music exclusively. He also plays a
wide variety of contemporary music, folk music, and lesser-
30 known works—sometimes by unknown composers.

Ma has jammed with Argentine tango bands, traded
tunes with bushmen in the Kalahari, and even performed
with the Muppets on Sesame Street. "I'm proud to say,"
he boasts a little, "that I knew Elmo before he became
35 Tickle-Me Elmo, the star. When he was starting the violin,
I helped him learn a very difficult note." Ma's appearances
on *Sesame Street*, with Mister Rogers, and as a giant
bespectacled gray bunny on *Arthur*, he says, are "the things
I am most proud of; I love being invited into the world of
40 children."

Early Beginnings

Ma's father, Hiao-Tsiun Ma, a violinist and a professor
at Nanjing University, left China for Paris in 1936. His
mother, Marina, a singer from Hong Kong and former
student of Hiao-Tsiun's, immigrated to Paris in 1949, where
45 she and Hiao-Tsiun were married. In 1955, Yo-Yo was born.
Some years ago, he told interviewer David Blum that "Yo,"
which in Chinese means "friendship," was the generational
character chosen for him and his sister, Yeou-Cheng, M.D.,
now a violinist and pediatrician, who is four years older
50 than he. "With me," he laughs, "they seem to have got lazy

recital

a formal
performance in front
of an audience

and been unable to think of anything else, so they added another Yo."

At his first public concert at the University of Paris when he was five, he played both the piano and cello. His
55 father "was the **pedagogue** of the family, very strict. I was born when he was 49, so he was an older parent, very old-world. He loved painting, and himself studied musicology, composition, and violin in Paris." Hiao-Tsiun tutored Yeou-Cheng and Yo-Yo in French and Chinese history,
60 calligraphy, and, of course, music. Each day, Yo-Yo had to memorize two measures of Bach; by the time he was four he was already playing a Bach suite.

At about this time, an important friend and advocate, violinist Isaac Stern, entered Ma's life. "When Yo-Yo was
65 about six," recalled Stern, "a good friend of mine in Paris said to me, 'You know, there's this young Chinese boy that you must hear.' I went to listen to him, six years old, and the cello was larger than he was. It was extraordinary." Stern was to be invaluable in helping the family get
70 established when they immigrated to the United States.

pedagogue
a teacher

Growing Up

When he was seven, Ma, his sister, and his parents moved to New York City, where the children would grow up. In New York, Ma continued his cello studies. Soon, the ever-watchful Isaac Stern buttonholed his friend, the
75 great cellist Leonard Rose. He said, "Lenny, you have to teach this boy," so Ma played for Leonard Rose, and Rose instantly took him as a student. He studied with Lenny for many years in the Juilliard precollege program. Isaac Stern recalled that everybody noticed Ma's extraordinary talent,
80 including his natural feel for being on stage, the way most people feel in their old clothes in their own living rooms.

As children, Ma and his sister played at a fundraiser in Washington D.C. The event, attended by President and Mrs. Kennedy, was hosted and conducted by Leonard
85 Bernstein. It was one of television's first specials. The film clips show a boy who is already displaying what Isaac

charisma

personal charm and appeal

Stern later called " **charisma** in spades." Yo-Yo Ma was introduced to the international music community. They loved him.

Working with Young People

90   Yo-Yo Ma recalls the difficulties of being young, and helping young people has become an important part of his life. He sees education as the key to young people's success. He brings young audiences into contact with music and allows them to participate in its creation. While touring, he
95 conducts master classes as well as informal programs for students—musicians and non-musicians alike.

"Often," he has said, "I meet young people getting really involved in music early. You know, the child-prodigy syndrome. Based on my own experience, I tell these kids
100 and their parents: 'Remember that what you do between the ages of, say, 12 and 21 is creating your emotional bank account. You'll be withdrawing from that account the rest of your life, so make sure you put in stuff that really counts. If you do nothing but tour during those years, if you are
105 center stage from concert hall to hotel to limo rides to the airport, that is what you will be withdrawing from because that is all you'll know.'" And competitions? He laughs. "Are you kidding? I lost every competition, except once when I was five. Today, I won't even be a judge. I'm against them."

Ma's Silk Road and Other Cultural Pursuits

110 His life has been about stretching boundaries; in 1998, he founded the Silk Road Project, his most ambitious stretch of all, a fusion of all his roads into one. Its goal is to study the ebb and flow of ideas among different cultures along the ancient Silk Road that connected Europe
115 to Asia, finding and performing traditional music and commissioning new works. "This is the most exciting thing I've ever done," he says. "The Silk Road is a metaphor for a number of things: as the Internet of **antiquity** , the trade routes were used for commerce, by religious people,

antiquity

ancient times

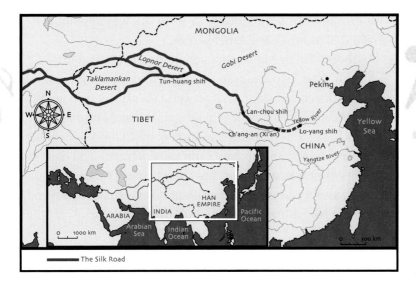

The Silk Road served as a trade route between China and the Mediterranean region for thousands of years.

120 adventurers, scientists, storytellers. Everything from algebra to Islam moved along the Silk Road. It's the local-global thing. In the cultural world, you want to make sure that voices don't get lost, that fabulously rich traditions continue to live, without becoming generic." Ma's Silk Road Project
125 has been called his "senior thesis, his grand unification, his Sistine Chapel."

Yo-Yo Ma founded the Silk Road Project to explore the musical currents of countries along the ancient Central Asian trade routes. His objective was to promote study of
130 the cultural, artistic, and intellectual traditions along the ancient Silk Road trade route, from the Mediterranean Sea to the Pacific Ocean.

One of Ma's life goals has been the exploration of music as communication and as a vehicle for the
135 migrations of ideas across cultures throughout the world. Ma says, "We live in a world of increasing awareness and interdependence, and I believe that music can act as a magnet to draw people together. . . . I'm seeking to join, to connect things that were not previously joined together:
140 from Bach to the Kalahari to music along the Silk Road, to country fiddling and the tango. . ." His large and diverse body of work is a testament to this idea. In recognition of

his cross-cultural diplomacy, in 2006 Ma was appointed a United Nations Peace Ambassador.

145   Today, Yo-Yo Ma is a household name. He and his wife, Jill, have two children, Nicholas and Emily. Jill and both children are musicians as well. Ma's life is full, with projects and goals beyond the imaginations of most people. Yo-Yo Ma's story includes a unique combination of prodigy,
150 celebrity, musicianship, and humanity. Recently, he has set dozens of new goals, exploring the worlds of folk, crossover music, and multimedia experimentation. This isn't the end of Yo-Yo Ma's life story. It's just getting good.

Excerpted with permission from "Yo-Yo Ma's Journeys" by Janet Tassel

Think About It

1. List reasons why Yo-Yo Ma's life is extraordinary.

2. Describe Yo-Yo Ma's father, Hiao-Tsiun.

3. Isaac Stern said that everybody noticed Ma's extraordinary talent, including his natural feel for being on stage, the way most people feel in their old clothes in their own living rooms. Analyze the meaning of Stern's statement. Why do you think some people are so comfortable, and others so ill at ease, on a stage?

4. What does Yo-Yo Ma say is the key to success for young people? Evaluate his statement. Is the key to success more complicated than he describes? Explain.

5. What is the Silk Road?

6. Cite any three of Yo-Yo Ma's life goals.

Young Playwright on Broadway:
Lorraine Hansberry's
A Raisin in the Sun

A Rave Review

New York City is world famous for the quality of its
theater productions. When a play opens on Broadway, a
playwright's dream comes true. That's what happened to
Lorraine Hansberry. Her play, *A Raisin in the Sun*, opened
5 on Broadway on March 11, 1959. But there was something
very different about this play. There was something very
different about its author. Hansberry was young, and she
was female. She was also African American. *A Raisin in
the Sun* was the first play by a black woman ever to be
10 produced on Broadway. *A Raisin in the Sun* became one of
the most highly regarded plays of all time.

Lorraine Hansberry.

    New York Times theater reviews are famous for making
or breaking a play. The famous theater critic, Brooks
Atkinson, wrote the play's first *New York Times* review. He
15 wrote:

    "In *A Raisin in the Sun*, which opened at the Ethel
Barrymore last evening, Lorraine Hansberry touches on
some serious problems. No doubt, her feelings about them
are as strong as anyone's.

20   But she has not tipped her play to prove one thing or
another. The play is honest. She has told the inner as well
as the outer truth about a Negro family in the South Side
of Chicago at the present time. Since the performance is
also honest and since Sidney Poitier is a candid actor, *A*

Raisin in the Sun has vigor as well as veracity and is likely to destroy the **complacency** of anyone who sees it.

complacency
satisfaction with the way things are

The family consists of a firm-minded widow, her daughter, her restless son, and his wife and son. The mother has brought up her family in a **tenement** that is small, battered but personable. All the mother wants is that her children adhere to the code of honor and self-respect that she inherited from her parents.

tenement
a low-rent and often rundown apartment building

The son is dreaming of success in a business deal. And the daughter, who is race-conscious, wants to become a physician and heal the wounds of her people. After a long delay the widow receives $10,000 as the premium on her husband's life insurance. The money projects the family into a series of situations that test their individual characters.

What the situations are does not matter at the moment. For *A Raisin in the Sun* is a play about human beings who want, on the one hand, to preserve their family pride and, on the other hand, to break out of the poverty that seems to be their fate. Not having any axe to grind, Miss Hansberry has a wide range of topics to write about—some of them hilarious, some of them painful in the extreme.

You might, in fact, regard *A Raisin in the Sun* as [an African-American] *The Cherry Orchard.*[1] Although the social scale of the characters is different, the knowledge of how character is controlled by environment is much the same, and the alternation of humor and **pathos** is similar.

pathos
a quality that brings out feelings of tenderness or sorrow

If there are occasional crudities in the craftsmanship, they are redeemed by the honesty of the writing. And also by the rousing honesty of the stage work. For Lloyd Richards has selected an admirable cast and directed a bold and stirring performance.

Mr. Poitier is a remarkable actor with enormous power that is always under control. Cast as the restless son, he

[1] In the play *The Cherry Orchard*, Anton Chekhov tells the story of the Ranevskaya family, and, in doing so portrays the major political, social, and economic shifts taking place in Russia at the beginning of the 20th century.

vividly communicates the tumult of a high-strung young
60 man. He is as **eloquent** when he has nothing to say
as when he has a pungent line to speak. He can convey
devious processes of thought as graphically as he can clown
and dance.

eloquent
movingly expressive

As the **matriarch**, Claudia McNeil gives a heroic
65 performance. Although the character is simple, Miss
McNeil gives it nobility of spirit. Diana Sands' amusing
portrait of the over-intellectualized daughter; Ivan Dixon's
quiet, sagacious student from Nigeria; Ruby Dee's young
wife burdened with problems; Louis Gossett's supercilious
70 suitor; John Fiedler's
timid white man, who
speaks sanctimonious
platitudes—bring variety
and excitement to a first-
75 rate performance.

matriarch
the female head of
a family or group

All the crises and
comic sequences take
place inside Ralph
Alswang's set, which
80 depicts both the poverty
and the taste of the family.
Like the play, it is honest.
That is Miss Hansberry's
personal contribution

A Raisin in the Sun
opened on Broadway in
1959 to rave reviews.

85 to an explosive situation in which simple honesty is the
most difficult thing in the world. And also the most
illuminating."

Raisin Plays On

More "firsts" awaited the young playwright. In 1959,
Lorraine Hansberry became the youngest playwright and
90 the first African American playwright to win the New York
Drama Critics Circle Award. She was the fifth woman and
the youngest American to ever have done so. (This award
was an even greater honor, knowing that two of America's
most celebrated playwrights, Eugene O'Neil and Tennessee

95 Williams, also had plays at that time on Broadway.) It was
ranked the best American play of the year.

Two years later, the play was turned into a film.
Hansberry wrote the screenplay for the film. For her
screenplay, she was nominated for the Screen Writers
100 Guild award. Then, in 1973, it became a musical, titled
Raisin. It won the Tony Award for the best musical of
1974. *A Raisin in the Sun* has been translated into over 30
different languages and is still produced on stages around
the country each year. Lorraine Hansberry has earned an
105 honored place in theater history.

Playing with the Title

Many theatergoers wondered about the play's title.
Where did Hansberry get the phrase "raisin in the sun"?
Half a century ago, many people were unfamiliar with great
literature composed by African Americans. Few outside
110 the black community knew the works of the brilliant
poet, Langston Hughes. Interestingly, when Hansberry
began to write this
play, she had titled
it "The Crystal
115 Stair," which is a
line from a different
Langston Hughes
poem—"Mother
to Son." Langston
120 Hughes' poetry sings
of the struggles of his
people. The phrase
"a raisin in the sun"
comes from his poem,
125 "Harlem," from his
poetry collection
*Montage of a Dream
Deferred*. Today,
things have changed.
130 Langston Hughes'
poems and Lorraine

Harlem
by Langston Hughes

What happens to a dream
deferred?

Does it dry up
like a raisin in the sun?
Or fester like a sore—
And then run?
Does it stink like
rotten meat?
Or crust and sugar over—
like a syrupy sweet?

Maybe it just sags
like a heavy load.

Or does it explode?

Hansberry's *A Raisin in the Sun* are recognized as great literature. Both are taught in schools and universities around the world.

The Playwright

135   On the night that *A Raisin in the Sun* opened on Broadway, Lorraine Hansberry must have thought about her journey. She was only 28 years old, and *this* was her first published play. Born in 1930 to a middle-class, African American family in Chicago, she was the youngest of four

140 siblings. Her father, Carl Hansberry, was a successful real estate broker. Her uncle was an African American scholar at Howard University. Many in her family were involved in civil rights. As a young girl, Lorraine had the opportunity to meet numerous famous African Americans of the time,

145 right in her parents' living room. Guests included the classical actor Paul Robeson, great jazz musician Duke Ellington, and Olympic gold medalist Jesse Owens.

When Hansberry was eight, her family moved into a home in an all-white neighborhood. At the time, Chicago

150 was a legally **segregated** city, so their arrival upset some of the neighbors. However, a lawsuit brought by Hansberry's father resulted in the end of Chicago's housing segregation laws. The Illinois Supreme court ruled that these discriminatory laws were unconstitutional. The experience

155 of living through this time influenced Hansberry.

segregated
divided or separated according to type

Hansberry attended the University of Wisconsin and studied art education. Later, she studied painting at the Art Institute of Chicago. In 1950, she moved to New York and worked at several different jobs—including reporting and

160 editing—while she continued to write plays and fiction. Before she finished her masterpiece, *A Raisin in the Sun*, she had written three plays and a novel.

After she had finished writing *A Raisin in the Sun*, Hansberry recalled that she could not quite believe what

165 she had accomplished. Later, in her autobiographical work, *To Be Young, Gifted and Black*, she described her feeling:

. . . I had turned the last page out of the typewriter
and pressed all the sheets neatly together in a pile, and
gone and stretched out face down on the living room floor.
170 *I had finished a play; a play I had no reason to think or*
not think would ever be done; a play that I was sure no one
would quite understand . . .

Hansberry began another play, *The Sign in Sidney*
Brustein's Window. Although it was less successful, it ran
175 on Broadway for over 100 performances. It closed on the
day of Hansberry's death, January 2, 1965. After a brief
illness, she died of cancer at the age of 35. These lines,
taken from her last play, adorn her tombstone:

I care. I care about it all. It takes too much energy not
180 *to care . . . the why of why we are here is an intrigue for*
adolescents; the how is what must command the living.

Adapted with permission from "Raisin in the Sun" by Vicki Hambleton

Think About It

1. Explain what the author means by ". . . reviews are famous for making or breaking a play."

2. What was unusual about Lorraine Hansberry writing this play?

3. Summarize Brooks Atkinson's review of "**A Raisin in the Sun**."

4. Explain why Lorraine Hansberry rewrote her play.

5. Explain how the play got its title. What was the source of the title?

6. List some reasons why Lorraine Hansberry was able to write a play that dealt with such difficult issues during that time period.

Join the Family

PlantFamilies

Imagine a tomato. Now imagine a potato. Did you know that these two common vegetables are cousins? This might sound weird, but it's true: plants have families, too. They're placed in families according to a "taxonomy." Taxonomy is
5 a system that organizes, classifies, and categorizes things. For scientists, taxonomies are very useful in helping them understand the natural world.

Scientists who study plants are called botanists. When examining a new kind of shrub, weed, or other plant,
10 botanists consider all parts. They ponder the stem, seeds, and flowers. They inspect the roots and overall structure. Some scientists also study plant genes on a microscopic level. What is their goal? They look for common features that will aid them in identifying a plant's "family tree."
15 A plant's flower often offers the best clues to its relatives. Flowers that are shaped like crosses might

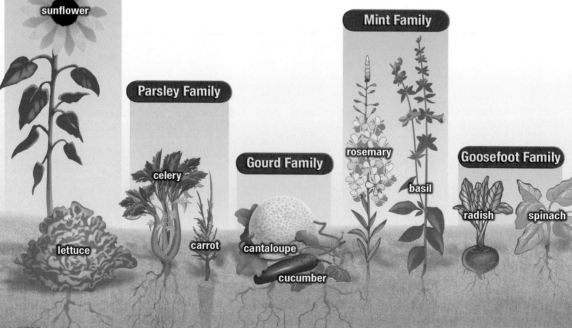

Sunflower Family — sunflower, lettuce

Parsley Family — celery, carrot

Gourd Family — cantaloupe, cucumber

Mint Family — rosemary, basil

Goosefoot Family — radish, spinach

indicate the *Cruciferae* or Cabbage family, for example. This scientific name comes from a word that means "cross."

20   It isn't always easy to spot plant cousins, however. As with human relatives, related plants don't always look alike. Think of a rose bush and an apple tree. Their appearances are very different, but these two plants are in the same family. Now, picture that potato again, and
25 compare it with a chili pepper. The potato grows below ground and has a mild flavor. The pepper grows above ground and tastes spicy. You guessed it—both belong to the same family.

Most vegetables belong to one of nine families. These
30 include the lily, mint, and pea families, as well as the gourd and goosefoot families. The parsley, sunflower, and cabbage families are vegetable families, too. Those chili peppers and potatoes are part of the ninth group—the nightshade family.

35   Go outside and look around. Even better, take a walk in the garden and look closely for plants with similar features. You might spot some family resemblances!

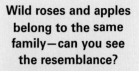

Wild roses and apples belong to the same family—can you see the resemblance?

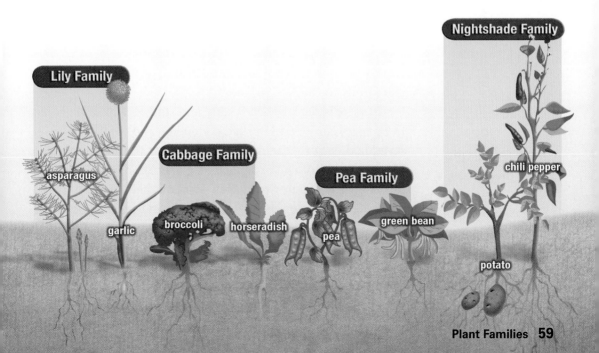

Nightshade Family

Lily Family

Cabbage Family

Pea Family

asparagus

garlic

broccoli

horseradish

pea

green bean

chili pepper

potato

A Family in Hiding:

Anne Frank's Diary

Anne Frank with her family.

Anne Frank started writing her diary when she was 13 years old.

Anne Frank was born on June 12, 1929, in Frankfurt, Germany. Her father, Otto Frank, was a respected businessman. For Anne and her older sister, Margot, the world of early childhood was a secure place inhabited
5 by loving parents and relatives. Beyond their family's comfortable home, though, the world was becoming increasingly unpleasant.

By 1933, the Nazi movement had gained control of the German government. Adolf Hitler became the chancellor
10 of Germany. Freedom of speech and assembly were suspended, and the Nazi government decreed a boycott of Jewish businesses. Because of these increasing tensions in Germany and the fact that the Frank family was Jewish, Anne's father decided it would be best to move his business
15 and family to the Netherlands.

In 1939, Hitler invaded Poland and started World War II. By 1940, Nazi Germany had conquered and controlled several other European countries, including the Netherlands. The Nazi government expanded its persecution of Jews. It
20 made Jewish citizens wear yellow stars on their clothing and began deporting them and others from these countries to concentration camps. The Holocaust[1]—the systematic destruction of Europe's Jews—gained momentum.

---

[1] The word "Holocaust" comes from the Greek word, *holokauston*, meaning "a sacrifice burned by fire." It refers to the destruction of the Jewish citizens in Europe during the Nazi regime. Over 6 million Jewish people along with many others were killed during World War II.

The Frank family was no longer safe. In 1942, Anne
25 celebrated her thirteenth birthday in Amsterdam with her
family. She received a diary as a birthday present. A few
weeks later, Anne, her parents, and her older sister were
forced into hiding. They moved into a secret annex of a
warehouse that was part of her father's factory.
30   While in hiding, Anne Frank wrote in her diary about
everything that happened to her and her family. She was a
girl who was experiencing all the emotions and conflicts of
a typical teenager, but she was doing so under very difficult
circumstances. Her family and four others lived for 25
35 months in cramped quarters, worrying every day about the
progress of the war and about what would happen to them
if they were discovered.
      These excerpts from her diary reveal some of Anne
Frank's feelings about her family and the events going on
40 around her.

Saturday, June 20, 1942

      Writing in a diary is a really strange experience for
someone like me. Not only because I've never written
anything before, but also because it seems to me that
later on neither I nor anyone else will be interested in the
45 **musings** of a thirteen-year-old schoolgirl. Oh well, it
doesn't matter. I feel like writing and I have an even greater
need to get all kinds of things off my chest. . . .
      My father, the most adorable father I've ever seen,
didn't marry my mother until he was thirty-six and she was
50 twenty-five. My sister Margot was born in Frankfurt-am-
Main in Germany in 1926. I was born on June 12, 1929. I
lived in Frankfurt until I was four. Because we're Jewish, my
father immigrated to Holland in 1933, when he became the
Managing Director of the Dutch Opteka Company. . . .
55   Our lives were not without anxiety since our relatives
in Germany were suffering under Hitler's anti-Jewish laws.
. . . In 1938 my two uncles (my mother's brothers) fled
Germany, finding safe refuge in North America. My elderly

musings
deep thoughts

grandmother came to live with us. She was seventy-three
60 years old at the time. . . . Grandma died in January 1942.
No one knows how often I think of her and still love her. . . .

**On July 5, Anne's sister, Margot, received a call-up to
be sent to a labor camp. The next day the Frank family
went into hiding in the Secret Annex. They were helped
65 by friends, who brought them food and news from the
outside. A week later, they were joined by another Jewish
family, Mr. and Mrs. van Daan and their fifteen-year-old
son, Peter. The seven of them, living so closely together,
became an extended family.**

Friday, August 21, 1942

70   Now our Secret Annex has truly become secret. . . . Mr.
Kugler thought it would be better to have a bookcase built
in front of the entrance to our hiding place. It swings out
on its hinges and opens like a door. . . .
        There's little change in our lives here. Peter's hair was
75 washed today, but that's nothing special. Mr. van Daan
and I are always at loggerheads with each other. Mama
always treats me like a baby, which I can't stand. For the
rest, things are going better. I don't think Peter's gotten any
nicer. He's an obnoxious boy who lies around on his bed
80 all day, only rousing himself to do a little carpentry work
before returning to his nap. . . .
        Mama gave me another one of her dreadful sermons
this morning. We take the opposite view of everything.
Daddy's a sweetheart. He may get mad at me, but it never
85 lasts longer than five minutes.

Friday, October 9, 1942

        Today I have nothing but dismal and depressing news
to report. Our many Jewish friends and acquaintances
are being taken away in droves. The Gestapo is treating
them very roughly and transporting them in cattle cars

90　to Westerbork. . . . It must be terrible in Westerbork. The
　　people get almost nothing to eat, much less to drink, as water
　　is available only one hour a day, and there's only one toilet
　　and sink for several thousand people. Men and women sleep
　　in the same room, and women and children often have their
95　heads shaved. Escape is almost impossible. Many people look
　　Jewish, and they're branded by their shorn heads.
　　　　　If it's that bad in Holland, what must it be like in those
　　faraway and **uncivilized** places where the Germans are
　　sending them? We assume that most of them are
100　being murdered. . . .

uncivilized
barbarous; primitive

　　　　**On November 16, Mr. Fritz Pfeffer joined the
　　others in the Secret Annex. (Anne changed his name
　　to Albert Dussel in her diary.) He became the last
　　member of this secret family.**

Thursday, November 19, 1942

105　　　Just as we thought, Mr. Dussel is a very nice man.
　　. . . The first day Mr. Dussel was here he asked me all
　　sorts of questions—for example, what time the cleaning
　　lady comes to the office, how we've arranged to use the
　　washroom, and when we're allowed to go to the toilet.
110　You may laugh, but these things aren't so easy in a
　　hiding place. During the daytime we can't make any
　　noise that might be heard downstairs. And when
　　someone else is there, like the cleaning lady, we have
　　to be extra careful. . . .

Saturday, November 28, 1942

115　　　Mr. Dussel, the man who was said to get along so
　　well with children and absolutely adore them, has turned
　　out to be an old-fashioned disciplinarian and preacher
　　of unbearably long sermons on manners. . . . Since I am
　　generally considered to be the worst behaved of the three
120　young people, it's all I can do to avoid having the same

old scoldings and admonitions repeatedly flung at my head and pretend not to hear. This wouldn't be so bad if Mr. Dussel weren't such a tattletale and hadn't singled out Mother to be the **recipient** of his reports. If Mr.
125 Dussel's just read me the riot act, Mother lectures me all over again, this time throwing the whole book at me. And if I'm really lucky, Mrs. van D. calls me to account five minutes later and lays down the law as well!

Really, it is not easy being the badly brought-up center
130 of attention in a family of nit-pickers. . . .

recipient

one who receives

Friday, February 5, 1943

. . . Margot and Peter aren't exactly what you'd call "young"; they're both so quiet and boring. Next to them, I stick out like a sore thumb and I am always being told, "Margot and Peter don't act that way. Why don't you follow
135 your sister's example!" I hate that.

I confess that I have absolutely no desire to be like Margot. She is too weak-willed and **passive** to suit me; she lets herself be swayed by others and always backs down under pressure. I want to have more spunk! But I keep ideas
140 like these to myself. They'd only laugh at me if I offered this in my defense.

passive

accepting without struggle

Monday Evening, November 8, 1943

I see the eight of us in the Annex as if we were a patch of blue sky surrounded by menacing clouds. The perfectly round spot on which we're standing is still safe, but the
145 clouds are moving in on us, and the ring between us and the approaching danger is being pulled tighter and tighter. We're surrounded by darkness and danger, and in our desperate search for a way out, we keep bumping into each other. We look at the fighting down below and the peace
150 and beauty up above. In the meantime, we've been cut off by the dark mass of clouds, so that we can go neither up nor down. It looms before us like an impenetrable wall, trying to crush us, but not yet able to. I can only cry out and implore, "Oh ring, ring, open wide and let us out!"

Friday, December 24, 1943

155 . . . Believe me, if you've been shut up for a year and
a half, it can get to be too much for you sometimes.
But feelings can't be ignored, no matter how unjust or
ungrateful they seem. I long to ride a bike, dance, whistle,
look at the world, feel young and know that I'm free, and
160 yet I can't let it show. Just imagine what would happen if all
eight of us were to feel sorry for ourselves or walk around
with the discontent clearly visible on our faces. Where
would that get us? . . .

Sunday, January 2, 1944

This morning, when I had nothing to do, I leafed
165 through the pages of my diary and came across so many
letters dealing with the subject "Mother" in such strong
terms that I was shocked. I said to myself: "Anne, is that
really you talking about hate? Oh, Anne, how could you?". . .

Wednesday Evening, January 19, 1944

. . . You know that I always used to be jealous of
170 Margot's relationship with Father. There's not a trace of my
jealousy left now. I still feel hurt when Father's nerves cause
him to be unreasonable toward me, but then I think, "I
can't blame you for being the way you are. You talk so much
about the minds of children and adolescents but you don't
175 know the first thing about them!". . .

Saturday, March 11, 1944

I haven't been able to sit still lately. I wander upstairs
and down and then back again. I like talking to Peter, but
I'm always afraid of being a nuisance. He's told me a bit
about the past, about his parents and about himself, but
180 it's not enough, and every five minutes I wonder why I find
myself longing for more. He used to think I was a real pain
in the neck, and the feeling was mutual. I've changed my
mind, but how do I know he's changed his? I think he has,
but that doesn't necessarily mean we have to become the
185 best of friends, although, as far as I am concerned, it would

make the time here more bearable. But I won't let this drive me crazy. . . .

Friday, March 17, 1944

    . . . For both of us [Anne and Margot], it's been quite a blow to suddenly realize that very little remains of the close
190 and **harmonious** family we used to be at home! This is mostly because everything's out of kilter here. By that I mean that we're treated like children when it comes to external matters, while, inwardly, we're much older than other girls our age. Even though I'm only fourteen, I know what I
195 want. I know who's right and who's wrong. I have my own opinions, ideas, and principles. And though it may sound odd coming from a teenager, I feel I'm more of a person than a child—I feel I'm completely independent of others. . . .

harmonious

working well together

Friday, March 24, 1944

    I often go up to Peter's room after dinner nowadays
200 to breathe in the fresh evening air. You can get around to meaningful conversations more quickly in the dark than with the sun tickling your face. It's cozy and snug sitting beside him on a chair and looking outside. The van Daans and Dussel make the silliest remarks when I disappear into
205 his room. . . . "Is it proper for a gentleman to receive young girls in his room at night. . .?" Peter has amazing presence of mind in the face of these so-called witticisms. My Mother, incidentally, is also bursting with curiosity and simply dying to ask what we talk about, only she's secretly afraid I'd refuse
210 to answer. Peter says that grown-ups are just jealous because we're young and that we shouldn't take their obnoxious comments to heart. . . .

Tuesday, April 11, 1944

    . . . None of us have ever been in such danger as we were that night. . . . Just think—the police were right at the
215 bookcase, the light was on, and still no one had discovered our hiding place! "Now, we're done for!" I'd whispered at that moment, but once again we were spared. . . .

I'm becoming more and more independent of my parents. Young as I am, I face life with more courage and have a better and truer sense of justice than Mother. I know what I want. I have a goal. I have opinions. . . . If only I can be myself, I'll be satisfied. I know that I'm a woman, a woman with inner strength and a great deal of courage.

Saturday, July 15, 1944

. . . So if you're wondering whether it's harder for the adults here than for the children, the answer is no. It's certainly not. Older people have an opinion about everything and are sure of themselves and their actions. It's twice as hard for us young people to hold on to our opinions at a time when ideals are being shattered and destroyed, when the worst side of human nature **predominates** . . . .

It's utterly impossible for me to build my life on a foundation of chaos, suffering, and death. I see the world being slowly transformed into a wilderness, I hear the approaching thunder that, one day, will destroy us too. I feel the suffering of millions. And yet, when I look up at the sky, I somehow feel that everything will change for the better, that this cruelty too will end, that peace and tranquility will return once more. In the meantime, I must hold on to my ideals. Perhaps the day will come when I'll be able to realize them.

predominates
has control over; overpowers

Tuesday, August 1, 1944, is the date of the last entry in Anne Frank's diary. On August 4, 1944, Gestapo officers and Dutch members of the Security Police arrested the eight people hiding in the Secret Annex and brought them to a prison in Amsterdam. They were then transferred to Westerbork, a transport camp for Jews. They

Auschwitz concentration camp in Poland.

were deported on September 3, 1944, on the last transport
to leave Westerbork. Three days later they arrived at the
Auschwitz concentration camp in Poland. The men and
255 women were separated. Margot and Anne were transferred
to Bergen-Belsen, another concentration camp in Germany.
A typhus epidemic broke out there in the winter of 1944–
45. Both Margot and Anne became ill and died that March.
Less than a month later, on April 2, 1945, the camp was
260 liberated by British troops.

Of the eight who had hidden in the Secret Annex, only
Anne's father, Otto Frank, survived the concentration
camps. A family friend had saved Anne's diary and
gave it to him. He published the first edition in 1947.
265 Anne Frank's *The Diary of a Young Girl* has since been
translated into 67 languages. It is one of the most widely
read books in the world.

Excerpted with permission from *The Diary of a Young Girl:
The Definitive Edition* by Anne Frank, edited by Otto H. Frank and
Mirjam Pressler, translated by Susan Massotty

Answer It

1. Judge why it is important for Anne to write in a diary.

2. Judge whether the Franks should have hid in the attic.

3. Critique Anne's initial impression of Mr. Dussel.

4. Assess why it would be important for all of the
people living in the attic to get along with each other.

5. Justify Anne's reasons for not wanting to be like
Margot.

6. Make a generalization about the type of person Anne
was becoming.

MY SIDE OF THE STORY

BY ADAM BAGDASARIAN

I was sitting at my desk in my bedroom practicing my signature when my brother came in and asked me if I wanted to throw the ball around or shoot baskets.

"No," I said. So he looked over my shoulder at the
5 signatures, went into the bathroom for a few seconds, came out, went to his own desk, unraveled an entire roll of Scotch tape and stuck it on my head.

Naturally, I was outraged. "What did you do that for?" I asked. It was a stupid question because I knew very well
10 why he had done it. He had done it for the same reason he had stuffed me in the laundry hamper and tied me to a chair with my best ties. He had done it because he was fourteen and had the great good fortune to be blessed with a little brother he could **bedevil** at will.

15 "Try to get it off," he said.

This I attempted to do, but he had rubbed the Scotch tape so hard into my scalp that it had become a part of my head.

"Let me try," he said.

bedevil
to torment; annoy

justice

fairness; rightness

righteous

guiltless; morally
justified

20   So he tried, and I yowled, and he stopped. Then he
gently pulled a piece of the Scotch tape off the side of my
head, along with six or seven of my temple hairs.
      Even at the age of nine I knew that I had been mightily
wronged; even at nine I knew that this violated every code
25 of **justice** and fair play that I had ever been taught. And so,
my heart full of **righteous** rage and indignation, I leaped
out of my chair, past my brother, in search of justice.
      In those days justice looked a good deal like my mother.
It had lovely brown hair, a warm enchanting smile, and
30 a soft, understanding voice. It was comforting to know
that in a matter of seconds my mother would hear the
evidence, weigh the evidence, and punish my brother.
Generally, things were murkier. Generally, I did something
by accident, then my brother did something back, and I
35 did something back, and on and on until it was impossible
to tell who was at fault. But this—this was the case of a
lifetime. And the best part of all was that the evidence was
stuck to my head.
      When I reached my mother's room, I saw that the door
40 was closed. For a moment I hesitated, wondering if she was
sleeping, but I was so sure of my case, so convinced of the
general rightness of my mission that I threw open the door
and burst into the room screaming, "Mom! Mom! Skip
put—"
45   And then I realized that I was talking to my father, not
my mother.
      In order to understand the **enormity** of the mistake
I had made, you have to understand my father. My father
was five feet seven and a half inches tall, stocky, powerfully
50 built, and larger than life in laughter, strength, character,
integrity, humor, appetite, wit, intelligence, warmth,
curiosity, generosity, magnetism, insight, and rage.
Consequently, he was not concerned with the little things
in life, such as sibling shenanigans, rivalries, or disputes.
55 His job, as he saw it, was to make us the best human beings
we could possibly be—to guide us, love us, and teach us
the large laws of honor, courage, honesty, and self-reliance.
He was the only man to turn to if you had a severed artery,

enormity

outrageousness;
vastness

integrity

honesty; faithfulness
to a code of good
conduct

broken ribs, or any serious disease or financial problems,
60 but he was not the kind of man one would knowingly burst
in upon screaming anything less than "The house is on
fire!" or "Somebody stole your car!"

I knew this, of course, which is why I had run to my
mother's room in the first place, and why, when I saw my
65 father, most of the color drained from my face. My first
impulse was to walk backward out of the room, closing
the door gently before me as I did so, but I had shifted so
suddenly from offensive indignation to defensive fear and
astonishment that I felt a little **disoriented**. For a moment
70 I considered telling him that I smelled smoke or saw
someone stealing his car, but I couldn't lie. I couldn't tell
the truth, either. In fact, for a moment, I couldn't speak.

"What on earth are you doing?" my father said.

I started to say, "I was sitting at my desk minding
75 my own business, when—" and I stopped. I stopped
because I knew instinctively that Scotch tape on my head
was not enough, not nearly enough to warrant my wild,
unannounced entrance into this room.

"When what?"

80   "Nothing."

"You ran in here screaming about something. What
happened?"

"I didn't . . ."

"You didn't what?"

85   "I didn't know you were here."

"So what! You knew someone was here! What did
Skip do?"

"Skip . . . uh. I was sitting at my desk, and Skip . . ."

"Skip what? Tell me!"

90   "Put Scotch tape on my head."

This apparently was all my father needed to set the
wheels of his anger in motion.

"You came running in here without knocking because
Skip put Scotch tape on your head?"

95   "No, I—"

"You didn't care that the door was closed? You didn't
care that your mother might have been sleeping?"

disoriented

confused;
bewildered

I wanted to explain to him that this had been going on
for years, that Mom and Skip and I had an understanding,
100 but I knew that we weren't having a discussion. I also knew
that he was working himself into a rage and that anything I
said would only make it worse.

"Is that what you do? You run into rooms screaming?"
He was on his feet now and advancing toward me. "You
105 don't knock?"

"No. Yes."

At this point my brother entered the room, saw what
was happening, and stood transfixed.

"Here!" my father said. "Here's what we do with Scotch
110 tape!" And with that he pulled the whole wad off my head,
along with fifty or sixty of my hairs.

I knew that he was only a few seconds away from his
closing arguments now, and my calculations were just
about right.

115   "You don't *ever* come in here without knocking! Do you
hear me?" my father bellowed. Silence. "Do you hear . . ."

At this point I heard a wheeze of escaping laughter
where my brother was standing, and saw him run out of
the room.

120   "Do you?"

"Yes, Pop, yes. I hear you."

"Are you ever going to come in here without knocking again?"

"No, no."

125   "Ever!"

"No."

"Now get out of here!"

And I got out and heard the door slam behind me.

There was not much to do after that but sit at my desk
130 and wonder what had happened. I had been signing my
name, Skip put Scotch tape on my head, I ran to tell Mom,
found Pop, and the lights went out. Where, I wondered,
was the justice in that? Obviously, when I burst into my
mother's room, I had entered a larger world of justice, a
135 world where screaming, whining, mother dependence, not
knocking on closed doors, and startling one's father were
serious crimes. That part I understood. The part I didn't
understand was the part about why my brother, who had
started the whole thing by putting Scotch tape on my
140 head, hadn't been punished. So, in the interest of a smaller
justice, I went over to his trophy shelf, picked up one of
his baseball trophies, and gradually wrested the little gold-
plated athlete off its mount.

With a little luck, my brother would want to tell Pop
145 about it.

Reprinted by permission of Farrar, Straus and Giroux, LLC

Answer It

1. Explain what the author meant when he wrote, "In those days, justice looked a good deal like my mother."

2. Explain why Adam thought he had "a case of a lifetime."

3. Describe some of the characteristics of Adam's father.

4. Assess how the story would have been different if the mother had been in the room instead of the father.

5. Make a judgment about which character caused the problem in this story.

Bringing Up BABY

Family Life in the Animal World

At some point in your life, an adult has probably
forbidden you from doing something or going somewhere,
explaining, "You just aren't old enough, yet!" That phrase,
reiterated by parents everywhere, can certainly be
5 annoying. However, there are valid reasons for parents
to evaluate their children's maturity before giving them
permission to jump into what might be a risky situation.

Among all animals, human beings take the longest time
to reach maturity—to achieve adulthood and independence.
10 That's because human babies and children have a tremendous
amount to learn before they can function on their own in
the world. In contrast, some members of the animal world
are ready for independence the moment they are born. Read
on to find out what "childhood" means to different kinds of
15 creatures and what family life is like for them.

You're On Your Own, Baby!

An eight-inch alligator hatches from an egg in a Florida
swamp. With the exception of its yellow markings, the baby
looks exactly like its parents—a miniature adult alligator.
From that moment on, the alligator is almost completely
20 on its own. Its mother's job is to protect the eggs from
predators, and she may defend the babies after they hatch.

However, the baby alligator already possesses the instincts and skills it needs to survive. Many animal babies are like the alligator. They do not necessarily need the protection
25 and nurturing of a parent. They are born with an **innate** ability for surviving in their environment.

Like alligators, most insects hatch ready to crawl out on their own. Even insects that develop through several stages of **metamorphosis** on the way to adulthood don't usually
30 need a parent to help them through the process. A female fly will simply lay her eggs in a safe spot and abandon them there, for example. She usually deposits those eggs, though, near a food supply. That way the baby bugs can eat immediately after emerging.

35 Most snakes, too, are ready to wriggle into the world as soon as they hatch. That's why a group of researchers were puzzled when they observed female black-tailed rattlesnakes in Arizona staying protectively near their young for nine days. The scientists speculated that the
40 mothers were waiting for the young snakes to shed their skin. Until these babies shed the opaque skin that covers their eyes, their vision is poor. Once the young snakes shed that skin and can see, the mother considers them old enough to fend for themselves. At that point she
45 unceremoniously slithers from the area.

Not So Fast

Some animal babies, though, come into the world with a lot to learn. In many species, parents must teach their young the skills they need to survive. Bears, lions, gorillas, and humans all go through a long period of **maturation**. In
50 order to live independently, they must learn how to obtain food, defend themselves, and relate to other members of their own species. These animals would die if left entirely to their own devices as youngsters. They need time to grow, as well as nurturing by their parents, in order to reach
55 adulthood.

Polar bear cubs are born with a very thin coat of fur in a snow den during the Arctic winter. This might seem like a particularly harsh entrance into a **frigid** world.

innate
natural; possessed at birth

metamorphosis
a change; transformation

maturation
the process of becoming fully grown

frigid
extremely cold

Bringing Up Baby: Family Life in the Animal World 75

The small cubs, however, never come into contact with
60 the sub-zero conditions outside the den. Their mother's
belly provides a place to sleep, eat, and stay toasty warm.
When they do venture into the world outside, the mother
bear keeps her babies away from male polar bears, who
sometimes attack and kill cubs. When spring comes, she
65 teaches her cubs how to hunt for seals and other animals.
Most polar bear cubs stay with their mothers until they are
two or three years old, have developed adequate hunting
skills, and have grown large enough to protect themselves
from the aggression of older bears.
70   Lion cubs are born blind and completely helpless.
When a lion mother goes to hunt, she skillfully hides her
young in tall grass. After about two months, the lion cubs
can accompany their mother wherever she goes. At this
point, a mother and her cubs usually rejoin the mother's
75 pride, or family of lions. Lion cubs begin to participate in
hunting by 11 months of age. However, they cannot survive
independently until their second year of life. Male cubs
are usually forced to leave the pride when they are about
three years old, and do not join a group again until they are
80 adults, at about age five.
    Gorilla babies are also born totally helpless. Mothers
carry their newborns in their arms for the first two or three
months of life. A young gorilla sleeps in its mother's nest
and rides around on her back. Until the age of four, baby

*A baby gorilla rides
on its mother's back.*

85 gorillas depend on their mothers and other adults in the group for all their needs.

A human being takes longer than any other animal to reach maturity. Childhood for humans lasts for 12 to 14 years. Scientists estimate that it would take about nine
90 years for a child to learn how to survive in the wilderness. More time, though, is needed for the child to learn the skills required for living in a complex social group. In fact, although most humans reach physical maturity by the age of 18 to 20 or so, many do not leave home until they are older.
95 For human adults, survival means much more than just knowing where to find food. Young people must also learn how to interact with other members of their communities. Learning to walk and talk, going to school, and acquiring life skills and job skills are just some of the
100 many tasks human youngsters must accomplish. Like polar bears, lions, and gorillas, humans are not born with the instincts, strength, or abilities to survive without assistance from their parents. As a rule, humans need the advice and support of many people to achieve full maturity.

Which Parent Does the Work?

105 In most animal families, females are the main caregivers for the young. In some animal species, however, the father enthusiastically takes on this role. After a female emperor penguin lays an egg in Antarctica, the male penguin begins to incubate it, keeping it warm for 60 days.
110 He rests the egg on his feet, covers it with a flap of skin, and does not move from the egg—not even to eat! When the chick hatches, the father finally excuses himself to eat a large fishy meal. But then he quickly returns to care for the chick, helping the mother feed it for the next six months.
115 The male unarmored threespine stickleback, a type of fish, also has fabulous fatherly instincts. In the spring, this stickleback male labors to create the perfect "nursery." After finding a sandy location in shallow water, he digs an **elaborate** nest. He lines the nest with water plants and
120 algae and then cements the walls with a sticky material produced by his kidneys. After he carves out a tunnel for

An emperor penguin father helps the mother take care of the baby for six months.

elaborate

highly detailed; complex

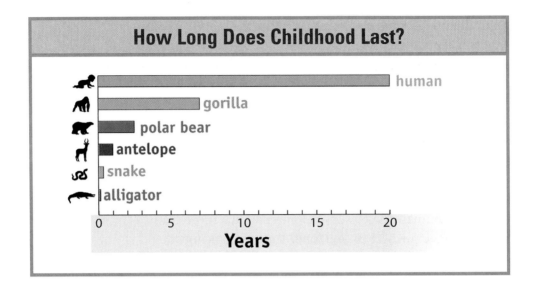

How Long Does Childhood Last?

human

gorilla

polar bear

antelope

snake

alligator

0 5 10 15 20

Years

entering and exiting the nest, he is finally ready to breed. He undergoes a color change from dull gray to brilliant dark green and orange-red. He uses this spectacular
125 coloration to attract a female fish to his nest, where she lays eggs. He then chases her away and fertilizes the eggs.

For the next seven days, the male guards the eggs. He cleans them with his mouth and circulates water over them by fanning them with his tail. Once the eggs hatch,
130 he continues to guard the babies for several weeks. He dutifully herds the baby fish to keep them together. If another male stickleback, or anything bearing the color red, appears, he may suck the babies protectively into his mouth to guard them from danger.
135 For some creatures, "family" doesn't just mean mom or dad—it includes the entire community. Wolves, gorillas, and elephants are all animals that raise their young collectively, as a group. Baby elephants are raised in family groups led by a female called the matriarch. All of the adult
140 females in the group look out for the elephant babies. As the youngsters grow, they become big sisters or big brothers who help raise the young.

Many insects have no family life, but there are a few exceptions. Ants, termites, and a few kinds of bees are
145 social insects. They live together in a community in which

each insect has a job, and all of the community members depend on each other for survival. Young honeybees spend 6 to 24 days in a special bee nursery. There, older bees feed the worm-shaped larvae a mixture of honey and pollen.

150 The young bees chew their way out of the wax cells once they have grown into adults. They spend the rest of their lives doing their assigned jobs for the hive.

Clearly, the length of time it takes living creatures to grow up and gain independence varies greatly. Family life 155 also differs from one animal species to the next. However, one thing is true for all creatures: most parents do their best to give their offspring what they need for survival, no matter how little or how much that may be.

Think About It

1. Why do some animals need to be raised by their parents?

2. Compare the responsibilities of a mother alligator to the responsibilities of a mother fly.

3. Explain why scientists think female black-tailed rattlesnakes stay near their young for nine days.

4. Describe the sacrifice that the male emperor penguin makes for his young.

5. How are elephants and bees similar?

6. Reread the last paragraph of the selection. Assess the generalization the author makes about animal and human parents.

Who Cares About Great-Uncle Edgar?

We come across an old family photograph. The photo is in black and white. It's faded and cracked. The person in the picture stands stiffly against a background of drapes, plants, and fancy furniture.

5   This old-fashioned studio portrait was taken in the early 1900s. Who is this person in the picture? Is it your great-grandfather's brother? He was the first member of the family to become a famous brain surgeon. He was fondly and respectfully known as Great-Uncle Edgar. Or is

10 it your great-grandfather himself, the most studious boy in his class? He had to drop out of school to work and never fulfilled his dream of becoming a brilliant lawyer.

Possibly you are wondering why you should even care about your ancestors. Your great-grandparents may

15 have died before you were born. Or, if they are alive, they may live in a distant place. The same may be true of your grandparents.

These days, it's easy to lose touch even with our own parents. They may have separated. They may be divorced.

20 One or both of them may have remarried. We may find ourselves part of a stepfamily, with a whole new set of

relatives. Or possibly we are being raised by just one parent or by our grandparents. Many young Americans today, though, can't even *name* all four of their parents' parents.

Yet, whether we know our ancestors or not, we are each a link in a human chain. We share our genes—the tiny units in our body's cells that are responsible for **inherited** traits—with our ancestors. And we'll pass on new combinations of these traits to our children and our children's children.

inherited
passed from parent to child

The word *genealogy* means the study of family lines of descent. It is related to the word *gene*. Our genes are what determine certain traits. Genes determine the color of our eyes and hair. Genes determine the shape of our bodies. They also determine the special workings of our brains. Genes are what give us our inborn talent for music, science, or sports. Even certain diseases, how long we will live, and what we will eventually die of may be traceable to our genes.

Scientists believe that there may be as many as 3,500 inherited, or genetic, diseases. Some are as mild as a mere tendency toward hay fever. Others are as serious as hemophilia. This disease is caused by the blood's failure to clot and can lead to uncontrollable bleeding from even a tiny cut or scrape. In many cases, healthy parents are the carriers of the disease-causing genes. Death in infancy or early childhood can result from genetic abnormalities passed on by healthy parents.

On a happier note, we can also inherit a trait such as great musical talent from our ancestors. An amazing example is found in the family of the famous composer Johann Sebastian Bach. Bach's earliest-known musical ancestor was born in the late 1500s. Forty out of sixty of this ancestor's descendants, many of whom lived during the 1700s, became accomplished musicians!

Heredity –the Bach "bloodline"—was an important factor in producing so much musical talent. But was it the only reason? The Bach family's children all grew up in strongly disciplined households. Music was at the center of family life. These surroundings helped their inborn abilities

heredity
the passing of genetic traits from generation to generation

60 to blossom. Similar abilities in children who were not
    exposed to music may have withered because their talents
    were never encouraged.

    In other words, our home, our schooling, and the time
    and place in which we live are all important influences
65 on how we develop. They form part of what we call our
    "environment." It isn't only sharing certain genes that leads
    to similarities among family members. We often are alike
    because of our shared experiences.

    Adopted children, for example, may be closer in

mannerisms

distinct behaviors

70 **mannerisms**, attitudes, and even appearance to their
    adoptive family than to their natural, or biological, family.
    They "take after" their adoptive parents to whom they
    have no "blood" ties. This may be due to their close family
    environment.

75 Does heredity or environment link us more closely to
    our ancestors? The answer is probably a combination of the
    two. You may grow up to have the tall, broad-shouldered
    build of your great-great-grandfather. That's heredity.
    On the other hand, when your ancestors came to North
80 America, this changed their environment significantly. It
    changed yours as well.

    Who were the very first people to keep records of
    their family lines? Why did they keep track? People have
    been searching for their "roots" and constructing their
85 "family trees" since earliest times. They have done so out of
    curiosity. They have done so out of a sense of family pride.

inheritance

property received
upon someone's
death

    And, often, they wish to establish **inheritance** claims.
    According to many traditions, rights to rulership, land
    holdings, and other possessions have been handed down
90 from parent to child.

    Even before they kept written records, many peoples
    relied on oral history to recall their ancestors. This was
    true among the ancient Scandinavians, Irish, Scots, and
    Welsh. Storytellers and poet-singers known as bards passed
95 on the names and heroic deeds of earlier generations to
    younger members of the clan or tribe. They wanted these
    stories to be memorized for safekeeping. We think of a
    generation as the time span between *our* being born and

the birth of our children—usually twenty-five to thirty
100 years. But there have been—and still are—peoples among
whom a new generation is produced as often as every
fifteen to twenty years.

Among certain Africans, Indonesians, and Pacific
Islanders, oral history is still very much alive. In recent
105 times, a chieftain of the Maori, the Polynesian people native
to New Zealand, recited a thirty-four-generation history
of his people. He did so as a claim to the inheritance of a
certain piece of land in that country. His recital was said to
have taken three days!

110 Oral history endures, of course, only as long as it
is both remembered and retold. In 1966, a group of
high school English students in Rabun Gap, Georgia,
interviewed the neighboring Appalachian mountain people.
Many, in fact, were older members of the students' own
115 families. Under the guidance of their teacher, the students
published a magazine called *Foxfire*. It contained the
spoken rememberings of the mountain dwellers.

As the wealth of material grew, the magazine developed
into a numbered series of best-selling *Foxfire* books. These
120 books covered traditional crafts and skills—from banjo
making to bear hunting. They contained stories, songs, and
other mountain lore. *Foxfire* not only preserved
the rich **heritage** of a fast-disappearing segment
of American life. It also enriched the young
125 people who collected the folkways of the southern
Appalachians.

Probably the most famous personal experience
with oral history in our time is the one that Alex
Haley wrote about in his book *Roots: The Saga of*
130 *an American Family*. Published in 1976, Haley's
story described what he learned as a result of his
successful search for his African ancestry.

Haley's first slave ancestor, as revealed in
Roots, was a man named Kunta Kinte. He had
135 been brought to America in the 1760s. During
Haley's childhood years, his grandmother had told
him stories she had heard as a child about a man

heritage
beliefs, history, and cultural traditions passed from one generation to the next

Author Alex Haley
published Roots *in 1976.*

called "Kintay." He had been kidnapped by slavers near the "Kamby Bolongo" in Africa and taken by ship to a place
140 called "Naplis" in the United States. There he was sold to a plantation owner who brought him to work in Virginia, under the slave name of Toby.

The spoken memories of Haley's grandmother made a deep impression on him. As a grown man, he began a
145 twelve-year search for his roots. "Naplis," he discovered, was Annapolis, a port city in Maryland. The "Kamby Bolongo" was the Gambia River in the West African country of Gambia. Haley learned that there were tribal historians in Gambia known as *griots*. He traveled to that country. There,
150 a *griot* recited for Haley the history of his family, the Kinte clan. The *griot* traced the line all the way back to the time of Kunta Kinte's grandfather in the early 1700s.

The people who kept the first written records of their ancestry were probably the ancient Egyptians and Chinese.
155 Such records were especially important to the wealthier classes in these civilizations because they had the most to gain through inheritance. At the very top of the heap were the royal families, known as dynasties. Dynasties ruled in both Egypt and China for thousands of years. Enormous
160 power and untold wealth were passed on to the members of those noble family lines.

Among the Chinese, the common people, too, kept detailed family records. This was because the devotion of sons to fathers and the worship of ancestors were
165 important parts of the teachings of Confucius. Confucius was a Chinese philosopher who lived twenty-five hundred years ago. Confucianism spread through all levels of Chinese society. Even the poorest homes had altars inscribed with the names of ancestors. It was the duty
170 of the eldest son in the family to burn incense and make offerings at the altar.

As European society developed, from the Middle Ages onward, members of the upper classes often referred to their family history as their "pedigree." Today this word
175 makes us think of some prize-winning animal, like a carefully bred racehorse or a fancy show poodle. Actually,

The Chinese philosopher, Confucius, worshiped his ancestors.

the word *pedigree* comes from the Middle French *pie de grue*, meaning "foot of a crane." This is because, on old genealogy charts, the lines showing who was descended
200 from whom formed a pattern. The pattern resembled the shape of a crane's foot.

In America, searching for a well-known ancestor didn't become fashionable until the 1800s. Once the Revolutionary War was over, some Americans who had
205 begun to enjoy increased wealth looked for a way to add to their family's **dignity**. One mark of distinction was to be able to say that they were descended from a passenger who had arrived on the *Mayflower*. The *Mayflower* was the ship that carried the first Pilgrims to America in 1620. Another
210 was to trace their roots to one of the "first families of Virginia." The first families formed a colony of the English king in 1624.

Being related to a signer of the Declaration of Independence or to someone who fought in the American
215 Revolution was also a great honor for a family to claim. Some Americans seeking a glorious past made some real mistakes, though. Imagine those who claimed that they were direct descendants of George Washington. History tells us that the famous "father of his country" never had
220 any children of his own!

Today many of us go ancestor hunting because we both appreciate and are proud of the struggles and achievements of the earlier generations of our family. At the same time, getting to know our roots gives us a sense of stability in an
225 uncertain and rapidly changing world. Finding out where we came from can help explain and clarify the present and may make it easier for us to look forward to the future.

dignity
self-respect;
inherent worth

Adapted and reprinted by permission of Houghton Mifflin Company
from *The Great Ancestor Hunt* by Lila Perl

Think About It

1. Define **genealogy** in your own words.

2. What role do genes play in determining our traits?

3. Summarize the role that social environment plays in determining our traits.

4. Describe the purpose of the student magazine *Foxfire*.

5. Explain how a **griot** helped Alex Haley trace his ancestry back to the early 1700s.

6. Assess the importance of keeping track of family history.

Solve the Puzzle

HOW TO MAKE A CROSSWORD PUZZLE

The crossword puzzle is based on a game called a word square. In a word square, words of the same length are written both across and down, with each
5 word appearing twice. The oldest word squares were found in the ruins of Pompeii, an ancient Roman city.

The first "word-cross" was published in 1913 by the *New*
10 *York World* and proved to be an instant hit. By following the steps here, you can make your own crossword puzzle.

Step 1: **Choose the words and write the clues.**

Pick six to eight words,
15 including a mix of shorter and longer terms. Write a simple clue for each word. At this point, don't worry about how to arrange the clues. Just write out a hint that
20 helps indicate each word.

A Word Square

T	A	N
A	P	E
N	E	T

STEP 1

My words
triangle
feather
weather
cattle
apple
example
title

Words & clues
triangle= three-sided shape
feather= what a bird has
weather= rain and shine
cattle= group of cows
apple= red fruit
example= for instance
title= a book's name

Step 2: "Cross" the words.

Use grid paper to figure out how the words will fit together. Start by writing one word that goes across the grid. Then
25 write another word that goes down, with one letter in the second word crossing a letter in the first word. Continue by adding the remaining words,
30 one at a time. Each word should cross at least one letter in another word. Use a pencil— you may need to erase a word and find another position for it.

Step 3: Number the words.

35 Number the words after all the words are in place. Start with the word at the top. Number the words from top to bottom and from left to right.

STEP 2

STEP 3

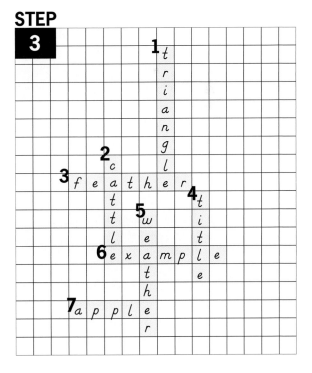

Step 4: Number and sort the clues.

40   Number the clues the same way you numbered the words. For example, let's say that the word "triangle" is number 1 in the puzzle; then the clue

45 for "triangle" should also be number 1. Now sort the clues into two groups: Across and Down.

STEP **4**

Across
3. what a bird has
6. for instance
7. red fruit

Down
1. three-sided shape
2. group of cows
4. a book's name
5. rain and shine

Step 5:

Make a blank puzzle.
     Draw a dark

50 outline around the shape of your puzzle. Create a blank version of it, making sure to insert the numbers.

STEP **5**

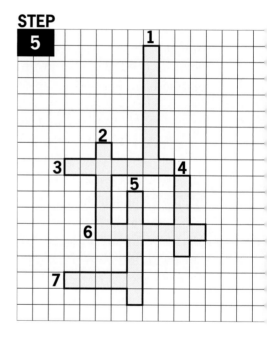

Step 6: Finish the puzzle.

55   The last step is to write out the clues for your crossword puzzle. Then give it to someone else to solve.

STEP **6**

Across
3. what a bird has
6. for instance
7. red fruit

Down
1. three-sided shape
2. group of cows
4. a book's name
5. rain and shine

A COLLECTION OF PUZZLING TALES

Around the world, people like to tell and hear stories. We especially like stories that challenge us to solve a puzzle. Puzzling stories seem to satisfy our natural **curiosity**. In many different cultures, such tales have been

5 told for centuries—often becoming folktales. Folktales are stories that usually teach some kind of lesson. They appeal to young and old alike, and are often passed down orally from one generation to the next.

Today, modern mystery writers puzzle us with their

10 stories. A mystery story presents us with some kind of confusing event. At the beginning of the mystery, we don't know what made the event happen. We read the mystery for clues, and the clues reveal the truth by the story's end.

Four puzzling tales follow. The challenge is to figure

15 out what happened and how it happened. **Visualize** the characters, imagine the settings, and think about the events. Listen to and read each story carefully. See if you can spot the clues that will help you solve each puzzle!

curiosity
a desire to know or learn

visualize
to form a mental image; imagine

The Sticks of Truth
—A Tale from India

Long ago in India, judges traveled from village to

20 village. One day, a judge stopped at an inn to rest. The innkeeper who greeted the judge was very upset. Someone had just that day stolen his daughter's gold ring. The judge told the innkeeper not to worry because he would find out who the thief was. The judge had all the guests gather in

25 one room so that he could question them. Their answers to his questions did not reveal the thief, so the judge decided

to use some old magic. He told all the guests he was going to give them the sticks of truth.

"These are magic sticks," he explained, "that will catch
30 the thief."

He kept a stick for himself and gave each guest a stick to keep under the bed during the night.

"The stick belonging to the thief will grow two inches during the night. At breakfast we will compare sticks, and
35 the longest stick will be the thief's."

The next morning the judge had the guests assemble at his table and hold their sticks up to his to see if the sticks had increased in length. But one after another, the sticks were the same length.

40   At last, there was only one woman left to show her magic stick. She held her stick carefully up to the judge's stick. The judge looked at it and then called out, "This is the thief! Her stick is shorter than all the rest."

confessed

admitted;
made known

Once caught, the woman **confessed** she was the thief
45 and returned the ring. But all the guests were confused about the sticks of truth. The judge had said the longest stick would belong to the thief, but instead she had the shortest stick. Why?

The Cleverest Son
—A Tale From Ethiopia

Once there lived an old man who had three sons. When
50 he grew old and ill and knew that he soon would die, he gathered his three sons in his room.

"There is no way I can divide the house and farm to support all three of you. The one who proves himself the cleverest will **inherit** the house and farm. There is

inherit

to receive from a
relative or friend,
often after death

55 a coin on the table for each of you. The one who can buy something that will fill this room will inherit all I own."

The eldest son took his coin, went straight to the marketplace, and filled his wagon full of straw. The second son thought a bit longer and then also went to the
60 marketplace, where he bought sacks and sacks of feathers. The youngest son thought and then quietly went to a little

shop. He bought two small things and tucked them into his pocket.

65   That night the father asked his sons to show him what they had bought. The eldest son spread his straw on the floor, but it filled only a portion of the room. The second son dumped out his sacks of feathers, but they filled only two corners of the room. Then the youngest son smiled, pulled the two small things out of his pocket and filled the
70 room with them from corner to corner.

    "Yes," said the father, "you are indeed the cleverest and have filled my room when the others could not. You shall inherit my house and farm."

    What had the youngest son bought and with what did
75 he fill the room?

which flower?
—A Tale from the Middle East

    Once long ago there lived two rulers named the Queen of Sheba and King Solomon. They were from different lands and were both famed for their wisdom. King Solomon paid a visit to the Queen of Sheba, and she decided to test
80 King Solomon's wisdom by a series of tests and riddles. He passed each one with ease until she led him to a room filled with flowers of every shape and color. The queen had directed the finest craftsmen and magicians in her land to **construct** the flowers so that they looked exactly like the
85 real flowers from her garden.

    "The test," she told King Solomon, "is to find the *one* real flower among all the **artificial** ones."

    King Solomon carefully looked from flower to flower and back again, searching for even the smallest of
90 differences. He looked for any sign of wilted leaves or petals but found lifelike leaves and petals on every flower. And fragrance was no help, because the room was filled with fragrances.

    "Please," said King Solomon. "This room is so warm.
95 Could we open the curtains and let in the breeze? The fresh air will help me think more clearly."

construct

to assemble; put together

artificial

manmade; fake

The Queen of Sheba agreed. Within minutes after the curtains were opened, King Solomon leaned over, picked the one real flower, and handed it to the queen.

100   How did he discover it?

Love and Pumpkins
—A Tale from the Philippines

When the king announced he was going to marry, stories of the bride quickly spread through the palace.

"She's beautiful," said one servant.

"With the voice of a bird," said another.

105   "More than that," said the third. "She can do anything! When the king dared her to get a large pumpkin inside a narrow-necked jar without cutting the pumpkin or breaking the jar, she did it. My cousin was there when the king broke open the jar."

110   "That's impossible. Your cousin tells lies," said a servant just joining the group.

"No, it's true," said another. "I heard the king announce it myself."

How did the bride do it?

Tales reprinted with permission from *More Stories to Solve: Folktales from Around the World* and *True Lies: 18 Tales for You to Judge* by George Shannon

Solution to "The Sticks of Truth": The thief, worried about being caught, cut off two inches of her stick during the night in an effort to hide its growth. But since the sticks were not magical, her stick was the only short one.

Solution to "The Cleverest Son": He bought a match and a candle and filled the room with light.

Solution to Which Flower?: A bee flew in the window and immediately went to the real flower.

Solution to Love and Pumpkins: Since the king did not say she had to start with a large pumpkin, the bride placed a tiny pumpkin inside the jar, then let it grow while it was attached to the vine.

Answer It

1. Describe how the judge found the thief in "The Sticks of Truth."

2. Plan a modern-day solution to the problem presented in "The Cleverest Son."

3. Summarize the problem in "The Cleverest Son."

4. Explain how a bee helped King Solomon pass the test in "Which Flower?"

5. Compose a different title for the folktale "Love and Pumpkins."

THE DISAPPEARING man

by Isaac Asimov

I'm not often on the spot when Dad's on one of his cases, but I couldn't help it this time.

I was coming home from the library that afternoon, when a man dashed by me and ran full speed into an alley
5 between two buildings. It was rather late, and I figured the best thing to do was to keep on moving toward home. Dad says a nosy fourteen-year-old isn't likely to make it to fifteen.

But in less than a minute, two policemen came
10 running. I didn't wait for them to ask. "He went in there," I said.

One of them rushed in, came out, and shouted, "There's a door open. He went inside. Go 'round to the front."

They must have given the alarm, because in a
15 few minutes, three police cars drove up, there were plainclothesmen on the scene, and the building was surrounded.

I knew I shouldn't be hanging around. Innocent bystanders get in the way of the police. Just the same, I was
20 there when it started and, from what I heard the police saying, I knew they were after this man, Stockton. He was a **loner** who'd pulled off some pretty spectacular jewel robberies over the last few months. I knew about it because Dad is a detective on the force, and he was on the case.

loner

someone who prefers to be alone

25   "Slippery fellow," he said, "but when you work alone, there's no one to double-cross you."

    I said, "Doesn't he have to work with someone, Dad? He's got to have a fence—someone to **peddle** the jewels."

    "If he has," said Dad, "we haven't located him. And why

30 don't you get on with your homework?" (He always says that when he thinks I'm getting too interested in his cases.)

    Well, they had him now. Some jeweler must have pushed the alarm button.

    The alley he ran into was closed on all sides but the

35 street, and he hadn't come out. There was a door there that was open, so he must have gone in. The police had the possible exits guarded. They even had a couple of men on the roof.

    I was just beginning to wonder if Dad would be

40 involved, when another car came up, and he got out. First thing he saw me and stopped dead. "Larry! What are you doing here?"

    "I was on the spot, Dad. Stockton ran past me into the alley."

45   "Well, get out of here. There's **liable** to be shooting."

    I backed away, but I didn't back off all the way. Once my father went into the building, I got into his car. The driver knew me, and he said, "You better go home, Larry. I'm going to have to help with the search, so I can't stay here to

50 keep an eye on you."

    "Sure, you go on," I said. "I'll be leaving in a minute." But I didn't. I wanted to do some thinking first.

    Nobody leaves doors open in New York City. If that door into the alley was open, Stockton must have opened it.

55 That meant he had to have a key; there wasn't time to pick the lock. That must mean he worked out of that building.

peddle

to sell things

liable

likely

I looked at the building. It was an old one, four stories high. It had small businesses in it, and you could still see the painted signs in the windows in the fading light.

60   On the second-floor window, it said, "Klein and Levy, Tailors." Above that was a theatrical **costumer**, and on the top floor was a jeweler's. That jeweler's made sense out of it.

    If Stockton had a key to the building, he probably worked with that jeweler. Dad would figure all that out.

65   I waited for the sound of shots, pretty scared Dad might get hurt. But nothing happened. Maybe Stockton would see he was cornered and just give in. I hoped so. At least they didn't have to evacuate the building. Late on Saturday, I supposed it would be **deserted**.

70   After a while, I got tired of waiting. I chose a moment when no policemen were looking and moved quickly to the building entrance. Dad would be hopping mad when he saw me, but I was curious. I figured they had Stockton, and I wanted to see him.

75   They didn't have him.

    There was a fat man in a vest in the lobby. He looked scared, and I guess he was the watchman. He kept saying, "I didn't see *any*body."

    Policemen were coming down the stairs and out of the
80 old elevator, all shaking their heads.

    My father was pretty angry. He said, "No one has anything?"

    A police sergeant said, "Donovan said no one got out on the roof. All the doors and windows are covered."

85   "If he didn't get out," said my father, in a low voice that carried, "then he's in the building."

costumer

a person who makes costumes

deserted

abandoned; empty of people

"We can't find him," said the sergeant. "He's nowhere inside."

My father said, "It isn't a big building—"

90 "We had the watchman's keys. We've looked everywhere."

"Then how do we know he went into the building in the first place? Who saw him go in?"

There was a silence. A lot of policemen were **milling** 95 about the lobby now, but no one said anything. So I spoke up. "I did, Dad."

milling
moving about randomly or in confusion

Dad whirled and looked at me and made a funny sound in the back of his throat that meant I was in for it for still being there. "You said you saw him run into the alley," he 100 said. "That's not the same thing."

"He didn't come out, Dad. There was no place else for him to go."

"But you didn't actually see him go in, did you?"

"He couldn't go up the side of the buildings. There 105 wouldn't have been time for him to reach the roof before the police—"

But Dad wasn't listening. "Did *anyone* actually see him go in?"

Of course no one said anything, and I could see my 110 father was going to call the whole thing off, and then when he got me home I was going to get the talking-to of my life.

The thought of that talking-to must have stimulated my brain, I guess. I looked about the lobby desperately, and said, "But, Dad, he *did* go into the building, and he 115 didn't disappear. There he is right now. That man there." I pointed, and then I dropped down and rolled out of the way.

There wasn't any shooting. The man I pointed to was close to the door—he must have been edging toward 120 it—and now he made a dash for it. He almost made it, but a policeman who had been knocked down grabbed his leg and then everyone piled on him. Later they had the jeweler, too.

I went home after Stockton was caught, and when my 125 father got home much later, he did have some things to say about my risking my life. But he also said, "You got onto that theatrical costume bit very nicely, Larry."

I said, "Well, I was sure he went into the building and was familiar with it. He could get into the costumer's if
130 he had to, and they would be bound to have policemen's uniforms. I figured if he could dump his jacket and pants and get into a policeman's uniform quickly, he could just walk out of the building."

Dad said, "You're right. Even after he got outside, he
135 could pretend he was dealing with the crowd and then just walk away."

Mom said, "But how did you know which policeman it was, Larry? Don't tell me you know every policeman by sight."
140 "I didn't have to, Mom," I said. "I figured if he got a policeman's uniform at the costumer's, he had to work fast and grab any one he saw. And they wouldn't have much of an assortment of sizes anyway. So I just looked around for a policeman whose uniform didn't fit, and when I saw one
145 with trouser legs stopping above his ankles, I knew he was Stockton."

Published by permission of the Estate of Isaac Asimov
c/o Ralph M. Vicinanza, Ltd.

Answer It

1. Summarize what the police knew when they arrived on the scene.

2. The police knew that the thief had run into the building. Design a strategy the police could have used for finding the thief.

3. Explain how Larry identified the thief.

4. Make a generalization about Larry's personality.

5. Compose a short newspaper article reporting the arrest of Stockton, the jewelry thief.

Puzzle People

The Spanish word for jigsaw puzzle, *rompecabezas*, literally translated means "broken heads." And no wonder! The mental challenges presented in puzzles can be so difficult—and entrancing—that they can make our brains, well . . . ache.

But, in fact, puzzles are good for our brains. Puzzles challenge our wits. We must concentrate intensely, think **logically**, and make connections by sorting through layers of information. And, once we solve them, puzzles make us feel proud and smart, too. There's a lot of satisfaction in that "Aha!" moment when we finally crack the code of a puzzle we've been laboring over for hours.

If it takes a determined person to solve a puzzle, what sort of person does it take to design a puzzle in the first place? Who are some of the people behind the puzzles?

Crossword Craze

In 1913, the crossword puzzle made its **debut** in print as the "word-cross." In no time at all, the country was hooked on this new form of amusement. During the 1920s, most of the major newspapers began publishing crossword puzzles. In 1924, the first published book of crossword puzzles sold nearly half a million copies in its first year.

Margaret Farrar was one of the editors of that first book of puzzles. She helped to develop many of the modern rules of the crossword puzzle, including the rule that a puzzle's pattern must look identical right side up and upside down. (This rule is usually applied only to advanced crossword puzzles.)

Farrar became the first crossword editor at *The New York Times*, one of the nation's most highly respected newspapers. There, Farrar instituted the tradition of making puzzles become gradually more difficult over

logically
sensibly; based on a set of rules

debut
first public appearance

the course of the week, a tradition that continues today. Monday's puzzle is the easiest, and Saturday's puzzle, as Farrar once explained, is "a two-cups-of-coffee puzzle."

35 When asked if mistakes ever appeared in the famous newspaper's crossword puzzles, Farrar replied, "Oh dear, yes!" She recalled that the *Times* once constructed a puzzle that asked for the defining characteristic of a famous character in the novel *Moby Dick*. The *Times* mistakenly

40 assumed that the answer was "wooden leg." But an eight-year-old boy wrote in to point out that the character in *Moby Dick* had an artificial leg fashioned from ivory, not from wood. Farrar explained, "Perfectly true, but I couldn't help wondering, rather testily, what an eight-year-old was

45 doing reading *Moby Dick*!"

The Cube Loved Round the World

The best-selling puzzle in history is a colorful cube made of plastic, known as Rubik's Cube. The Cube is made up of 26 brightly colored smaller cubes, which can be rotated. The objective is to **align** the smaller cubes so that

50 each side of the Cube is all one color.

This puzzle looks deceptively simple—almost like a child's toy. But, in fact, the Cube is extremely difficult to solve. The Cube can be rotated into 43 quintillion possible configurations—only one of which is correct.

55 The Cube's difficulty adds to its **allure**. During the peak of the Cube's popularity in the early 1980s, people all over the world became obsessed with solving the colorful puzzle. Some people even developed "Rubik's wrist," an injury developed from the **repetitive** motion involved in

60 rotating parts of the cube.

Even the inventor of the Cube, a Hungarian named Erno Rubik, was stunned when he realized how difficult it was to solve his own puzzle. Here's how he describes his first experience trying to solve the Cube:

65 "It was wonderful to see how, after only a few turns, the colors became mixed. . . . It was tremendously satisfying to watch this color parade. Like after a nice walk when you have seen many lovely sights you decide to go home, after a

align
to arrange in a line

allure
attractiveness

repetitive
done again and again

while I decided it was time to go home, let us put the cubes
70 back in order. And it was at that moment that I came face
to face with the big challenge: What is the way home?"

Maize Mazes

Most of the time, we do everything we can to keep
ourselves from getting lost. We ask for directions. We travel
with maps. Some of us even travel with a GPS (Global
75 Positioning System), which uses satellites to tell us our
exact location on the planet. On the other hand, sometimes
we go to great lengths to become lost—very lost—just for
fun in the winding paths of mazes.

Mazes have been around for centuries. Recently,
80 though, they have made a comeback in an unexpected
place: cornfields. Viewed from above, these maize mazes
appear as intricate patterns, and some are even designed
to represent images. One maze was designed to look like
Oprah Winfrey! But from the inside of a corn maze at
85 ground level, little can be seen at all. Walls of corn stalks
tower on all sides and **envelop** those who dare to wander
inside. The challenge is to first get lost and then find the
way out. What makes getting lost in a corn maze so fun?

Ask Adrian Fisher, who helped design one of the first corn
90 mazes. He has since built over 500 mazes in 30 countries.
According to Fisher, one the world's premier maze designers,
the challenge—and fun—of mazes is in the numerous
decisions required to find the way out. He says, "A roller
coaster . . . will give you a great number of . . . thrills, but the
95 only decision you make is to stand in line for 28 minutes and
then be strapped in. Here, you're making choices all the time."

A Puzzle from Behind the Iron Curtain

When Alexey Pajitnov invented the computer game
Tetris, he might not have foreseen how successful his game
would become, but he certainly had an understanding of
100 how addictive the game can be. While writing its code,
Pajitnov says he spent many hours "testing the system."

In the game of Tetris, different geometric shapes fall
from the top of the screen and pile up at the bottom.

envelop
to enclose;
surround

Players have a second or two to rotate the shapes to fit them
105 together. Rows disappear if there are no gaps between the
shapes. But if there are gaps, the screen quickly begins to fill
up with jumbled shapes, and in short order, the player loses.

Pajitnov invented Tetris in the Soviet Union in 1985,
at the end of the Cold War, a period of tense relations
110 between the Soviet Union and Western countries, including
the United States. By that year, the Soviet Union's leader,
Mikhail Gorbechev, had begun loosening trade restrictions
with the United States and Europe. Tetris was exported
to other countries and marketed as "the first game from
115 behind the Iron Curtain."

Tetris began to gross millions of dollars, but Pajitnov
did not at first profit from his own invention. In the Soviet
Union, the government, not individuals, owned inventions.
Pajitnov did not begin to make money from Tetris until
120 1996, when the game's license was renewed. Pajitnov has no
regrets, however. "You could always make a little more, but
I never seriously think about this stuff. I live as I live." More
than 70 million copies of his game have now been sold.

What will the next great puzzle sensation be? Who
125 knows? Could you or someone you know be the one to
create the next world-challenging puzzle?

Adapted with permission from "The Puzzling Business of Sam Loyd
& Erno Rubik" by Natalie Rosinsky

Think About It

1. Why did Margaret Farrar refer to Saturday's *New York Times* crossword puzzle as a "two-cups-of-coffee puzzle"?

2. Explain the objective of Rubik's Cube.

3. Describe Erno Rubik's reaction to his own puzzle the first time he tried to solve it.

4. Summarize Adrian Fisher's statement about mazes and roller coasters.

5. Compare Tetris and Rubik's Cube.

6. If you were to invent a puzzle, what type of puzzle would it be? Why?

THE ROSETTA STONE:
KEY TO A LINGUISTIC PUZZLE

The Discovery

In 1798, Napoleon and his army landed in North Africa intending to conquer Egypt for the glory of France. Napoleon brought soldiers with him, of course, but he also brought biologists, **linguists**, mathematicians, and
5 archeologists to explore and study Egypt's rich culture and history.

In 1799, French soldiers were restoring a fort in the small port city of Rosetta, also known as el-Rashid. They uncovered a large, flat piece of stone made of black basalt.
10 The surface was inscribed with three bands of **script**. As soon as the officer in charge saw the stone, he realized that it was an important discovery. He had the soldiers pack the stone carefully, and it was transported to French scholars in Cairo. There it would undergo further study.
15 French scientists and scholars were excited when they saw the stone. They knew almost immediately that the Rosetta Stone could be a key for unlocking one of history's most **tantalizing** linguistic puzzles—how to read ancient Egyptian hieroglyphs. Part of the Greek script
20 along the stone's bottom implied that each of the three inscriptions on the rock was the same text. The top part of the stone contained hieroglyphs. The middle part of the stone was written in demotic script. Demotic script was

linguists
people who study languages

script
handwriting

tantalizing
tempting; teasing

The Rosetta Stone was inscribed with three bands of writing.

Hieroglyphs

Demotic Script

Greek

a cursive version of hieroglyphic writing. The appearance
25 of these three sets of writing together seemed to suggest
a straightforward way to solve the mystery of how to read
Egyptian hieroglyphs. However, it would be 23 more years
before European scholars would finally unlock this puzzle.

The Puzzle

Before the discovery of the Rosetta Stone, scholars
30 in Europe had worked for centuries to decipher ancient
Egyptian hieroglyphs but had met with limited success.[1]
The writing was made up of pictures carved and painted on
Egyptian monuments, tombs, buildings, vessels, and other
items. It also appeared on papyrus, a type of paper.
35 The symbols fascinated many scientists and linguists.
They knew this writing could open great windows of
understanding into this ancient civilization, which had
flourished for thousands of years. Ancient Egyptians
had used hieroglyphs for writing as early as 3100 BC. The
40 last known hieroglyphic inscription dates from AD 394.
After that time, the knowledge of how to write or read
hieroglyphs faded, and experts believed it had been lost.
Egyptian hieroglyphs picture the animals, plants,
and household items that ancient Egyptians saw around

flourished

thrived; grew

[1] About 600 years earlier, it seems that Muslim scholars had succeeded in deciphering
these hieroglyphs. European scholars, though, were not aware of this breakthrough.

45 them every day. In the following centuries, people tried to decipher the pictures as symbols of objects. For example, a circle would represent the sun, and so on. The system of language behind hieroglyphs was much more complicated than that, however. Thus, early attempts at deciphering
50 the code failed. Earlier scholars, though, did conclude that there was a connection between ancient hieroglyphs and the later phases of Egyptian writing.

Phases of Ancient Egyptian Writing. Ancient Egyptian writing passed through several distinct phases.
55 The oldest version dates to around 5,000 years ago. This version consisted of what appears to be pictographs. Clearly, this form of writing required a tremendous amount of time to produce. As a result, an easier cursive form of writing, known as hieratic, was developed.

60 **Hieratic.** In hieratic writing, the letters corresponded to the original picture-type symbols of the earlier script. However, hieratic writing simplifies the hieroglyphic signs so that they can be written much more quickly. Both hieroglyphic and hieratic writing were used from about
65 3,000 to 600 BC, or even later. Hieroglyphs were often reserved for the inscriptions of names and messages on monuments and buildings. Hieratic writing was primarily written on papyrus documents.

Demotic. Demotic script derived from hieratic writing
70 and first appeared about 600 BC. It was an even more cursive style than hieratic and was used primarily for business documents. Hieratic writing continued to be used for religious and literary purposes. The middle portion of the Rosetta Stone contains demotic script.

Unlocking the Puzzle

75 In 1801, the French began to surrender Egypt to British and Turkish forces. In doing so, the French also surrendered the Egyptian antiquities they had collected. The Rosetta Stone, along with many other artifacts, was shipped to the British Museum. Prints and copies of the stone were sent to
80 top scholars in hopes that someone would solve the puzzle of what was written on it. The demotic text looked more like

words than pictures, and that helped some scholars start to identify word groups.

The frequently repeated name of a king written on the
85 Rosetta Stone offered an important clue. Scholars identified the Greek royal name *Ptolemaios* in the demotic text. Then, around 1816, an Englishman named Thomas Young compared that name with a word written in hieroglyphs. The word appeared within an oval called a *cartouche*. This
90 oval was used to surround royal names. He concluded that the name *Ptolemaios* as written in Greek (PTΩLΞMΔΦΩS) was the same as that in the hieroglyphic writing. Young correctly concluded that the royal name was written alphabetically, in other words, that each sign represented a
95 sound. However, he still incorrectly believed that the other hieroglyphs were symbolic.

The European credited with the final decipherment is the French linguist Jean-François Champollion. Champollion had mastered many Eastern languages at a
100 very young age. When he was 16 years old, he presented a paper tying the Coptic language of contemporary Egypt with the language of ancient Egypt. He traveled to Egypt. He took voluminous notes. He had access to additional **bilingual** writings on other artifacts and monuments.
105 After reading Young's work, Champollion speculated that all hieroglyphs could be phonetic, not just those contained in the cartouches. He used his knowledge of Greek, demotic, and Coptic words as guides. In doing so, Champollion solved the puzzle of hieroglyphic writing.
110 Again working with names, he matched the signs in "Ptolemy" on the Rosetta Stone to the name that he found on another monument. He let the hieroglyphs represent *sounds*, rather than *symbols*. In this way, he was able to read: **? + l + e + o + p + a + t/d + ? + a.**
115 He guessed correctly that the second name was *Cleopatra*. He continued to successfully decipher other hieroglyphs on the Rosetta Stone and translated hieroglyphs on other Egyptian artifacts as well. In 1822, he presented his **thesis**. He proposed that hieroglyphs were a
120 combination of phonetic and nonphonetic signs. His years

Jean-François Champollion.

bilingual

in two languages

thesis

a proposed explanation; theory

of dedicated work opened up an important way for us to understand the world of Ancient Egypt.

The Hieroglyphic Puzzle Solved

Today, we know that in hieroglyphic writing there are about 800 commonly used hieroglyphic signs. These signs
125 are called glyphs. Most common are the 24 glyphs that represent single consonant sounds. Hieroglyphic signs can be divided into four categories. First, as alphabetic signs, they can represent a single sound—usually a consonant sound. Second, as syllabic signs, they can represent a
130 combination of two or more consonants. Third, as word-signs, they are the pictures of objects—in this case they are used as the words for those objects. And fourth, as determiners, they are used in relationship to other hieroglyphs to explain their meanings.
135 Breaking the code of a written language is like breaking any other code. First, the basis of the code must be found. For centuries, European scholars had presumed that

Champollion proposed that hieroglyphs were a combination of phonetic and nonphonetic signs.

hieroglyphic writing was based on a pictographic code. After all, pictures of familiar objects were used in the
140 writing. But as every scientist knows when trying to solve a puzzle, a multitude of possibilities must be considered. In this case, the code was primarily alphabetic. It was much like the kind of code we use in English today.

Jean-François Champollion, Thomas Young, and
145 dozens of other linguists, historians, and Egyptologists were persistent. They never gave up in their pursuit of cracking the code, and their hard work made it possible for the Rosetta Stone's hieroglyphs to be decoded. Today, the term "Rosetta Stone" is used as a metaphor to refer
150 to anything that is a critical key to figuring out a difficult problem. The real Rosetta Stone sits in the British Museum in London. It is on view to the world as the solution to one of the greatest language puzzles of all time.

Think About It

1. Describe the appearance of the Rosetta Stone.

2. The bottom band of script on the Rosetta Stone was in Greek. How did this help linguists unlock the puzzle of the Rosetta Stone?

3. Compare and contrast hieratic and demotic scripts.

4. Trace the history of the Rosetta Stone from the time it was discovered until it reached the British Museum.

5. Early scholars of hieroglyphic writing made an incorrect assumption about the writing, which prevented them from breaking its code. Summarize that assumption.

6. Explain the significance of understanding the Egyptian hieroglyphic writing.

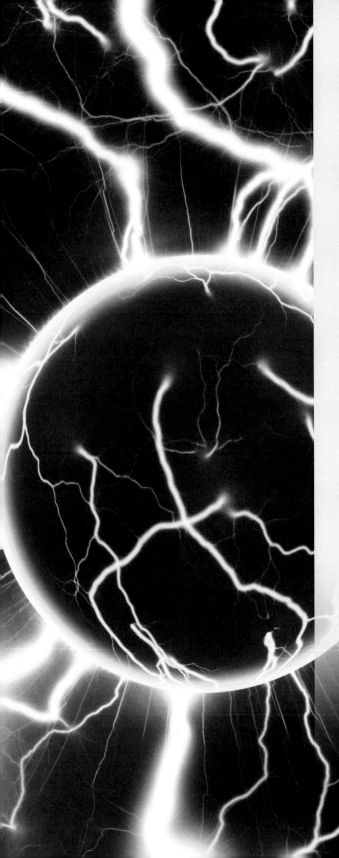

Unit 23

Power Up!

We can measure length by using a ruler. We can measure heat and cold with a thermometer. We can measure how fast a car is going with a speedometer. But what if we want to measure a car's power? What would we
5 use? Believe it or not, we would use horses.

Cars are often described as having "horsepower." Why do we compare the power of cars to the power of horses? It helps to know some history. The rise of many civilizations throughout the world has happened with the help of horses.
10 Approximately 50,000 years ago, some of the earliest people kept horses for food.

When early humans started farming, they tamed the horse. They used the horse for riding. The first draft horses appeared in the Near East between 3,000 and 2,000 BC.
15 People have been using them to move things ever since. They rode the horse to travel. They used horses for war. They attached them to carts and plows to provide pulling power. Horses turned millstones, grinding grain into flour. In many places, horses became the key to producing food.
20 They also became symbols of money and power. The

number of horses that people owned could make them important in the eyes of others.

James Watt was the person who coined the term "horsepower." He invented a new kind of steam engine in
25 the 18th century. When he was ready to sell it, he needed a way to describe how much power the engine had. He wanted to say that the engine could do the work of so many horses. To do this, he had to figure out the power of one horse doing a task. By watching a horse pull a mill,
30 Watt calculated that one horse could pull 33,000 pounds, one foot, in one minute. This became the definition for "horsepower."

Today, we talk about how much horsepower a car has. We can measure the car's horsepower by hooking its engine
35 up to a dynamometer. The device puts stress on the engine for the engine to work against. Then the dynamometer measures the amount of pulling power the engine can produce.

We now measure the power of cars, lawn mowers,
40 vacuums, and many other machines using horsepower. And today, people still love the power of horses. They also love the horsepower of their cars. But it's funny today to see cars pulling trailers carrying horses. As we progress into the future, we are still taking horses for a ride.

Adapted with permission from "Horsepower Helped"
by Brigid Casey-Meyer

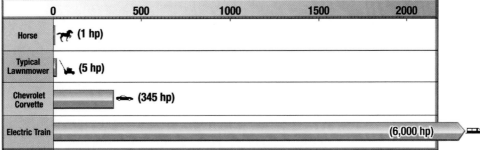

Horsepower Produced

	0	500	1000	1500	2000
Horse	(1 hp)				
Typical Lawnmower	(5 hp)				
Chevrolet Corvette	(345 hp)				
Electric Train				(6,000 hp)	

Zaaaaaaaap!

a science fiction story

Prologue

crisis
an emergency

    The year is 2160. Thirteen-year old Maitn and her family are living at the end of "The Dark," a period of history when the world faced a serious energy **crisis** *. Many factors contributed to this dark period. Fossil fuel supplies on Earth*
5 *suddenly ran out in 2080. At the turn of the century, a severe drought in the Northern Hemisphere limited the use of hydroelectric power. Alternative energy sources—such as solar, wind, and ocean wave power—were in development but not ready for powering whole cities. To respond to the*
10 *crisis, many nuclear power plants were built as quickly as possible. A massive earthquake in the Pacific Ocean in 2152 damaged nuclear power plants in several countries and exposed thousands of people to unhealthy doses of radiation. Maitn's best friend, Josha, suffers from radiation exposure.*
15   *However, this time period has not been all dark. Scientists have made advances in medical research as a result of a whole new field of study called "* **organic**

organic
biological; related to living things

engineering." Organic engineering of some kinds of fruit has raised the hope of finding a cure for radiation sickness and
20 *some types of cancer. This cure is still being tested, however, and is not ready for public use.*
    A major breakthrough in energy generation has also made it possible to harness the power of lightning. The system isn't perfect, but, overall, it seems to be much
25 *safer than nuclear power. But watch out when a lightning storm comes!*

Zaaaaaaaap!

    Maitn shimmied up the branches of the pear tree, her feet feeling for a firm hold. She saw what she was looking for almost ten feet farther above. The fruit glimmered

30 huge and welcoming, a feat of organic engineering and the world's next miracle cure.

The pear was for Josha, so the fact that picking it from the tree was illegal meant little to her. Josha was close enough to be family. He had been getting weaker. On his
35 last trip to the clinic, the doctor had told his family that his exposure to radiation eight years earlier was slowly killing him. Josha had been visiting a friend near the Powell Nuclear Power Plant when the accident happened. The earthquake damaged the plant's cooling system, and the
40 radiation leak made many people in the area sick, including Josha. Ironically, both of his parents now worked at the same plant although no power had been produced by it since the accident. Josha's parents were part of a team responsible for assisting in the cleanup after the nuclear
45 accident.

Lost in thought, Maitn didn't see the cracked branch above her. As her left hand went to grasp it, the branch split, and she skittered almost halfway down the trunk. Intent on her goal, Maitn **deftly** climbed back up to the
50 pear. She picked the ripened fruit off the branch and dropped it into the duffel bag that hung at her side.

The task complete, she sighed and looked off to the west. There was a storm brewing; the clouds on the horizon hung dark and heavy. In the distance, she could see the
55 flashes that could only be lightning. The lightning meant that her mom would be working this evening. Her mom had a job at the new Lightning Power Corral.

Maitn looked toward the lightning corral that was right next to the experimental orchard. It consisted of a
60 huge web of thin metal wires. Thousands of thin metal wires connected to the web were lifted into the sky. The wires were held up by small weather balloons that sent meteorological data to the power plant operators on the ground. Just before the lightning was right above the corral,
65 Maitn's mother would flip the vacuum switch. The energy from the lightning bolts would funnel down the wires to be stored in giant batteries and then doled out and shipped to the surrounding counties.

deftly
quickly; skillfully

"Hey!" a voice yelled.

70 Maitn glanced down. It was her brother, Mriel.

"Get down from there! A storm is coming!"

Maitn let gravity take her down the branches until she hung just five feet above the ground. Then she dropped and dusted off her pants.

75 "What're you doing? Trying to get killed?"

Maitn pointed to the duffel bag. "For Josha."

Mriel let out a sound that was half smug, half **aggravated**.

"That won't do him any good. Don't you know that 80 radiation poisoning is **irreversible**?"

"I know that," Maitn said, shuffling her feet. "But at least he'll have some hope. At least that's something he can hold on to."

"You're a saint, you know that? Come on, Mom's getting 85 ready to go to work, and she said she has permission for us to go with her and watch."

They made it home just before the warning siren sounded. It **reverberated** off the buildings surrounding the corral. A friendly voice advised them, "Stay indoors or 90 don a rubber suit. Leave all electrical appliances on standby for the duration of the storm."

Mom was leaving the house. Maitn and Mriel ran after her. The three of them mounted the four-seater trike and pedaled to the corral. The wind started picking up as they 95 neared Demante Avenue, and now it blew dust in their eyes and rustled in their jackets.

They parked the trike and hurried toward the building. Her mother used a key card to get into the power plant next to the corral. Mriel followed closely behind her, but 100 Maitn stopped and turned. Her eyes fell on the same pear tree she had climbed earlier that bordered the station. As they were pedaling, she thought she had seen someone in that tree. "Mom!" she shouted, above the wind.

But Mom and Mriel were now locked inside the 105 power plant. As a safety precaution, the doors locked automatically when a storm was very close.

aggravated

bothered; irritated

irreversible

impossible to undo; permanent

reverberated

echoed

The flashes of lightning grew brighter. The clouds loomed darker overhead. It wouldn't be long before her mom had to activate the switch so that the storm's energy

110 was sucked down into the power corral.

Maitn ran over to the tree and strained to see through the wind-whipped branches. There was someone up there, all right, and it didn't take long to see who it was. Quickly, Maitn climbed up the tree.

115 "My sleeve is stuck!" Josha yelled when he saw her.

His eyes were sunken and his face was pale, but in his hands he held a pear even larger than the one Maitn had picked.

"Great minds think alike," she muttered.

120 Josha started to speak, but she waved him to be quiet. She had heard a sound that made her stomach lurch. It was the loud hum of the vacuum switching on. In less than a minute, more than a billion volts of electricity would be spewing through the atmosphere, striking the spiderweb's

125 wires helter-skelter. Though not many volts would stray, some would, and a tree 40 feet tall would be a great bull's-eye.

Maitn climbed above Josha and ripped his jacket loose from the branch that held it tight.

130 "Hurry up!" she screamed, pulling at him as she went down. Another flash of lightning lit up the sky and painted

spots in front of her eyes. As her heart pounded in her throat, she jumped from the tree, pulling Josha with her.

Their landing was rough, but necessity jerked them
135 instantly to their feet. Suddenly, the air changed texture. The hairs on the back of Maitn's neck stood on end. It was coming. The incredible power was coming.

The pair ran as fast as they could, the sound of crackling electricity filling their ears. They spotted a
140 concrete drainage pipe 20 yards from the tree, and dived into it. They lay there while the storm crashed around them, breathing heavily and watching the spectacular fireworks as the corral collected the lightning's power.

Then, after what seemed like an eternity, the storm
145 moved on, and the hum of the wires died down. The plant's workers emerged to inspect the corral. The captured energy would soon be transported to the hundreds of thousands of people in the state who needed it.

Josha took a huge bite from his prize pear, and offered
150 one to Maitn, his way of thanking her for his rescue. She took the bite willingly, and tucked her smaller pear into his pocket for later. Energized by the power of hope, the two headed home.

Adapted with permission from "Zaaaaaaaap!" By Jennifer A. Ratliff

Zap! ... ka-BOOM!

For years, people have speculated about capturing lightning and turning it into usable electricity. Such powerful displays of energy easily could power a city for a long time, right?

Unfortunately, that's not the case. According to scientists, there are several natural and technical reasons why lightning is unlikely to ever power our homes, schools, and businesses.

Believe it or not, lightning doesn't produce that much electricity to begin with. Most of its energy is used up in making the flash of light and thunderous noise, according to the National Aeronautics and Space Administration (NASA). The electricity generated by a bolt of lightning is substantial, but it lasts for a very short time—a fraction of a second. Altogether, a typical lightning strike only contains enough electricity to light one 100-watt light bulb for about six months.

Lightning strikes are infrequent and unpredictable. Committing vast resources of money and technology to harness such an unreliable power source would cost more than it's worth.

Technically, collecting and storing the huge, brief surge of electrical current from lightning is dangerous and unrealistic.

Capturing and using the energy in lightning has been the subject of many imaginative proposals over the years. The idea might be an exciting source of energy in science fiction tales, but it is highly unlikely that it will ever become reality.

Answer It

1. Make a hypothesis about how Maitn and Josha know each other.

2. Revise the prediction you made earlier of how the story would end.

3. Summarize the factors that contributed to the energy crisis during the era of "The Dark."

4. Assess the level of danger that Josha and Maitn are exposed to during the storm.

5. Paraphrase Maitn's explanation of how a pear can help Josha.

SATYAGRAHA:
Power for Change
by Alden R. Carter

Ramdas Bahave met me at the sidelines. "In what part of the body are you wounded, Kenneth?" he asked.

"Hand," I gritted.

"The smallest finger again?"

5   "Yeah."

"Let me see it, please."

I held out my right hand, the dislocated little finger already twice normal size and rapidly turning purple.

Rollin Acres, my best buddy and the team's fullback,
10   made a barfing sound. "Jeez, I wish you'd stop messing up that finger, Ken. It's disgusting."

"Just watch the game, Rollin."

"Sure. But, you know, if you had a little more vertical you could catch a pass like that."

15   "I've got more vertical than you do."

"You're supposed to. You're a tight end. Who ever heard of a fullback with vertical leap?"

Ramdas interrupted. "Would you like me to correct this problem now?"

20   "Yeah, do it," I said.

Ramdas took my pinkie in his strong, slender fingers and pulled. Pain shot up my arm and my eyes teared. Dang! This time he really was going to pull it out by the roots. Then there was a pop and sudden easing of the pain. He felt

25 gently along the joint. "It is back in place. Are you all right? Feel faint, perhaps?"

"I'm okay. Just tape me up and get me back in."

He made a disapproving sound but started buddy-taping my pinkie and ring fingers. Out on the field we'd
30 covered the punt and held Gentry High to four yards on two running plays. Still time to win if we could hold them on third down. "Come on, Patch," I yelled. "Now's the time."

"Please hold your hand still, Kenneth," Ramdas said.

The Gentry quarterback dropped back to pass as Bill
35 Patchett, our all-conference defensive end, bull-rushed their left tackle. Bill slung the kid aside, leaped a shot at his ankles by the fullback, and buried the quarterback. The ball popped loose and Bill dove on it, but the ref signaled no fumble, down by contact. Bill jumped up and started yelling
40 at the ref, but a couple of the other seniors pulled him away before he got a flag.

Ramdas handed me a bag of ice. "Here. Sit down. Rest."

"I can't sit down. We're getting the ball back."

While Gentry set up to punt, Coach Carlson strolled
45 down the line to me. "Finger again?"

"Yes, sir."

"Can you play?"

"Yes, sir."

Coach looked at Ramdas, who shrugged. "It is a
50 dislocation like the other times. I think he should keep ice on it."

Coach looked at me. "Right hand?"

I nodded.

"Hard for you to hold on to a football, then. I'll put in
55 Masanz."

So that was it for me for that game. We got the ball back on our thirty with two minutes to go. Marvin Katt, our quarterback, got two quick completions against their prevent defense but couldn't connect on the big pass
60 downfield. Final score: 16–10. Yet another loss for ol' Argyle High.

Bill Patchett spent his usual five minutes bashing his fists, forearms, and head into lockers. At six four, 240, that's

a lot of frustration on the loose, and the rest of us stayed
65 out of his way. "Hey, Bauer," he yelled at me. "Where were
you on that last series?"

I held up my bandaged hand. "Dislocated a finger."

"And so little doc Ramdas wouldn't let you play, huh?"

"It wasn't like that, Bill."

70 He didn't listen. Instead he grabbed a roll of tape and
fired it at Ramdas, who was straightening up the training
room, his back to us. The roll of tape flew through the
open door and did a three-cushion bank shot around the
room. Ramdas jumped out of the way and looked at us in
75 confusion.

"Hey, Ramboy!" Bill yelled. "Your job is to get people
back in, not keep them out!"

Ramdas didn't answer, only stared. That just made Bill
madder, and he started for the door, fists balled. "The idea
80 is to win. No matter what it costs. So unless a guy's got an
arm ripped off, you get him back in!"

Rollin stepped in front of him. "Come on, Bill. We all
feel terrible about losing. You played—"

"He doesn't feel terrible! He doesn't care one way or the
85 other as long as he gets to play with his bandages and his
ice packs."

"Yeah, yeah, sure, Bill," Rollin said. "Just let it alone
now. Go take a shower. You'll feel better."

Bill **stalked** back to his corner, smashing another
90 locker door, and started pulling off his uniform.

I got into the passenger seat of the Toyota pickup
piloted by my **liberated**, non-committed, female friend,
Sarah Landwehr. (You can call her my girlfriend if you've
got the guts. I don't.) "Tough loss," Sarah said.
95 "Aren't they all? A couple more, and we'll have to start
replacing lockers."

"Billy Patchett took it out on poor, defenseless
inanimate objects again, huh?"

"Yep. He got after Ramdas too. Rollin broke it up."
100 "What's with Bill, anyway? It's not Ramdas's fault you
guys lost."

stalked

walked angrily

liberated

independent; freed
from the influence
of others

inanimate

not alive; unmoving

"Well, Ramdas would rather sit a guy down than risk making an injury worse. Bill doesn't think that's the way to win football games."

105 Sarah snorted. "So he thinks you should risk permanent injury just to win a stupid game?"

"Something like that. Let's go to Mac's. I'm hungry." I started fiddling with the radio dial, hoping she'd let the subject drop.

110 She didn't, which is pretty typical of her. "I still don't get it. There's got to be more to it than that."

I sighed. How to explain? "Ramdas doesn't seem to care if we win or lose. And that drives Bill nuts. I mean, look at it from his standpoint. Here he is, the best player on a lousy 115 team. He's been all-conference, but he could have been all-state if he'd played in a winning program. And all-state means a scholarship and the chance to play for a Division One or a Division Two school. All-conference doesn't guarantee anything."

120 "None of that **justifies** being mean to Ramdas."

"No, but it explains it a little."

She harrumphed, unimpressed. "So what's going to happen next? Is Bill going to start punching him?"

"I don't think it'll come to that."

125 "Well, I think it might! And I think you'd better do something about it, *team captain*."

"Only one of four."

"Still—"

"I know, I know. I'll keep an eye on things."

130 She glared at me. "You should do a heck of a lot more than that, Kenny."

Maybe she was right, but I didn't plan on doing anything. If Ramdas felt there was a big problem, he should go to Coach Carlson. Me, I was going to ignore the whole 135 thing as long as possible.

We didn't have practice Monday, and I didn't see anything of Ramdas or Bill until Tuesday morning.

justifies

explains; gives
reasons for

Rollin and I were coming down the east corridor maybe twenty feet behind Bill when Ramdas turned the corner.

140 Bill took a step to his left and put a shoulder into him. Ramdas bounced off the lockers, skidded on the slippery floor, and only just managed to keep his balance. Bill didn't even look back.

"Oh-oh," I said. "I hope Bill doesn't make a habit of that."

145 "He already has," Rollin said. "Started yesterday morning. Every time he sees Ramdas, *wham*, into the lockers."

"Wow, did you say anything to him?"

"To Bill?"

150 "Yeah."

"I said something. Asked him why. He says he's gonna get Ramdas's attention one way or another."

"I don't think getting his attention is the problem."

"Neither do I, but are you going to argue with someone

155 as big and ornery as Billy Patch?"

No, and it wouldn't do any good if I did. Besides, I had a couple questions of my own for Ramdas.

At noon I found him sitting by himself in the cafeteria, a textbook open beside his tray. I sat down across from

160 him. "Hey, Ram," I said.

"Hello, Kenneth." He marked his place, closed the book, and looked at me expectantly.

"Why do you always use people's full names?"

He smiled, shrugged slightly. "I like their sound. I do

165 not like to use contractions either. I like the full words."

"It makes you sound like a professor or something."

"Sorry."

"Uh, well, not a problem. But, look, you've got to do something about this thing between you and Bill Patchett."

170   "What would you suggest?"

"For starters you could act like you care if the team wins or loses."

"But I do not care. Football is a lot of pointless violence as far as I can see."

175   "Then why'd you volunteer to be a trainer?"

"To help with the wounded."

I shook my head. "Well, maybe you could at least stop being so passive about everything."

He laughed. "You would have me fight William

180 Patchett?"

"Well, not exactly, but—"

"Because I will not fight. It goes against everything I believe."

"I don't expect you to fight him, but you can stand up to

185 him in other ways."

"But I am."

"How's that?"

"By not reacting with force. Force is never justified."

"Well, maybe not in this case, but—"

190   "No, Kenneth, in all cases. Never, no matter how good the cause."

"Oh, come on. How else are we supposed to keep other people or other countries from taking what's ours? Sometimes you've got to use force."

195   He sighed. "I guess that is what a lot of you Americans believe. But I believe that you can **resist** in another way. Mahatma Gandhi called it *satyagraha*, to stand firmly for truth and love without ever resorting to force."

I stared at him in disbelief. I mean, Bill was about to

200 turn him into a smear of jelly and Ramdas was talking about some dead holy man! "Well, that may be very cool, Ram, but—"

"You have heard of Gandhi, have you not?"

resist
to oppose; fend off

"Sure. I mean, the name, anyway. And I'd love to hear
205 more. But right now I think you'd better tell me what you're
planning to do about Bill Patchett."

"I am telling you. The Mahatma used *satyagraha* to
free all of India from the British. I think I can use it to
control Mr. William Patchett."

210 Oh, sure. But I bet Gandhi never had to face down six
foot four, 240 pounds of crazed defensive end. "Ram, listen—"

He interrupted gently. "Let me tell you a story. Under
British rule it was illegal for Indians to make their own
salt. Everyone had to buy expensive government salt, and
215 that was very hard on the poor. Three thousand of the
Mahatma's followers went to protest the law at a place
called the Dharasana Salt Works. They stepped four at
a time up to a line of soldiers, never lifting a hand to
defend themselves, and let the soldiers beat them down
220 with bamboo clubs. Those who could got up and went
to the back of the line. All day they marched up to the
soldiers until the soldiers were so tired they could not lift
their arms."

"What did that prove?"

225 "It proved that the Mahatma's followers were willing to
suffer for what they believed without doing hurt to others.
Their example brought hundreds of thousands of new
recruits to the struggle for independence. Eventually, the
jails were full and the country did not work anymore and
230 the British had to leave."

It was my turn to sigh, because this had gotten a long
way from football or figuring out a way to keep Bill from
turning Ramdas into an ooze of pink on a locker door.
"Look, Ramdas, that might have worked in India, but in this
235 country—"

"Your Martin Luther King made it work in this country."

"Okay, point taken, but what are you going to do about
Bill?"

"Just what I am doing. I am going to answer his violence
240 with *satyagraha*. Someday, his arms will get tired."

"If he doesn't kill you first."

Ramdas smiled faintly. "There is always a risk."

Ramdas didn't get it. OK, he was Indian, had moved
here with his family only a couple of years ago. But
245 somehow he must have gotten this *satyagraha* thing
wrong. No way could it work. During study hall I went
to the library, figuring I could find something that would
prove it to him. All the Internet computers were busy, so
I went to the shelves. I found a thick book with a lot of
250 photographs of Gandhi and sat down to page through it.
And . . . it . . . blew . . . me . . . away. Here was this skinny
little guy with thick glasses and big ears wandering around
in sandals and a loincloth, and he'd won! And I mean big
time: freed his country without ever lifting his hand against
255 anybody. Incredible.

Now, I'm not the kind who tosses and turns half the
night worrying about things. I'm a jock. I need my sleep.
When I hit the pillow, bam, I'm gone. But that night I
lay thinking until well past midnight. Hadn't Jesus said
260 to turn the other cheek? Ramdas was living that, and he
was a Hindu or something, while most of the guys I saw
in church on Sunday would prefer to beat the other guy
to a pulp. Man, oh, man, I didn't need this. Let Sarah
and Ramdas talk philosophy; I was just a jock. But like it
265 or not, I was going to have to do something or feel like a
hypocrite forever.

Wednesday morning I went to see Coach Carlson
with my plan. He didn't like it. "Look, I'll get Patchett's
attention," he said. "I'll tell him to quit giving Ramdas a
270 hard time."

"Coach, I really want to do this. For a lot of reasons."

We talked some more and he finally agreed, though he
still didn't like it much.

Next I talked to Rollin. He shook his head. "Man, you
275 could get hurt. And I mean *bad*."

"I'll take that chance. Just tell the other guys not to step
in. And if Ramdas starts, you stop him."

Finally, I told Sarah. She studied me for a long minute.
"You're not really doing this for Ramdas, are you?"
280 "I'm not sure."

hypocrite

a person who
claims to believe
one way, but acts
differently

"Can I shoot Bill with a tranquilizer dart if things get out of hand?"

"I guess that wouldn't be too bad an idea. But I don't think they will. He's big, but I'm pretty big too."

285 Bill Patchett takes everything seriously, which makes it all the scarier practicing against him. Bill is, by the way, not a moron. He maintains a 4.0 in a full load of honors classes and is the only kid in school with the guts to carry a briefcase. On the football field, he studies an opponent,
290 figures out his moves, and then pancakes him or blows by him. Believe me, I know; I've been practicing against him for years. But as I'd reminded Sarah, I'm big too, and I'd seen all his moves.

We lined up for pass rushing/blocking drill. The center
295 hiked the ball to Marvin Katt, who was back in the shotgun. Billy Patch hit me with a straight bull rush. I took it, letting him run over me. When I got up and took my stance for the next play, he gave me a funny look. "Ready this time?"

"Yep," I said, and set my feet to make it just as hard as
300 possible for him.

Cat Man yelled, "Hut, Hut, HUT!" and there was the familiar crash of helmets and shoulder pads. Bill hit me so hard my teeth rattled. Every instinct told me to bring up my arms to defend myself, but I just took the hit. I landed
305 flat on my back, the air whooshing out of my lungs.

He glared down at me. "C'mon, Bauer. Get with the program, huh?"

He must have figured I was trying to sucker him, because the third time he took a step to the right, as if he expected me to come at him hard. Instead, I took a step to my left to get in front of him and let him run me down.

After that play he didn't talk and he didn't try to go around me. He just came at me as hard as he could. After a while the other players stopped practicing and just watched. Cat Man would yell, "Hut, Hut, HUT!" and the same thing would happen again. I lost count how many times Bill decked me. Finally, he hit me so hard my ears rang and the back of my helmet bounced two or three times on the turf. I just lay there, almost too stunned to move, as he stalked off toward the locker room. But it wasn't quite enough. Not yet.

Somehow I managed to stumble to my feet. "Hey, Bill, I can still stand, Bill. Can still stand up to you." He turned and came at me with a roar. And it was the hardest thing I'd ever done in my life to take that hit without trying to protect myself. He hit me with every ounce of his 240, drove me into the turf, and the world flashed black and then back to light.

We lay a yard apart, panting. "Okay," he gasped. "I give up. What's this all about?"

"It's about standing up without fighting back."

"Don't give me puzzles, man. I'm too tired."

"It's about Ramdas. He doesn't want to fight."

"The little weasel should stand up for himself."

"He is, just like I did now. He calls it *satyagraha*. I don't know if I'm even pronouncing it right, but it means standing firm without using force. He won't fight no matter what you do."

"That's dumb."

"It's what he believes. I think he's got a right to that."

We sat up, still breathing hard. Bill took off his helmet and wiped sweat from his face. "You were driving me crazy. This was harder than a game. I'm whipped."

I took a breath. "Ramdas told me a story." I told him about the three thousand guys who'd walked up to the soldiers at the Dharasana Salt Works and let themselves get beaten down with clubs.

Bill listened. "And that worked, huh?"

"Yeah, it did."

350 He shook his head. "I couldn't do that. I don't have the guts." He struggled to his feet and plodded toward the sidelines where Sarah, Ramdas, Coach Carlson, and most of the team were watching. Passing Ramdas, he laid a hand briefly on his shoulder. It wasn't much, but a start maybe.

355 Ramdas met me halfway to the sideline. "In what part of the body are you wounded this time, Kenneth?"

"All over, but nothing special."

"Your hand. It is all right?"

"Fine."

360 He hesitated. "And your spirit? How is it?"

I looked at him, saw his eyes shining with something that might have been laughter or maybe a joy I didn't quite understand but thought I recognized from the old black-and-white pictures of Gandhi and his followers.

365 "Feeling not too bad," I said. "Not bad at all."

Used by permission from Penguin Group (USA)

Answer It

1. Make a generalization about Bill Patchett.

2. Explain Ramdas's response to Bill Patchett.

3. Hypothesize why Kenneth changes his mind about the best way to deal with Bill Patchett.

4. Explain Kenneth's approach to using **satyagraha** on the football field.

5. Compose an alternate ending to the story.

Mohandas Gandhi: SOUL FORCE

In 1947, India overcame nearly 200 years of British rule. Though many countries, such as the United States, won their revolutions with long, bloody wars, India won its independence using an entirely different kind of power.

5   According to Mohandas K. Gandhi, the man who led the struggle for India's independence, it was the combined powers of courage, nonviolence, and truth that won freedom from Great Britain.

If a war is fought with nonviolence, then what are the

10   weapons? In India, with Gandhi's leadership, the weapons were ordinary things like spinning wheels and a pinch of salt.

Gandhi would never have frightened anyone passing him in a dark alley. He was a slight man with a bald head. He wore round, wire-rimmed glasses. He covered his body

15   with only a couple pieces of homespun cloth. He often carried a walking stick.

Born in Porbandar, a small town on the west coast of India, on October 2, 1869, Gandhi was a very timid little boy. He was afraid of the dark and insisted on sleeping with

20   the lights on. According to his religious tradition, Gandhi was married when he was 13 years old. Even though Gandhi did poorly in his studies, a family friend thought he might **excel** as a lawyer, and so when Gandhi was 19 years old, he departed for London, where he enrolled in law school.

25   In Great Britain, Gandhi tried hard to look and behave like a successful man. Not only did he acquire flawless

> *"You* must be the **change** *you wish to see in the* **world."**
>
> — Mohandas Gandhi

excel
to perform better than others

English, he wore fancy clothes, rented rooms that were beyond his means but gave the **impression** of wealth, and even took dance lessons.

30 After a while, though, he realized that none of these affectations made him any happier, and so he began discarding them. He started cooking for himself, and rather than taking expensive taxis, he walked to his destinations. Gandhi felt a little better living more simply, and he
35 managed to pass his law exams.

Returning to India, he began to practice law. Due to a number of factors, he struggled as a lawyer and found little success. His career suffered, and so again, his family stepped in to provide assistance. This time, they found him
40 a job practicing law in South Africa.

Gandhi was shocked when he experienced the prejudiced ways that Indians were treated in South Africa. One time, when he was riding in the first-class section of a train, another passenger demanded that he move to third
45 class. Gandhi possessed a first-class ticket and refused to move, and so the passenger fetched a steward who threw him off the train in the middle of the winter night. Gandhi spent that long, cold night reflecting on what had happened to him, especially wondering how Indian people who were
50 subjected to this kind of racism could fight back.

Gandhi lived in South Africa for over 20 years and become a leader in the Indian community there. Though some people might have planned wars or violent uprisings after experiencing injustice, Gandhi **devised** another kind
55 of power. He called it *satyagraha.*

In practicing *satyagraha*, a person never gives in to violence when trying to resolve conflicts; instead, he or she uses nonviolent resistance. Translated as "soul force," *satyagraha* means holding fast to truth or firmness in
60 a righteous cause. Gandhi wrote, "... determined spirits fired by an **unquenchable** faith in their mission can alter the course of history." He dedicated the rest of his life to demonstrating how *satyagraha* worked.

When he returned to India, one of Gandhi's biggest goals
65 was Indian independence. Surely millions of Indians could

overtake the handful of British ruling India! Why not stage a forced revolution and win back the country? According to Gandhi, not only did violence fan the flames of hatred, but war always led to more war. Gandhi believed in the power of
70 nonviolent resistance to overcome corrupt systems.

So instead of war, Gandhi thought up creative ways to resist unfair British laws. For example, Indians were forced to buy cloth made in English factories. Gandhi organized a mass movement in which the people throughout India used
75 spinning wheels to make their own homespun cloth and sew their own clothes. The British could no longer make money selling their factory-made cloth to Indians, and even better, the Indians were learning **self-sufficiency**.

There were also severe laws against Indians making
80 their own salt. In hot India, salt is a very important part of the people's diet, but with the salt laws in place, Indians were forced to buy expensive salt from the British. Again, Gandhi suggested using the power of resistance. In 1930, he began a 240-mile walk to the sea.
85 As he walked, spreading the word about resisting this unjust British law, thousands of people left their villages and joined him. When they reached the ocean, Gandhi bent
90 down and pinched up a bit of salt from the beach.

self-sufficiency

the ability to provide for one's self; independence

Gandhi and his followers walked 240 miles to protest salt laws.

The British arrested him for breaking their salt laws, but they were beginning to suspect that they were losing their grip on the Indian people. How could they stop people
95 from making their own clothes and salt? Even better, these simple acts of resistance empowered the Indian people, giving them control over their own lives.

Even so, Indian society was not free from its own conflicts. An ancient caste system in India divided people
100 into categories of importance, with the priests at the top and a group called the "untouchables" at the bottom. Not only were the "untouchables" not allowed to enter temples or use wells, but people in other castes literally would not touch them. Gandhi knew that even if India gained independence
105 from Great Britain, it would not be a free country if a group of people were treated with inequality and cruelty. He gave the "untouchables" the name *Harijan*, or "people of God," and throughout his life, he used techniques of nonviolent resistance to gain rights for the *Harijan*.

110 One of the biggest obstacles in the struggle for Indian independence was the conflicts between the Hindu and Muslim people in that country. Each group was worried that the other would have more power in a newly independent India. On several occasions, violent fighting
115 broke out between the Hindus and Muslims. To stop the violence, Gandhi would go on a fast, refusing to eat so long as there was violence. Many people on both sides of this conflict, Hindu and Muslim, respected and loved him. They did not want Gandhi to die, and so they promised
120 to keep the peace. By this time, Gandhi's followers were calling him Mahatma, which means "great soul."

Gandhi used fasting with the British, as well. Many times they threw him in prison for his acts of resistance, and there he would quit eating. The British knew that if the
125 Mahatma died in prison, chaos would break out in India, and so time and again, they released him from prison and gave in to his requests.

In 1947, when India finally won its independence from Great Britain, most people celebrated, but Gandhi's heart
130 was broken. The Muslim and Hindu people had not been

able to forge a working **alliance**, and so India was divided into two countries: Pakistan was Muslim, while the rest of India was Hindu.

alliance

an agreement to work together; a group of people joined for a purpose

135   On January 30, 1948, Gandhi walked to his evening prayer meeting. Each night hundreds, sometimes even thousands, of people joined him for prayer. As he was walking to the meeting place, a man rushed up to him and dropped to his knees in front of Gandhi, as if he were about to pray. Instead, this Hindu man, who didn't like Gandhi's

140 attempts to bring peace between Hindus and Muslims, pulled out a gun and fired.

    Gandhi died right away, but no one could kill his spirit. His deep belief in the powers of courage, nonviolence, and truth has continued to inspire people around the

145 world. A few years later, Dr. Martin Luther King Jr. used those powers to lead the nonviolent movement for African American civil rights in the United States. Gandhi's *satyagraha* also inspired Nelson Mandela, who led the anti-apartheid movement in South Africa.

150   Gandhi once said, "You must be the change you wish to see in the world." The power of his "soul force" lives on in those who use nonviolent means for positive change. Dedicated to truth and armed with courage, they strive to make the world a better place for us all.

Adapted with permission from "Mahatma Gandhi and the
Untouchables of India" by Veena Talwar Oldenburg

Think About It

1. Explain why Gandhi was thrown off the train in South Africa.

2. Define **satyagraha**.

3. Summarize Gandhi's plan for resisting Britain's rule through the use of spinning wheels.

4. Explain why Gandhi gave the "untouchables" the name **Harijan**.

5. Summarize the way that Gandhi used fasting to bring about change.

6. Gandhi once said, "You must be the change you wish to see in the world." Put that message into your own words.

BLACKOUT!

On August 14, 2003, people all over the northeastern United States were powering up for ordinary activities. In Cleveland, Ohio, David turned on his computer to write his final paper for summer school. In New York City, Julian
5 plugged in the vacuum cleaner because he had promised his mom he'd vacuum the apartment before she got home from work. In Detroit, Consuelo happily climbed into the seat of a Ferris wheel next to her best friend.

The activities of David, Julian, and Consuelo were all
10 **dependent** on one thing: electricity as power. Probably none of them even thought about this at the time. But when David's computer suddenly shut down, Julian's vacuum cleaner died, and Consuelo's Ferris wheel stopped in mid-air, they probably all knew they'd lost electricity. What they
15 didn't know was why they'd lost electricity.

In fact, on that day in the summer of 2003, power went out over a region covering eight American states and parts of Canada. Roughly 50 million people lost power. What happened?

How Power is Produced

20   To understand what causes a power failure of this kind, it helps to know how electricity is produced. In 1882, Thomas Edison built the first electrical generating plant; it used steam power to generate electricity to light parts of New York City. By 1896, electricity created by the force of
25 water turning **turbines** at Niagara Falls was transmitted to the city of Buffalo, 20 miles away.

For almost 100 years, the same basic system was used. Power plants were built next to the cities where the demand was highest. Electricity was distributed from these local

dependent
reliant upon

turbines
machines that
produce power

30　plants across transmission lines that connected the power
　　plants to the cities. Today the system is much more complex.
　　In an effort to serve more and more customers, power plants
　　cooperate to serve areas that cover many thousands of
　　square miles. They form an **interconnected** system that
35　supplies power to millions of buildings and homes.

　　　　So how does electricity get from this complex system to
　　David's computer, Julian's vacuum cleaner, and Consuelo's
　　Ferris wheel? First, electrical power is created by generators
　　in power plants. The generators must turn in order to
40　produce electricity, and this is done in many different ways.
　　Some power plants use hydroelectric dams or nuclear
　　reactors; others use large diesel engines, gas turbines, or
　　steam turbines. Burning coal, oil, or natural gas is another
　　way to power generators.

45　　　　Once the electrical power is generated, it is distributed
　　through transmission lines. These are the tall metal
　　structures often built along highways with wires strung
　　between them. These lines are connected to power
　　substations, which lead out to other poles and lines, and
50　eventually are connected to the power poles that run down
　　roads and streets. The lines then run from the power poles
　　straight into buildings and homes. (Some neighborhoods
　　now have their power lines underground, so these lines
　　cannot be seen.) These wires run through the walls of the
55　buildings and are attached to the outlets—the places to
　　plug in appliances, such as David's computer or Julian's
　　vacuum cleaner. The electricity running Consuelo's
　　Ferris wheel traveled a similar path, only its end was an
　　amusement park rather than a home or an apartment
60　building.

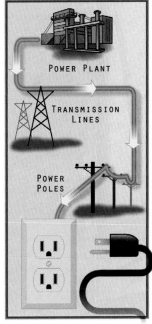

POWER PLANT

TRANSMISSION LINES

POWER POLES

　　　　Today, all of these parts—power plants, transmission
　　lines, substations, and power poles—are interconnected and
　　make up what is called the grid. In the United States, there
　　are three main grids. One serves most of the United States
65　and Canada east of the Rocky Mountains. Another serves
　　most of Canada and the United States west of the Rockies
　　(except Alaska and Hawaii). Texas has its own grid system.

Failures in the Grid

Small failures in these grids happen frequently. Tree limbs can fall on power lines, knocking them out. Brush
70 fires can burn down power poles. Lightning can strike a power line. A power line insulator has failed more than once because a bird landed on it!

When part of the grid fails, other parts of the grid take up the slack. For example, if a power plant in Ohio
75 shuts down, another one on the same grid in New York or Michigan could take over and send power to the same customers. Small failures in the grid usually go unnoticed as a result of this interconnected system. However, when several breaks or disturbances occur at once, the rest of the
80 grid is put under pressure. When too much pressure is put on an **isolated** part of the grid, it will overload and shut down. Before long, cascading failures result, like a chain reaction, and an entire area loses power. This is called a blackout.

isolated

separated

What Happened on August 14, 2003?

85 The biggest blackout in North American history began with a series of failures that caused a massive chain reaction. A joint U.S.-Canadian government investigation into the outage blamed an Ohio utility company for starting the chain reaction.

90 First, the company's computer system failed, preventing it from being fully aware of the problem as it began. Second, workers hadn't trimmed some overgrown tree limbs that were too close to key transmission lines. When these lines became overloaded, they sagged on the tree
95 limbs and shorted out. Finally, when the utility did become aware of the problem, they should have reduced the load of the remaining lines by cutting off power for a short time period to some customers. They also should have notified other power plants on the grid so they could **compensate**
100 by producing more power. The Ohio company didn't take these steps, and so more overloaded lines tripped off, and soon the chain reaction was out of control.

compensate

to offset;
counterbalance

With more and more of the grid out, enormous amounts of power were trying to travel through fewer lines. Shortly after 4:10 p.m., huge power surges swept through Michigan and then into New York, knocking out power from Manhattan to Toronto to Detroit. These surges overwhelmed the system, and generators in the U.S. and Canada began automatically shutting down to avoid damage. By the evening commute, 263 power plants had gone offline.

Elevators didn't work, so workers in New York and in many other cities had to walk down dozens of flights of stairs to exit their buildings. The stairwells were dark and crowded, so the going was very slow in some places. Once on the streets, there were no trains or subways running. Some people had to walk many miles to get home. Electric pumps didn't work in some areas, so drinking water wasn't available either.

There were many heroes during the Blackout of 2003. Volunteers stood in busy intersections and directed traffic. Folks who had cars ferried as many walkers home as possible. At least one ice cream store owner gave away as many free ice cream cones as he could before his ice cream melted. People gathered with their neighbors on that hot August night, lit candles, and shared what food they had in their warming refrigerators.

What happened to David, Julian, and Consuelo? David had to write his paper out by hand and type it into the computer the next day. Julian couldn't vacuum for his mom. He waited for her in the dark and was happy when she finally arrived after walking all the way home from work. After some nerve-wracking moments, Consuelo and her friend were rescued off the Ferris wheel.

During the Blackout of 2003, people had to walk many miles to get home.

The Future of Power

135   The need for electrical power—to run our televisions, refrigerators, computers, heating systems, lighting, and much more—is not likely to decrease in the future. Many people are asking if our existing grid system can continue to meet increasing demand.

140   Other forms of generating electrical power could be used to reduce the strain on the existing grid. For example, fuel cells convert chemicals such as oxygen and hydrogen into water to produce electricity. Wind turbines use wind to make electricity. These and other **alternative** sources
145 of power could be installed locally. They could serve as backup power sources when the grid goes down.

alternative
different; additional

Before Thomas Edison invented the electric light and built the first electrical generating plant a little more than a century ago, people went about their business without
150 electricity. But Edison's inventions led to a new and more productive world. The Blackout of 2003 reminds us how dependent we are on electrical power and how much we take for granted that it will always be there. The Blackout of 2003 should remind us to use this resource wisely so that our
155 future remains bright.

Adapted with permission from "Blackout!" by Kathiann M. Kowalski

Think About It

1. Compare how power is produced today to how it was produced a hundred years ago.

2. Explain what a grid is and how its parts are interconnected to help bring electrical power into homes and businesses.

3. List two things that can cause part of a power grid to fail.

4. Explain how the problems of one utility company in Ohio could lead to power outages in places as far away as New York and Canada.

5. Describe the effects of the Blackout of 2003.

6. Imagine you are in charge of a national task force set up after the Blackout of 2003. What are some of the things you would do to ensure that a blackout of such magnitude does not occur again?

Have a Dream

Dream While You Sleep

Sleep. Benjamin Franklin warned it could be a waste of time. Playwright William Shakespeare disagreed, calling sleep the soother of "hurt minds" and the bath that heals the pains of work. He described it as the most nourishing
5   food "in life's feast."

According to recent research, it looks like Shakespeare was closer to the mark than Franklin. Not only is sleep not a waste of time, it's essential to a happy, healthy life. We can't live without its healing effects. And it's not just the
10 body that requires it—the brain needs it, too!

During sleep, something fantastic happens in our minds: we dream. Some people remember their dreams in great detail. Others claim that they never dream. Everybody has dreams, though—it's just that we don't always
15 remember them. Before we can begin to explore the subject of dreaming, though, we need to understand sleep.

The Stages of Sleep

What happens during sleep? Among other things, our brains go on a roller-coaster ride of activity. On a typical night of sleep, we experience varying stages of brain activity
20 that occur in several cycles. During stages 1 through 4, sleep gets deeper. By the REM stage of sleep, our minds become more active.

Stage 1:   We drift into slumber, but we're in and out of sleep.

25 Stage 2:   We are still easily awakened, but deep sleep is approaching.

Stage 3:   Deep sleep has begun, and we're difficult to wake at this point.

Stage 4:   Sleep is deepest now. If we wake up, we feel
30 groggy and disoriented. It's during Stages 3 and 4 that the body does most of its healing. The immune system increases its efforts to battle illnesses and repair injuries.

REM Stage: Rapid eye movement, or REM sleep,
35 begins. Our eyelids are closed, but our eyes dart back and forth. Breathing is rapid and shallow; heart rates increase and blood pressures rise.

The graph below represents how we cycle through the
40 various stages of sleep in a typical eight-hour night.

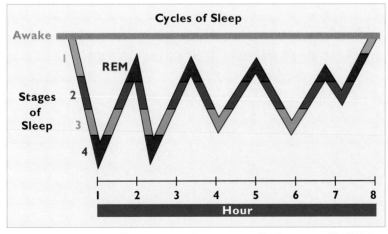

Color Key: ■ = Stage 1 sleep ■ = Stage 2 sleep ■ = Stage 3 sleep ■ = Stage 4 sleep ■ = REM sleep

What are Dreams?

Dreams can happen during any stage, but REM sleep is usually the time when they are most vivid and dramatic. During REM, the brain's nerve impulses increase while the brain's logic centers take a nap. The limbic system

45 gets involved, inserting more emotions and memories into dreams. The "big sleep" of dreamtime happens in part of the cortex, the region of the brain that controls logic, planning, and sequential thinking. Maybe that's why dreams often don't make sense. It's also probably why our

50 dreaming brains don't care.

Beyond the science of sleep, however, Shakespeare had it right. "Sleep," says one of his characters, "knits up the raveled sleeve of care."

Adapted with permission from "The Brain Never Sleeps," by
Faith Hickman Brynie

"To sleep, perchance to dream."

—William Shakespeare, 16th century playwright

Dreaming
the Night Away

by Judith Herbst

You have been asleep for perhaps an hour. Your muscles are relaxed. Your chest rises and falls with the slow, even rhythm of your breathing. There is a calm, almost angelic expression on your face. Silence and peace surround
5 you. The clock on your dresser ticks out the minutes to showtime. Four . . . three . . . two . . . one . . .

And suddenly the curtain is up! Your eyes are rolling back and forth, back and forth, back and forth behind your closed lids. This is it! This is REM, the amazing,
10 mysterious Rapid Eye Movement that signals a dream is in progress. You appear to be watching something, but your eyes are not looking at anything at all. Blind people also display REM.

REM begins quite early in our development as human
15 beings. It seems to be controlled by a part of the brain called the "pons," which is located in the brain stem. Research has shown that as soon as the brain stem develops in the fetus, there are signs of REM. So it looks as though we all start dreaming even before we're born, but what fetal
20 dreams are like is anybody's guess.

. . . back and forth, back and forth, back and forth . . .

This is the dance of REM. Somewhere deep inside your mind you are creating a little drama for an audience of one.

dialogue

a conversation

Your story, though, can hardly be called one of the year's
25 ten best. It's almost impossible to follow. The events are
confusing and disconnected. The characters come and go
for no apparent reason. The **dialogue** doesn't make any
sense. It's a mess, all right, but you don't seem to notice it.
On and on you dream, accepting even the most ridiculous
30 situations without question, thoroughly convinced that
it's all really happening. Furthermore, you are not just a
sleepy member of the audience, you're a participant, and
you react to everything that goes on. A frightening dream
in particular catches you like a hook, and you actually
35 experience fear.

    OH MY GOSH! *You're in the back of a speeding car
and there's no driver! You try desperately to reach the
steering wheel, but you can't move. Crazily, the car swerves
off the road. The brake! You've got to reach the brake!*

40   Meanwhile, back in your bedroom, your heart is
thundering. Your breath is coming in quick, shallow bursts.
Beads of perspiration break out, soaking your pajamas and
pasting your hair to your forehead. Your blood pressure
has shot up, and the **adrenaline** is pumping, pumping,
45 pumping.

adrenaline

the chemical
produced by the
body when
frightened, angry,
or excited

    *Suddenly the car is on a high cliff. The speedometer
needle is climbing . . . 90 . . . 100 . . . 110 . . . You can see the
edge of the cliff just ahead. It's an endless drop to nowhere.
Do something! DO SOMETHING!*

50   Your terror in this dream is very real. You are not
pretending to be scared; you are scared, and all the
readouts in the sleep laboratories prove it. The readouts
also show something else. You are almost completely
paralyzed. With a few exceptions, your muscles have lost so
55 much tone, they are literally immovable. We do indeed toss
and turn and roll around quite a bit while we're sleeping
but not during a dream. During a dream we have about as
much ability to get up and walk around as our pillow does.
Scientists believe the purpose of this strange paralysis is to
60 prevent us from acting out our dreams.

Although sleepwalkers appear to be giving a dream performance, they are not. In fact, sleepwalkers are in an entirely different level of sleep. They are sound asleep but strangely **mobile** . No one knows why some people—
65 several million in North America alone—sleepwalk. This bizarre activity may begin at any time in a person's life and without any apparent cause. Sleepwalkers are completely unaware of what they are doing and usually remain ignorant unless they are told about it. And even then, they
70 will strenuously deny it. They'll insist they've been asleep all night, as, of course, they have. But while they've been snoozing upright, they have been involved in some very strange activities.

Like fleshy robots, they will suddenly open their eyes,
75 swing their legs over the side of the bed, and head off on some mysterious midnight errand. Talk to them and they won't answer. Wiggle your fingers in front of their eyes and they won't see you. They will, however, steer their way around furniture, take the dog for a walk, do their grocery
80 shopping, and even drive a car.

But sleepwalking is only funny in the cartoons. Some people have been injured during a walk because they managed to climb out onto window ledges thinking they were stepping onto the front porch. Members of the family
85 have been taken for intruders and attacked. It is a ridiculous myth that if you awaken a sleepwalker he or she will get lockjaw, die of a heart attack, or become paralyzed. The danger, instead, lies in what the sleepwalker is doing, since these people have been known to get themselves
90 into some pretty scary situations. [EDITOR'S NOTE: New medications have proven effective in treating people prone to sleepwalking.]

Of course, sleepwalkers dream, just like everybody else, which makes for a pretty active night. They can return to
95 bed, settle in, and slip easily into the next level of sleep. Before long, they are involved in more excitement, but this time their muscles are holding them prisoner. Now

mobile

capable of moving from place to place

Dr. Stephen La Berge.

phenomenon

an unusual event; marvel

conscious

awake; alert; aware

illusion

a false thought or idea; an unreal image

they have to be content to stay put while a whole series of strange events unfolds before them in their dreams.

100   Sleep researcher Stephen La Berge has identified something about our dreams that most of us experience but few of us are aware of. La Berge calls the **phenomenon** "lucid dreams." A lucid dream is one that you recognize as a dream. You almost say to yourself, "Hey! Hold on, here.

105 This is a dream. All this stuff is fake. I'm dreaming!"

La Berge believes that once we know we are dreaming, we have the ability to control the outcome of the dream on a **conscious** level. We can change whatever we don't like. He says he has learned to alter his dreams while he's asleep,

110 and he can teach others to do the same. But if dreams, as they unfold naturally, are important in some way, perhaps we shouldn't be fiddling with them. Perhaps we should let nature take its course. Who knows? Maybe dreams are serving a very definite purpose, whether we remember

115 them or not.

Dreams seem to be speeded-up versions of events, like a movie run in fast forward, but actually, dreamtime often parallels real time quite closely. If it takes you three seconds to open a door in real time, that's how long it will take you

120 to open a door in your dream. The speed at which you do things in a dream is only an **illusion**, because you edit the scene. If you begin to walk across a bridge in your dream, each step will match your waking steps, but you get to the other side faster than normal because you have edited

125 out most of the steps. They are not necessary to the plot, so to speak. That's why you are able to be in a wheat field one minute and standing on a street corner the next. You simply eliminate the travel time for the sake of the "real" action.

130   You are also able to put your dream into slow motion. You can slow down an attacking tiger to keep him from grabbing you. If you're running through deep snow, you can slow down the steps to make the event very frustrating. Why you do this, however, is unclear, although it may have

135 to do with the purpose of the dream itself.

In our lifetime we will crank out about 125,000 dreams. No one knows why. . . . Most scientists today admit that dreams are far more complex bits of mind stuff than we ever, well . . . than we ever dreamed. Nature has provided

140 us with a truly bio amazing mechanism. Now, if we could just figure out what it's for. . . .

Reprinted with permission of Atheneum Books for Young Readers, an imprint of Simon and Schuster's Children's Publishing Division

Answer It

1. The author compares dreams to stories. Explain why dreams are like unusual stories.

2. Summarize what happens to our bodies when we dream.

3. Justify the author's concern about sleepwalking.

4. Assess why lucid dreaming is not necessarily a good thing.

5. Hypothesize why our muscles are immovable when we dream.

DREAM TEAM

by Ron Jones

*Based on a
True Story

Every basketball coach hopes to encounter a "benny"
somewhere in their coaching career. A benny is one of
those special kids that come along once in a lifetime. A
kid that won't leave the gym until you've turned out the
5 lights and locked the door. And after it's locked will have
fourteen ways and nine friends ready to re-enter. They
possess all the natural skills and instincts of a great player.
A desire to work hard perfecting the most elementary
moves. And work even harder to help their teammates
10 experience success. Perhaps that's the invisible quality that
makes a benny. The unselfish willingness to share the art of
basketball with anyone that cares to listen or participate in
the game. Whatever that spirit is, it's the quality each coach
looks for. It's the thing to build around and learn from. It's
15 a winning season and perhaps a lot more.

    At Cubberly High School in Palo Alto, where I was
basketball coach, the presence of a benny was extremely
unlikely. The students at Cubberly were white middle-class
children of professionally oriented parents. For the most
20 part, these kids mirrored their parents. They were striving

to become successful at something; what that something might be was never made clear. Without an objective in mind, the striving became all important. At Cubberly it meant getting in "advanced ability" groups, getting good
25 grades, getting accepted into a good university. Getting ahead. Getting through school. Getting. There was little time for intensity or giving to any one thing, especially a sport.

By a strange series of events it turned out I was wrong
30 about ever finding a benny at Cubberly. It started when school integration came to Palo Alto.[1] Black students volunteered to be bused across the freeway tracks. Cubberly High School as "host" school received its allotment of twenty-three "guest" students. As the basketball coach I
35 waited anxiously to see if any athletes might be a part of this transfer. Of course I was looking for a benny. Three days after the transfer students arrived I called the first basketball practice.

The turnout was excellent. Our basketball program had
40 been successful during the past few years and it gradually became known that if you turned out, you would get a chance to play. The prospect of gaining some new players from Ravenswood High School in East Palo Alto added to the tension and excitement of the first practice.

45 As the players came out onto the floor for the first time, I noted some familiar kids that had started on last year's team. In fluid movement they began the slow and graceful art of shooting their favorite shot. Dribbling a few steps and rearing up to take another shot. Rebounding
50 and passing out to a fellow player. Reliving past plays. Moving to the fantasy of future game-winning shots. Eyeing the new players.

At the baskets on each side of the central court the new players are assembled. They dribble the available
55 basketballs in place and watch the players moving on the center court. They don't talk much and look a little

[1] In the 1960s, efforts were made to reduce school segregation in many cities. In the early years of integration, students were often bused into different neighborhoods to achieve more racial balance.

frightened. Then as if on cue they begin to turn and shoot at the available baskets. They too have a private shot and a move to the basket. Soon the entire gym is alive with
60 players outwitting invisible foes and arcing up game winning shots. Another season is beginning.

Midway into this first practice Cubberly High School basketball met Huey Williams. He came rushing into the gym. In fact he ran around the entire court three times. He
65 didn't have a basketball. He was just running. And smiling. Nodding his head to the dumbstruck players. He didn't speak a word. Just smiled and nodded hello. By his third lap, everyone knew we had our first black athlete.

Huey Williams wasn't exactly the transfer student
70 coaches dream about. He was short, about the shortest player on the club. With stocky frame and bowed legs and radar-like hair, he seemed like a bottle of soda water, always about to pop. His shots were explosions of energy that pushed the ball like a pellet. When he ran, he couldn't
75 stop. He'd race in for a layup and instead of gathering his momentum and softly placing the ball against the backboard, he raced straight ahead, full speed, ejecting the ball in midair flight like a plane letting go a rocket. The ball usually slammed against the backboard or rim and
80 careened across the gym. To say it simply, Huey was not a basketball player. He was something else.

Every player carries to the game a personality. That's part of what makes basketball so interesting. That personality is directly reflected in the way a person plays.
85 Now, Huey brought with him a personality I had never quite seen before. He loved life, people, school, anything and everything. "Mr. Jones, how are you today?" he'd say. "Fine I hope." You would have to agree with Huey. His view of the world was contagious. He always had a smile
90 that burst out when you least expected. "Mr. Jones, I didn't shoot too well did I?" He'd be smiling, getting ready to shoot again.

As the first black player on our team, Huey was well received. After all he didn't represent a threat to any of
95 the white players. If anything he was a puzzlement. How

could anyone try so hard, smile so much, and play so bad? Weren't all blacks supposed to be super athletes? How come he doesn't know his place, isn't solemn, and I like him?

You couldn't help but root for Huey and want to be around 100 him. Carnegie and the make-you-feel-good folks could take lessons from Huey. He was a good human being that shared his optimism about life with anyone that ventured in his path. With a smile Huey started every practice with "We're going to win this whole thing, Mr. Jones. Just watch!"

105 I didn't share Huey's enthusiasm. It was the most unusual group of kids I had ever coached. In fact the team really constituted three distinct groups. Huey represented one of these groups. This was a collection of five kids who had never played before. They couldn't shoot or dribble, let 110 alone jump. Passing was iffy. When they were on the court my greatest fear was that they might run into each other. Although lacking skill, they **personified** Huey's faith and willingness to work hard. My gosh how they tried.

A second group of kids on the team had all played 115 together the past year. They were typical Palo Alto kids. I guess Chris Martin most exemplified the personality of this group. Chris was a class officer, good student, achievement oriented and serious about winning and of course playing. Chris just tolerated Huey and most everything else. His 120 attention was on the future. Basketball at Cubberly was like the Pony League, Little League, and Junior League he had participated in so well. It was one more right step to some mythical big league called Hilton, or perhaps Standard Oil.

Chris knew all the lessons and skills of basketball. 125 His jump shot was a picturebook example of perfection. He released the ball at the peak of his jump and followed through with his hands guiding the path of the ball as it slid into the basket. The closest parallel to Chris' behavior might be described as that of a little old man. He was 130 "finicky" at the age of sixteen. If things weren't just right, his voice would stretch several octaves and literally squeak. For Chris things going just right meant a championship and of course a star role. I liked and felt sorry for Chris all

personified
represented an idea; embodied

at the same time. He reminded me of myself. A little selfish
135 and awfully conceited. Extremely insulated from feelings.

A third group of kids making up the team can best
be described as outlaws. Dave Warnock characterized
this group. Whereas Huey had a **reverence** for life and
Chris was busy controlling life, Dave seemed always on
140 guard and challenging the heck out of it. He was always in
trouble. Usually a team is composed of kids like Huey who
can't play and kids like Chris who have played throughout
childhood. Kids like Dave rarely show up on a team. To
have five kids like him on the same team was most unusual.
145 If not intolerable.

Dave's style of life and play was outside prediction.
Dave reminded me of a stork trying to play basketball.
His arms and legs flayed at the air as he stormed up and
down the court. His shots were what players call "watch
150 shots." He would crank up the ball without facing the
basket from some unexpected place and yet it would go
right in. Prompting the defensive player to say, "Look in the
other hand . . . you might find a watch." Dave was always
a surprise. A surprise if he showed up for practice and a
155 surprise that he stayed with it. In a strange way he was also
a breath of fresh air. He lived to the fullest. He didn't stop
to explain his actions. He just acted.

So there you have it. Not exactly a dream team.
Five kids charging around looking for the pass they just
160 dropped. Five kids straining for an expected championship.
And five kids who might not even show up for the game.
The entire team tilted on the verge of combustion. The kids
that centered around Chris and Dave openly hated each
other. Huey and his troop of warriors became the grease
165 that kept the team moving together. Happy and delighted
to be playing they were **oblivious** to the conflict. In their
constant attempt to mimic a Warnock pass or a Chris jump
shot they inevitably made the originals look ridiculous.
Huey with his intensity and honesty put everything in
170 perspective. It was simply impossible to get angry or serious
about yourself with Huey around. He had girlfriends to tell
you about, a cheer for a good play, a hand for someone who

reverence

great admiration;
respect

oblivious

lacking awareness

had fallen, and a smile for everything. And if all that failed, he always had his "new shot" to show you.

175   It wasn't long before everyone was working to help Huey and the other inexperienced players. Chris was telling players about the right way to shoot. Dave was displaying one of his new trick passes. I was working hard to teach defense. If you don't have the ball, go get it. Don't wait for

180 someone to put it through the basket or even start a play. Go get the ball. Chase it. Surround it. Take it.

    We worked on how to press and trap a player with the ball. How to contest the inbound pass. Double team. Use the full court. Cut off the passing lane. Work together

185 with teammates to break over screens and sag into a help position. Work to keep midpoint vision. Block out. Experience the feeling of achievement without having the ball or scoring the winning point. Take pride in defense.

    The intensity and intricate working of defense was

190 something everyone on the team could do, and something new for everyone to learn. Defense is something most basketball teams just do not concentrate on. It's the unseen part of the game. Working hard on the techniques of team defense began to slowly draw the team together with a

195 common experience. As for offense, well, I taught the basic
passing pattern, but the shooting was up to whoever was on
the court. Chris and his group ran intricate patterns for the
layup or percentage shot. Dave with his team took the ball to
the hoop usually after three dribbles and a confederate yell.
200 Huey's team did their best just to get the ball up the court.

   By the start of the season we had one spectacular
defense and three offenses. In fact I divided the team
into the three distinct groups. In this way everyone could
play. It confused the heck out of opponents. According to
205 basketball etiquette you're supposed to play your best five
players. We played our best fifteen. You are also supposed
to concentrate on scoring. We emphasized defense. Finally,
a good team has a mark of consistency. We were the most
inconsistent team you could imagine.
210   We would start each game with Huey's bunch. They
called themselves "the Reverends." With their **tenacity** for
losing the ball and swarming after it plus their complete
inability to shoot, they immobilized their opponents.
The starting fives they encountered couldn't believe the
215 intensity and madcaps of Huey's Reverends. By the time
they realized they were playing against all heart and very
little scoring potential, it was time to send in Chris' group.
Chris' team called themselves the "A Train." That they
were. They methodically moved down the floor, executed a
220 series of crisp passes, and scored. By this time in the game
Huey was smiling his all-knowing smile, and the coach
from the other team was usually looking over at our bench
in a state of confusion. Just as the other team adjusted
to systematic and disciplined play, we sent in Dave's "G
225 Strings." Dave's team played with reckless abandon. They
were always in places they weren't supposed to be. Doing
things that weren't in the book. Playing their game.

   By the middle of the season we were undefeated. Oh, I
had to suspend Dave for breaking rules in the locker room
230 and once for smuggling a girl onto the travel bus. And
on occasion I had to remind Chris that I was the coach,
not him. But all in all the team was actually becoming
friends. It was a joy to witness this chemistry. Huey's group

tenacity

determination;
persistence

gradually improved. They started believing they could
235 beat anyone. The basketball still didn't go in the basket,
but in their minds and actions they were "starters." As
for Chris, he was actually beginning to yell for someone
besides himself. And Dave, well he didn't change much
in an outward way. He was still frantic on the basketball
240 court. It was off the court that he was becoming a little less
defensive. He started telling me of things he wanted in life.
Things not that much different than those securities and
accomplishments sought by others. In fact it was something
as simple as friendship.

245   Our first defeat of the year came not on the basketball
court but at the hands of the school superintendent. With
twelve games already played, the superintendent declared
that all transfer students were **ineligible** for interscholastic
sports. It was a knee-jerk reaction to other coaches in
250 the league who feared we might "raid" Ravenswood High
School of its top black athletes. No one worried about us
stealing away their intelligent students or class leaders, yet
that's just what we did. No one thought to ask the students
and parents how they felt. This was a coaches' decision.
255 Coaches who thought only about winning.

        The superintendent ordered Huey off the team
immediately. The announcement of this decision came
not in a telephone call or personal visit, but in a ten
word directive. "No transfer students will be eligible for
260 interscholastic athletic teams."

        The announcement came on a game day. The team was
already suited up waiting for the last minute game plan. I
read the superintendent's decision to the team. They were
stunned. And angry. Ideas and plots for Huey's survival
265 rang out against the white-tiled dressing room walls. Dave
slammed his shoe against a locker. "It's a bad decision."
Chris agreed. "We can appeal . . . let's go to the board
of education." Dave snapped. "When—in three weeks?"
Everyone joined the argument. "Let's give Huey a new
270 number." "Yeah, but can we also change his color?" "We
can play against ourself . . . can't we?" "Let's make up our
own league." In the din my own thoughts were welling up.

ineligible
disqualified by rule

I didn't know when I started verbalizing my feelings, but I became aware of it as my whispers all of a sudden
275 were audible in the now silent locker room. As my personal decision became clearer so did my pronouncement of it. "Huey's dismissal is wrong. It's unfair to defer the decision or obey it. I think we should forfeit all our remaining games. Huey is a part of this team. If you are willing to
280 give other teams an automatic win over us in exchange for having Huey play . . . raise your hand." Fifteen players leaped to their feet. Dave was yelling, "Well, all right then, we've got a game to play!" It was unanimous.

The players streamed onto the floor to begin their
285 warm up. I could hear a few rebel yells and even that high pitched squeak of Chris'. Huey still brought gasps of surprise with his high velocity layup. When he did his latest new shot, a sweeping, running hook, the assembled fans roared approval. Huey grinned and promised more.
290 As the players finished their warmup, the school principal came by to remind me of the superintendent's decision. "Ron," he said, "I'm sorry about Huey, but he hasn't scored many points for you has he?" "No," I replied, "Huey hasn't scored a point." "Things will be different next year," he
295 confided. I agreed.

As the game was about to start they huddled for final instructions. "Any after-thoughts?" I asked. "There is still time." We were all bundled together in a knot. Hands thrust together in a tight clasp. Everyone looked up. Eyes
300 all met. Every single kid was smiling. My gosh, I've got fifteen Hueys.

The horn sounded calling for the game to start. I took the entire team to the scoring desk and informed the league official. "We formally forfeit this game." The opposing
305 coach from Gunn High School rushed over to see what the commotion was about. "What are you doing?" he asked. I told him of our decision. "That doesn't make sense. You guys are undefeated," he stammered. "We let two of *our* players go today." "It's our decision," I explained. "We're
310 here to play basketball, all of us."

And we did. All of us. Huey did his patented dash.
Chris his jump shot while Dave relied on surprise. It was
a combination hard to beat. We poured in twenty more
points than Gunn and, more importantly, displayed a
315 constant hustle. Players ran to shoot free throws. Ran
to take a place in the game. Ran off the floor on being
replaced. It reminded me of that first practice with this
strange kid running around the gym. Perhaps we had
learned more from Huey than we taught. At the close
320 of the game the Gunn coach stopped to comment,
"Congratulations, you've got quite a team there." I reminded
him that we had forfeited the game, that his team had won.
He turned, "No, your kids won. They're a bunch of bennys."
   Dave Warnock was dead. Chris brought the message
325 to me. His father was a school official and he heard of
the news from the police. Dave had been at a party and
suffocated inhaling hair spray. Like a tape recorder erasing
its content I couldn't think or act. Then in forced flashes
I began to retread the past days. Searching for glimpses of
330 Dave. His face. His antics. Was there something there? A
warning? A plea? What did I miss?
   The school community for the most part remained
ignorant of Dave's death and its self-destructive cause.
There were faculty murmurs, "That crazy kid." Other than
335 side glances at what had happened there was no marking
of Dave's death. Drugs and death are not part of the
curriculum. It was improper to alarm parents. The school
didn't stop its parade. Even for a moment of respect or
some such other platitude. Nothing. Everything as usual.
340 Including basketball.
   The team gathered for practice out of habit. The season
actually had only a few days left. It had been a corrugated
course. Our protest to allow Huey the right to play had
sparked a boycott of all team sports. The boycott led to
345 a change in the rules allowing transfer students to play
with the condition that "due to the disruptions" no league
championship would be awarded. It was ok with us. We
declared ourselves champions. Actually it was Dave's idea.

Oh man, it didn't seem fair. Dave was a storm. He kicked
350 and dared the world. And lost. Or did he? I don't know.

One good thing about sports is that you can lose
yourself in physical exertion. Push yourself into fatigue. Let
the body take over the crying in the brain. I informed the
team that this would be our last practice. We would have a
355 game, full court scrimmage.

It was then that I realized Dave wasn't there. It's funny,
Dave was dead yet I expected him to come prancing into
the gym, the final trick on death itself.

Being short one player I joined in the scrimmage.
360 First Chris' bunch against Huey's team and then Dave's
group to play Chris'. I stood in for Dave. The play was
strangely conservative and sluggish. Perhaps this measured
play was in deference to Dave. Were we all letting our
thoughts wander? Just doing mechanical steps? Or was it a
365 subconscious statement that Dave's life was errant and not

emulated

imitated

to be **emulated**? Whatever, the play moved from one end
of the gym to the other like the arm of a ticking clock. Up
and down the floor.

It was Chris that broke the rhythm and silence.
370 Without warning he sliced across the floor, stole a pass,
dribbled the length of the court and slam dunked. Then
in an unexpected leap he stole the inbound pass. Taking
the ball in one hand he pivoted up a crazy sweeping hook
shot. It was a "watch shot" if I'd ever seen one. Out of the
375 blue as the ball cut through the net Chris erupted with a
shrill guttural yell that pierced the stillness. It was a signal.
The game tempo picked up, and became frantic. Everyone
pushed to their maximum. Straining for that extra effort.
Hawking the ball. Diving for a loose ball. Blowing tension.
380 Playing with relaxed abandon.

It felt wonderful. The game was fierce. Everything
learned in years of play was used. New moves were tried.
I crashed for a rebound, dived, elbows flying after a loose
ball and got it. Sprinted full tilt on a fast break. Yelled full
385 voice as I fed Huey with a behind-the-back pass that he
laid up for two. Everyone is moving as if driven by some

accelerating spell of power and will. Everything goes in. We can play forever. Play Forever.

390 The scrimmage raged on. The afternoon became evening and still we played. The gym glowed in the yellow light, warm and wet. We were racing now back and forth. Exploding for shots. Playing the toughest defense. Jumping over a screen. Blocking out. Back for one more sensation of excellence.

395 My chest heaved for relief. Body throbbed. I couldn't stop playing. And didn't want to. Didn't Want To. Down the court. Set up. That's it. Feed the cutter. Fantastic. Now the defense. Keep low. No. Take it away. That's it. Steal the ball. Now go. Fly.

400 In a heap I collapsed. Legs simply buckled. I was shaking. Head not able to move. In slow motion the team centered around my crumpled form. I'm all right. The air is rushing back into an empty body. Giving life and movement. "I'm all right." Everyone is breathing hard,

405 pushing out air and taking it back in. Grabbing their knees and doubling over. Letting the body know it can rest.

Without any words everyone gathered themselves, then silently headed for the locker room and home. It's over. The scrimmage was ended. Practice finished. The season 410 complete.

I slowly shower and dress, waiting for the locker room to empty. Walking through the silenced place I stop to look and say goodbye. There is Chris' locker. A good kid. Hope his life goes well. He has changed and matured. Been a part 415 of other lives. Huey's locker is still open. Gosh, even his locker has a smile. What a person. I'll never forget. Dave's place. Empty. I hate you for leaving us. I love you.

I push up a twenty-five foot jump shot that is five feet beyond my range. It goes in. Rush to chase the ball. Try 420 again. Seek the magnificent feeling of doing the undone. The unplanned. The unexpected.

There is a sign that hangs over the exit from the locker room. It reads, "There Is No Substitute For Winning." Someone scratched out the word winning and replaced it. 425 "There Is No Substitute For Madness."

Adapted with permission from "Winning" by Ron Jones

Answer It

1. What is a **benny**?

2. Describe the events that led Huey to attend Cubberly High School.

3. Justify the team's decision to forfeit the game.

4. Assess how Chris changed throughout the course of the story.

5. What was the coach's dream? Did it come true?

Pursuit *of a* Dream

The Dream

A woman stood over a developing tray. Gradually, black spots appeared in the shape of an X. Dr. Rosalind Franklin, an X-ray **crystallographer**, held the mystery of DNA in her hands. Yet, she didn't see it—not yet. She couldn't know
5 that it would lead to a Nobel Prize in Medicine—one of the most prestigious awards in science. As a scientist, she was **methodical** in her experiments; she was confident that eventually the truth would become clear. This was her work as well as her dream.

10 In 1952, it was known that physical characteristics were inherited. It had been proven that a genetic code was responsible for specific characteristics, such as the color of a child's eyes or the short tail of a Manx cat. It was strongly suspected that the code would be found buried in
15 the molecule called DNA, or deoxyribonucleic acid. Yet no one knew this with certainty because no scientist had yet unlocked the structure of DNA. What did the molecule look like? How was it organized? Once its structure was identified, a mystery would be solved. Many scientists
20 dreamed of finding the structure of DNA since its structure held the keys to larger mysteries. It could potentially unlock the cause of hereditary diseases. But the story of the search for the structure of DNA became a mystery in itself, and Rosalind Franklin was one of the players in that mystery.

Oil and Water

25 Rosalind Franklin worked at King's College in London. Franklin, an Englishwoman, was known for her success in using X-ray crystallography—a process that uses X-rays to

crystallographer
one who studies the formation and structure of crystals

methodical
systematic; in a step-by-step manner

Dr. Rosalind Franklin.

photograph molecules. Franklin had been hired to apply her method to the structure of DNA.

30   Maurice Wilkins, a British biophysicist who had begun X-ray work on DNA, had been traveling when Franklin arrived. He may have expected to **supervise** Franklin's work, but she had joined the lab as an independent researcher with her own projects. She was already a highly
35 respected scientist who had developed her own techniques. Franklin and Wilkins quickly came to dislike one another and **collaboration** became impossible.

     Rosalind Franklin wasn't afraid to argue. She was an assertive woman who stood up for herself. Before arriving
40 in London, she had spent time at a lab in Paris where her argumentative style was accepted, and she got along well with her colleagues.

     In England, however, her frankness isolated her. Though they came from similar backgrounds, Wilkins and
45 Franklin had somewhat opposite natures. He spoke quietly and responded to her not with argument, but with silence. The two were like oil and water. She kept to herself in the lab, while he interacted with others. Wilkins shared ideas with other colleagues at King's College and with scientists
50 in Cambridge. Eventually, his decision to share Rosalind Franklin's work—without her permission or knowledge— would give him a huge advantage in the quest to figure out the structure of DNA.

Collaboration at Cavendish

     Eighty kilometers away, at Cavendish Laboratory in
55 Cambridge, American scientist James Watson had begun work with Francis Crick, a graduate student. They believed that the Nobel Prize would belong to the first group to publish an accurate description of the DNA structure, so they were determined to use every available piece of
60 information to help them build a molecular model.

     This is what they knew: It was a long molecule made up of building blocks called nucleotides. The nucleotides contained a sugar, a phosphate, and a base. The nucleotides were probably combined in such a way that part of them

---

supervise

to oversee; manage

---

collaboration

the act of working together toward one goal

---

65 formed a backbone for support. Four different bases were
   present: there were two purines, adenine and guanine,
   and two pyrimidines, thymine and cytosine—called A, G,
   T, and C, for short. They knew that these four bases were
   flat molecules, and they learned from Austrian biochemist
70 Erwin Chargaff that the number of As was equal to the
   number of Ts and that the number of Cs was equal to the
   number of Gs. But they didn't know how all these pieces fit
   together. What was the structure of the DNA molecule?

Clues from Crystallography

   Rosalind Franklin's work began to expose many clues.
75 In November 1951, Watson attended a seminar during
   which Franklin described her latest findings. Watson
   didn't bother to take notes, but based upon what Watson
   thought he had heard Franklin say at the seminar, he and
   Crick rushed to produce a DNA model. Franklin, with the
80 group from King's College, went to Cavendish to look at
   their model. She was quick to point out their errors. This
   incident confirmed Franklin's conviction that guesswork
   was no substitute for hard work.
   Franklin continued her experiments by mounting
85 a piece of DNA on a platform and pointing a beam of
   X-rays at it. When X-rays hit atoms in a molecule, they
   bounce back. Atoms in crystalline material are arranged
   in regular patterns, so when X-rays bounce back, they do
   so in regular, predictable ways. They provide
90 information about the molecule's structure
   that is called a "diffraction pattern." It can be
   captured on photographic paper, but X-rays are
   used instead of visible light. X-rays are smaller
   than the molecules, whereas the wavelength of
95 visible light is longer than molecules. Trying to
   see molecules with visible light would be like
   trying to measure a flea's leg with a yardstick!
   Franklin worked with two forms of DNA,
   which she called the A and B forms. Through her
100 photos, she had been the first to show that there were two
   forms of DNA. The A form was drier, and more crystalline.

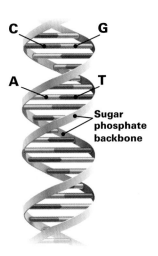

C   G
A   T
Sugar
phosphate
backbone

The structure of DNA resembles a twisted ladder.

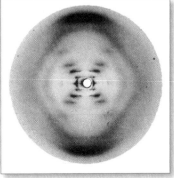

Rosalind Franklin's photograph of the B form of DNA.

It gave more distinct patterns than the B form, which was created when she moistened the DNA and spun it into a thin fiber. This gave a cloudier picture, but the spots were 105 arranged in simpler patterns that were easier to interpret. It was Franklin's intention to learn as much as she could from the A form first, before turning her attention to the B form.

At the end of February 1953, James Watson paid a visit to Maurice Wilkins. Watson wanted to get the latest news 110 on Rosalind Franklin's work, and Wilkins showed him what he had obtained from Franklin a few days before—her photo #51. Franklin had developed this photograph of the B form months earlier. Its X-shaped lines of spots spoke eloquently of a **helical** molecule, which Franklin clearly 115 understood. However, because the A form didn't seem to show this pattern, she didn't want to draw conclusions until she had done more work.

The moment he saw the photograph, Watson realized that Franklin had identified the missing piece of the puzzle. 120 He took her findings back to his own lab. Using cardboard cutouts and metal rods, Watson and Crick built their model and cracked the code. With its complementary double strands forming the sides of a twisting 125 ladder, and its flat, tightly packed bases forming the rungs, here was a molecule whose simplicity 130 and **elegance** were worthy of its simple design function.

James Watson and Francis Crick with their DNA model.

helical

shaped in a spiral

elegance

precision; neat, simple design

Rosalind Franklin went to view the model. As a
scientist, she took great pleasure in the beauty of the
135 structural truth of DNA. She showed no disappointment
because to her, it had been about the process of discovery.

Shortly afterward, Rosalind Franklin moved to
Birkbeck College in London. Five years later, in 1958, she
died of cancer at the age of 37. She never knew that Wilkins
140 had shown Watson her photo. She never knew that it had
been used by Watson and Crick to construct their model.

In 1962, four years after her death, the Nobel Prize in
Medicine was awarded for discovery of the structure of
DNA. The Nobel Prize is not awarded to someone who
145 has died or to more than three people for one discovery.
Watson thought Franklin would have been included in the
prize instead of Wilkins if she had lived. The prize instead
went to James Watson, Francis Crick, and Maurice Wilkins.

Adapted with permission from "Out of Her Hands: The Woman Who
Didn't Win the Nobel Prize" by Barbara Eaglesham

Think About It

1. In 1952, what aspect of DNA remained a mystery?

2. Describe some of the characteristics of Rosalind Franklin.

3. Explain how Maurice Wilkins helped Watson and Crick
   make the first accurate model of DNA's structure.

4. Who won a Nobel Prize for discovering the structure
   of DNA?

5. Do you think that Maurice Wilkins's actions were
   ethical? Why or why not?

6. Assess the author's point of view regarding the
   accomplishments of Watson and Crick.

Martin Luther King, Jr.:
The Freedom Dreamer

boycott

the refusal to do
business with
a company

Martin Luther King, Jr., grew up in Atlanta, Georgia. Highly motivated, King worked hard at school and was an outstanding student. He skipped two grades and enrolled at Morehouse College at age 15. From Morehouse, he went
5 to Crozer Theological Seminary. He became a minister like his father and grandfather before him. Dr. King went on to head a congregation in Montgomery, Alabama.

In 1955, King gained national recognition when he employed nonviolent methods of protest in the Montgomery
10 Bus **Boycott**. He led the Montgomery Improvement Association, the group that had been formed to publicize and raise money to support the boycott. He took this opportunity to practice the principles of nonviolent protest. Gandhi had used nonviolent protest to help win India's
15 independence from Great Britain in the 1940s. King had dreamed about the possibility of using Gandhi's "soul force" as a way to battle racial segregation. King had the ability to inspire others, and many joined him. The peaceful boycott, with his leadership, changed the law that had required
20 African Americans to ride in the backs of buses.

After the success of the Montgomery Bus Boycott, Dr. King continued to preach nonviolence, and he directed his efforts at challenging other discriminatory laws. King urged activists to use sit-ins to protest segregated
25 restaurants. They also conducted marches, demonstrations,

and freedom rides. Gradually, their efforts won greater freedom and equality. Several times, Dr. King was arrested for breaking discriminatory laws, and was sent to jail. His courage and commitment, though, won recognition and
30 support from around the world.

Others followed his example by protesting peacefully and successfully against unjust laws. Churches formed the center of the African American community. It was no accident that black ministers stood at the forefront of
35 the civil rights movement. Among them, King stood out. He was a brilliant **orator**. He held a strong belief that Americans of all colors have a basic sense of decency. He believed they would respond to nonviolent protests.

His movement led to far-reaching success. Martin
40 Luther King, Jr., spoke to television cameras as effectively as to church congregations. Thousands of people—black and white, young and old, educated and uneducated— responded to his call. They risked losing their jobs, their homes, and their lives in the civil rights struggle. They
45 looked to him as an inspiration. He became their beacon of hope for a brighter future.

In the summer of 1963, King helped plan the March on Washington. About 250,000 people came to Washington to support civil rights legislation and the end of racial
50 segregation in public schools. During the march, King touched the heart of the nation. His "I Have a Dream" speech is now recognized as one of the great speeches in U.S. history.

Time magazine named Dr. King the "Man of the Year"
55 for 1963. A few months later, the international community recognized his contributions to history when he was awarded the Nobel Peace Prize. Tragically, Martin Luther King was assassinated in 1968. His legacy, though, lives on. Each January, a national holiday honors him and the
60 influence he exerted during this crucial time in history.

The following is Dr. King's "I Have a Dream" speech, delivered on August 28, 1963. Dr. King spoke on the steps of the Lincoln Memorial in front of a huge crowd during the March on Washington.

orator

a public speaker

65   I am happy to join with you today in what will go down in history as the greatest demonstration for freedom in the history of our nation.

Five score years ago, a great American, in whose symbolic shadow we stand today, signed the Emancipation
70 Proclamation. This momentous decree came as a great beacon light of hope to millions of Negro slaves who had been seared in the flames of withering injustice. It came as a joyous daybreak to end the long night of their captivity.

But 100 years later, the Negro still is not free. One
75 hundred years later, the life of the Negro is still sadly crippled by the manacles of segregation and the chains of discrimination. One hundred years later, the Negro lives on a lonely island of poverty in the midst of a vast ocean of material prosperity. One hundred years later, the Negro
80 is still languished in the corners of American society and finds himself an exile in his own land. And so we've come here today to dramatize a shameful condition.

In a sense we've come to our nation's capital to cash a check. When the architects of our republic wrote the
85 magnificent words of the Constitution and the Declaration of Independence, they were signing a promissory note to which every American was to fall heir. This note was a promise that all men—yes, black men as well as white men—would be guaranteed the unalienable rights of life,
90 liberty, and the pursuit of happiness.

It is obvious today that America has defaulted on this promissory note insofar as her citizens of color are concerned. Instead of honoring this sacred obligation, America has given the Negro people a bad check, a check
95 that has come back marked "insufficient funds."

But we refuse to believe that the bank of justice is bankrupt. We refuse to believe that there are insufficient funds in the great vaults of opportunity of this nation. And so we've come to cash this check, a check that will

give us upon demand the riches of freedom and security
of justice. We have also come to this hallowed spot to
remind America of the fierce urgency of now. This is no
time to engage in the luxury of cooling off or to take the
tranquilizing drug of **gradualism**. Now is the time to
105 make real the promises of democracy. Now is the time to
rise from the dark and desolate valley of segregation to
the sunlit path of racial justice. Now is the time to lift our
nation from the quicksands of racial injustice to the solid
rock of brotherhood. Now is the time to make justice a
110 reality for all of God's children.

It would be fatal for the nation to overlook the urgency
of the moment. This sweltering summer of the Negro's
legitimate discontent will not pass until there is an
invigorating autumn of freedom and equality. Nineteen
115 sixty-three is not an end but a beginning. Those who
hoped that the Negro needed to blow off steam and will
now be **content** will have a rude awakening if the nation
returns to business as usual. There will be neither rest
nor tranquility in America until the Negro is granted his
120 citizenship rights. The whirlwinds of revolt will continue to
shake the foundations of our nation until the bright day of
justice emerges.

But there is something that I must say to my people
who stand on the warm threshold which leads into the
125 palace of justice. In the process of gaining our rightful
place we must not be guilty of wrongful deeds. Let us not
seek to satisfy our thirst for freedom by drinking from the
cup of bitterness and hatred. We must forever conduct
our struggle on the high plane of dignity and discipline.
130 We must not allow our creative protest to degenerate
into physical violence. Again and again we must rise to
the majestic heights of meeting physical force with soul
force. The marvelous new militancy which has engulfed
the Negro community must not lead us to a distrust of all

gradualism
achieving a goal in
slow, small steps

content
satisfied; pleased

135 white people, for many of our white brothers, as evidenced by their presence here today, have come to realize that their destiny is tied up with our destiny. And they have come to realize that their freedom is inextricably bound to our freedom. We cannot walk alone.

140 And as we walk, we must make the pledge that we shall always march ahead. We cannot turn back. There are those who are asking the devotees of civil rights, "When will you be satisfied?" We can never be satisfied as long as the Negro is the victim of the unspeakable horrors of police

145 brutality. We can never be satisfied as long as our bodies, heavy with the fatigue of travel, cannot gain lodging in the motels of the highways and the hotels of the cities. We cannot be satisfied as long as the Negro's basic mobility is from a smaller ghetto to a larger one. We can never

150 be satisfied as long as our children are stripped of their selfhood and robbed of their dignity by signs stating "for whites only." We cannot be satisfied as long as a Negro in Mississippi cannot vote and a Negro in New York believes he has nothing for which to vote. No, no we are not

155 satisfied and we will not be satisfied until justice rolls down like waters and righteousness like a mighty stream.

I am not unmindful that some of you have come here out of great trials and tribulations. Some of you have come fresh from narrow jail cells. Some of you have come from

160 areas where your quest for freedom left you battered by storms of persecution and staggered by the winds of police brutality. You have been the veterans of creative suffering. Continue to work with the faith that unearned suffering is redemptive.

165 Go back to Mississippi, go back to Alabama, go back to South Carolina, go back to Georgia, go back to Louisiana, go back to the slums and ghettos of our northern cities, knowing that somehow this situation can and will be changed.

170 Let us not wallow in the valley of despair. I say to you today my friends—so even though we face the difficulties of today and tomorrow, I still have a dream. It is a dream deeply rooted in the American dream.

I have a dream that one day this nation will rise up
175 and live out the true meaning of its **creed**: "We hold these
truths to be self-evident, that all men are created equal."
I have a dream that one day on the red hills of Georgia
the sons of former slaves and the sons of former slave
owners will be able to sit down together at the table of
180 brotherhood.
I have a dream that one day even the state of
Mississippi, a state sweltering with the heat of injustice,
sweltering with the heat of oppression, will be transformed
into an oasis of freedom and justice.
185 I have a dream that my four little children will one day
live in a nation where they will not be judged by the color of
their skin but by the **content** of their character.
I have a dream today.
I have a dream that one day down in Alabama, with its
190 vicious racists, with its governor having his lips dripping
with the words of interposition and nullification—one day
right there in Alabama little black boys and black girls will
be able to join hands with little white boys and white girls
as sisters and brothers.
195 I have a dream today.
I have a dream that one day every valley shall be
exalted, and every hill and mountain shall be made low,
the rough places will be made plain, and the crooked places
will be made straight, and the glory of the Lord shall be
200 revealed and all flesh shall see it together.
This is our hope. This is the faith that I go back to the
South with. With this faith we will be able to hew out of
the mountain of despair a stone of hope. With this faith
we will be able to transform the jangling discords of our
205 nation into a beautiful symphony of brotherhood. With
this faith we will be able to work together, to pray together,
to struggle together, to go to jail together, to stand up for
freedom together, knowing that we will be free one day.
This will be the day, this will be the day when all of
210 God's children will be able to sing with new meaning "My
country 'tis of thee, sweet land of liberty, of thee I sing.

creed
a formal statement
of belief

content
what is contained
in something

exalted
elevated in rank;
honored

Land where my fathers died, land of the Pilgrim's pride, from every mountainside, let freedom ring!"

And if America is to be a great nation, this must
215 become true. And so let freedom ring from the prodigious hilltops of New Hampshire. Let freedom ring from the mighty mountains of New York. Let freedom ring from the heightening Alleghenies of Pennsylvania.

Let freedom ring from the snow-capped Rockies of
220 Colorado. Let freedom ring from the curvaceous slopes of California.

But not only that; let freedom ring from Stone Mountain of Georgia.

Let freedom ring from Lookout Mountain of Tennessee.
225   Let freedom ring from every hill and molehill of Mississippi—from every mountainside.

Let freedom ring. And when this happens, and when we allow freedom to ring—when we let it ring from every village and every hamlet, from every state and every city,
230 we will be able to speed up that day when all of God's children—black men and white men, Jews and Gentiles, Protestants and Catholics—will be able to join hands and sing in the words of the old Negro spiritual: "Free at last! Free at last! Thank God Almighty, we are free at last!"

Adapted with permission from Haskins, Roop, and Whitman. "I Have a Dream" reprinted by arrangement with The Heirs to the Estate of Martin Luther King, Jr., c/o Writers House as agent for the proprietor, New York, NY.

Think About It

1. Explain the meaning of the term **soul force** used in lines 16 and 132–133.

2. Describe how Dr. King worked to change discriminatory laws.

3. According to Dr. King, list what the Constitution guarantees Americans.

4. Explain what Dr. King meant when he said, "Let us not seek to satisfy our thirst for freedom by drinking from the cup of bitterness and hatred."

5. Describe the dream that Dr. King had for his own children.

6. Discuss the purpose of Dr. King's speech.

Resources

abroad (ə-brôd') *adverb*

    having to do with a foreign country

    During his travels **abroad**, Perry visited Denmark, Sweden, and Norway.

accurate (ăk'yər-ĭt) *adjective*

    precise; without error

    Practice is the only way to become an **accurate** free-throw shooter.

adrenaline (ə-drĕn'ə-lĭn) *noun*

    the chemical produced by the body when frightened, angry, or excited

    That movie is so scary that it really gets your **adrenaline** pumping.

against (ə-gĕnst') *preposition*

    in opposition to; not in favor of

    Ms. Wang voted for the proposal to eliminate summer break, but Mr. Stoppard voted **against** it.

aggravated (ăg'rə-vāt′ĭd) *adjective*

    bothered; irritated

    Juno was **aggravated** by the kids yelling in the hallway.

align (ə-līn') *verb*

    to arrange in a line

    Let's **align** the dominoes along the edge of the table.

alliance (ə-lī'əns) *noun*

    an agreement to work together; a group of people joined for a purpose

    The United States and France formed an **alliance** during the American Revolution.

allure (ə-lo͝or') *noun*

    attractiveness

    The red paint job on the sports car adds to its **allure**.

alternative (ôl-tûr'nə-tĭv) *adjective*

    different; additional

    If you don't like pumpkin pie, chocolate cake is an **alternative** dessert.

antiquity (ăn-tĭk'wĭ-tē) *noun*

    ancient times

    The museum displayed many tools that the ancient Greeks and Romans had invented in **antiquity**.

artificial (är'tə-fĭsh'əl) *adjective*

    manmade; fake

    The **artificial** turf looks just like real grass.

audacity (ô-dăs'ĭ-tē) *noun*

    overconfidence; fearless daring

    The princess had the **audacity** to think she could fight the giant alone.

beautiful (byōo'tə-fəl) *adjective*

very pretty

The **beautiful** horse won three blue ribbons at the county fair.

beauty (byōo'tē) *noun*

the quality of being very pretty

The **beauty** of the mountain view made many tourists pull off the road to take pictures.

bedevil (bĭ-dĕv'əl) *verb*

to torment; annoy

If you camp near the lake, the mosquitoes will **bedevil** you.

bilingual (bī-lĭng-gwəl) *adjective*

in two languages

The **bilingual** sign at the zoo told about tigers in English and Spanish.

blurred (blûrd) *adjective*

unclear; hazy

Because Tony wasn't very good at using his new camera, most of his pictures were **blurred**.

boycott (boi'kŏt´) *noun*

the refusal to do business with a company

Angry at the cut in pay, workers organized a **boycott** of the company's products.

business (bĭz'nĭs) *noun*

the type of work or trade someone does for a living

Mrs. Billing's **business** sells carpet to companies that build office buildings.

busy (bĭz'ē) *adjective*

occupied; working on something

Troy was too **busy** with homework to go to the ballgame.

cables (kā'bəlz) *noun*

heavy, braided ropes, usually made of metal or plastic

The radio station's antenna was held in place by 20 steel **cables**.

caloric intake (kə-lôr'ĭk ĭn'tāk) *noun*

the amount of calories eaten

Before Maylin runs a race, she increases her **caloric intake** to give her enough energy.

captain (kăp'tən) *noun*

leader

The **captain** ordered the sailors to steer the ship toward Hawaii.

cellists (chĕl'ĭst) *noun*

musicians who play the cello

There were five **cellists** in the school orchestra.

charisma (kə-rĭz'mə) *noun*

personal charm and appeal

Franklin used his **charisma** to impress people during his campaign for class president.

collaboration (kə-lăb'ə-rā'shən) *noun*

the act of working together toward one goal

The three students decided that **collaboration** on the science project was their best chance of getting an A.

colleague (kŏl'ēg') *noun*

associate; fellow worker

Professor Tutu's new **colleague** moved into the office across the hall.

communications (kə-myōō'nĭ-kā'shənz) *noun*

ways of sharing information

Modern **communications** include television, cell phones, and the Internet.

compensate (kŏm'pən-sāt') *verb*

to offset; counterbalance

After nights when they have a ballgame, Sarah and Nataya **compensate** for the study time they miss by waking up early to do their homework.

complacency (kəm-plā'sən-sē) *noun*

satisfaction with the way things are

The **complacency** of the restaurant customers was broken when they heard the cook yell "Fire!" in the kitchen.

confessed (kən-fĕst') *verb*

admitted; made known

Micah **confessed** that he had taken the last apple.

conscious (kŏn'shəs) *adjective*

awake; alert; aware

Breathing is not a **conscious** action; your body does it automatically.

construct (kən-strŭct') *verb*

to assemble; put together

Grandpa plans to **construct** a tool shed from the extra lumber.

content (kən-tĕnt') *adjective*

satisfied; pleased

Tara was **content** with one scoop of ice cream and did not ask for more.

content (kŏn'tĕnt') *noun*

what is contained in something

The **content** of a purse says a lot about its owner.

convenient (kən-vēn'yənt) *adjective*

easy to use; useful

A folder is a **convenient** way to organize your homework.

costumer (kŏs'tōō'mər) *noun*

a person who makes costumes

The director talked with the **costumer** about what each of the actors should wear.

courage (kûr'ĭj) *noun*

the ability to face danger or unpleasantness

It took **courage** for the shy student to give his speech.

course (kôrs) *noun*

direction; path

The **course** for the cross-country race took the runners through the park.

creed (krēd) *noun*

a formal statement of belief

A nation's beliefs, or **creed**, is usually described in its constitution.

crisis (krī'sĭs) *noun*

an emergency

The village faced a **crisis** when it ran out of food.

crystallographer (krĭs'tə-lŏg'rə-fər) *noun*

one who studies the formation and structure of crystals

The **crystallographer** worked late at the lab, zapping the test tube with x-rays.

cuisine (kwĭ-zēn') *noun*

food; French for "food" and "kitchen"

Rashida likes making spaghetti and other Italian **cuisine**.

curiosity (kyŏŏr'ē- ŏs'ĭ-tē) *noun*

a desire to know or learn

The trip to the space museum sparked the class's **curiosity** about planets.

curtain (kûr'tn) *noun*

material that acts as a screen or cover

When the play began, the **curtain** opened but the stage was empty.

debt (dĕt) *noun*

something owed

The woman paid off her **debt** quickly because she worked two jobs.

debut (dā-byōō') *noun*

first public appearance

Benicio has never sung publicly before, so Friday night will be his musical **debut**.

deftly (dĕft'lē) *adverb*

quickly; skillfully

The woman **deftly** crossed the log that had fallen across the creek.

dependent (dĭ-pĕnd'dənt) *adjective*

reliant upon

Your final grade is **dependent** on how well you do on this test.

Vocabulary

deserted (dĭ-zûrt'ĭd) *adjective*

abandoned; empty of people

The ghost town had been **deserted** since the gold mine closed.

devised (dĭ-vīzd') *verb*

created; thought of

Coach Wilson **devised** a new kind of kickball game so that the whole class could play at once.

dialogue (dī'ə-lôg') *noun*

a conversation

In the play, the two main characters have a **dialogue** about their favorite books.

dignity (dĭg'nĭ-tē) *noun*

self-respect; inherent worth

Mr. Moran's dignity kept him from asking for help.

disdain (dĭs'dān') *noun*

a feeling of contempt

The knights disliked the prince and did not hide their **disdain**.

disoriented (dĭs-ôr'ē-ĕnt'ĭd) *adjective*

confused; bewildered

Tanya always carries a compass in case she gets **disoriented** in the woods.

distribution (dĭs'trə-byoo'shən) *noun*

the act of supplying products to stores and customers

Her uncle oversees nationwide **distribution** of his company's hair products.

egocentric (ē'gō-sĕn'trĭk) *adjective*

selfish; self-centered

She seems **egocentric**, but she's always been generous and kind to us.

elaborate (ĭ-lăb'ər-ĭt) *adjective*

highly detailed; complex

The **elaborate** model at the museum looked just like a real spacecraft.

elegance (ĕl'ĭ-gəns) *noun*

precision; neat, simple design

Their house was not fancy, but it had a simple **elegance** that impressed people.

eloquent (ĕl'ə-kwənt) *adjective*

movingly expressive

The artist's **eloquent** sculpture captured all the beauty and grace of a great dancer.

emulated (ĕm'yə-lāt'ĭd) *verb*

imitated

Paco was a great role model, whose work ethic and success I **emulated**.

enormity (ĭ-nôr'mĭ-tē) *noun*

outrageousness; vastness

The **enormity** of the fire could only be seen from above.

entranced (ē'gō-sĕn'trĭk) *adjective*

fascinated; enchanted

Lee had never seen fireworks before and was **entranced** by the colorful flashes of light.

envelop (ĕn-vĕl'əp) *verb*

to enclose; surround

Be careful when walking in the swamp, or the mud will **envelop** your boots.

exalted (ĭg-zôl'tĭd) *adjective*

elevated in rank; honored

Judge Ferris is a simple man, but he is the most **exalted** member on the town council.

excel (ĭk-sĕl') *verb*

to perform better than others

Stella studied hard so she could **excel** on her algebra test.

extraordinary (ĭk-strôr'dn-ĕr´ē) *adjective*

unusual; remarkable

The bloodhound is one kind of dog that has an **extraordinary** sense of smell.

exuberant (ĭg-zoo'bər-ənt) *adjective*

enthusiastic; joyful

The **exuberant** crowd cheered loudly when their team won the game.

flourished (flûr'ĭsht) *verb*

thrived; grew

The tomato plant **flourished** after Johari gave it some fertilizer.

friend (frĕnd) *noun*

a person you know, like, and trust

After Miko got to know him, the new neighbor became a good **friend**.

frigid (frĭj'ĭd) *adjective*

extremely cold

Scientists studying the **frigid** Antarctic environment wear specialized coats and hats.

gesture (jĕs'chər) *noun*

an act meant to convey meaning

Sending a get-well card to a sick friend is a thoughtful **gesture**.

glumly (glŭm'lē) ad*verb*

sadly; unhappily

Asa failed to find his lost book and walked **glumly** home.

gradualism (grăj′ōō-ə-lĭz′ əm) *noun*

achieving a goal in slow, small steps

Some leaders think **gradualism** is the best way to solve difficult problems, but sometimes dramatic steps are necessary.

guarantee (găr′ən-tē) *noun*

a promise to do something; a promise that something is the way you say it is

The light bulb came with a **guarantee** that it would shine for 10,000 hours without burning out.

guard (gärd) *verb*

to protect from harm

The soldier's job was to **guard** the palace.

guess (gĕs) *verb*

to predict with little information; to be unsure of but answer anyway

Emma didn't remember the answer to the history question, so she took a **guess**.

guest (gĕst) *noun*

a welcome visitor

We invited Jeri to be our **guest** at the picnic.

half (hăf) *noun*

one of two equal parts that make a whole thing

She only had one orange, so she gave her brother a **half**.

harmonious (här-mō′nē-əs) *adjective*

working well together

Elle and Brad rarely got along, but they were surprisingly **harmonious** in our study group.

helical (hē′lĭ-kəl) *adjective*

shaped in a spiral

The **helical** shape of the main staircase reminded Phil of a seashell.

herb (ûrb) *noun*

a plant used in medicine or to flavor cooking

The chef went to the store to shop for a special **herb** for her pasta sauce.

heredity (hĕ-rēd′ĭ-tē) *noun*

the passing of genetic traits from generation to generation

Ranchers study the **heredity** of cattle so they can produce a strong herd.

heritage (hĕr′ĭ-tĭj) *noun*

beliefs, history, and cultural traditions passed from one generation to the next

Their great-grandmother's quilt is a cherished reminder of their family's **heritage**.

honest (ŏn′ĭst) *adjective*

truthful; genuine

Mr. Alvarez asked the **honest** old judge for advice.

honor (ŏn'ər) *noun*

mark of respect; award

The Nobel Prize in Physics is the highest **honor** a physicist can receive.

hour (our) *noun*

one of the 24 segments of a day; 60 minutes

Algebra class starts at ten o'clock and lasts one **hour** each day.

hypocrite (hĭp'ə-krĭt) *noun*

a person who claims to believe one way, but acts differently

If Fiona tells you to wear your seat belt but doesn't buckle up herself, then she's a **hypocrite**.

illusion (ĭ-lōō'zhən) *noun*

a false thought or idea; an unreal image

The sun's reflection on the hot pavement looked like a pool of water, but it was just an **illusion**.

impression (ĭm-prĕsh'ən) *noun*

an idea; effect

The sporty look of the car gave the **impression** that it was fast.

inanimate (ĭn-ăn'ə-mĭt) *adjective*

not alive; unmoving

The statue looked lifelike, but it was still an **inanimate** object.

indignantly (ĭn-dĭg'nənt-lē) ad*verb*

angrily

Kali didn't think the rules of the game were fair, so she stomped away **indignantly**.

indolently (ĭn'də-lənt-lē) ad*verb*

lazily

After work, his sister usually comes home and lounges **indolently** on the couch.

ineligible (ĭn-ĕl'ĭ-jə-bəl) *adjective*

disqualified by rule

Sandy won the essay contest two years in a row, but this year she is **ineligible** because she turned 18.

inherit (ĭn-hĕr'ĭt) *verb*

to receive from a relative or friend, often after death

When the company president dies, her son will **inherit** the business.

inheritance (ĭn-hĕr'ĭ-təns) *noun*

property received upon someone's death

When Kate's dad died, part of her **inheritance** was the house he had built.

inherited (ĭn-hĕr'ĭt-ĭd) *adjective*

passed from parent to child

His red hair and freckles are **inherited** traits from his dad's side of the family.

innate (ĭ-nāt') *adjective*

natural; possessed at birth

Young kittens seem to have an **innate** ability to stalk and hunt.

integrity (ĭn-tĕg'rĭ-tē) *noun*

honesty; faithfulness to a code of good conduct

Everyone believes what Nancy said because her **integrity** is well known.

interconnected (ĭn'tər-kə-nĕkt'ĭd) *adjective*

linked; joined together

An **interconnected** system of trails runs through the park.

interpret (ĭn-tûr'prĭt) *verb*

to explain the meaning of

The archeologists could not **interpret** the mysterious carvings found in the ancient tomb.

iron (ī'ərn) *noun*

a type of metal

The rusty old wagon wheels were made of **iron**.

irreversible (ĭr'ĭ-vûr'sə-bəl) *adjective*

impossible to undo; permanent

A tattoo is **irreversible**, so a person should think carefully about getting one.

isolated (ī'sə-lā'tĭd) *adjective*

separated

The mean dog was **isolated** in its own pen to protect the other dogs.

jouncing (jouns'ĭng) *verb*

moving with bumps and jolts

We saw Luella **jouncing** down the old road on a nervous horse.

journal (jûr'nəl) *noun*

a written personal record; a diary

Every day, Renaldo wrote in his **journal**.

journey (jûr'nē) *noun*

lengthy travel; voyage

The travelers bought a map to help them on their **journey** to Alaska.

justice (jŭs'tĭs) *noun*

fairness; rightness

There is no **justice** in punishing Billy for something he did not do.

justifies (jŭs'tə-fīz') *verb*

explains; gives reasons for

Coretta **justifies** borrowing her brother's new baseball glove by saying she's breaking it in for him.

language (lăng'gwĭj) *noun*

communication of thought using speech or writing

Navajo is not an easy **language** to learn, though Erin knows a few words.

leopard (lĕp'ərd) *noun*

a large, dangerous, spotted cat of Africa and Asia

A **leopard** will hide in trees to ambush deer and other animals.

lethargy (lĕth'ər-jē) *noun*

a lack of energy; inactivity

After a quick nap, Jeff shook off his **lethargy** and went back to work.

liable (lī'ə-bəl) *adjective*

likely

If you eat junk food every day, you're **liable** to gain weight.

liberated (lĭb'ə-rāt´ĭd) *adjective*

independent; freed from the influence of others

After being cooped up in the house all morning, Eli felt **liberated** to get outside.

limousine (lĭm'ə-zēn') *noun*

a large, fancy vehicle driven by a hired driver

Mrs. Kelly likes to show off her wealth by riding in a **limousine** to the office.

linguists (lĭng'gwĭsts) *noun*

people who study languages

The **linguists** spent countless hours studying the language of the remote tribe.

listen (lĭs'ən) *verb*

to hear; pay attention to sound

The man liked to **listen** to Tejano music on his radio.

logically (lŏj'ĭk-lē) ad*verb*

sensibly; based on a set of rules

After thinking **logically** about how to solve the puzzle, Aleta put her plan into action.

loner (lō'nər) *noun*

someone who prefers to be alone

The book's hero starts out as a **loner** who rarely reaches out to others.

luxurious (lŭg-zhŏŏr'ē-əs) *adjective*

extremely enjoyable; self-indulgent

When Joy came in from the cold, she wrapped herself in a large, **luxurious** blanket.

mannerisms (măn'ə-rĭz´əmz) *noun*

distinct behaviors

One of his **mannerisms** was to chew on his pencil eraser during class.

matriarch (mā'trē-ärk´) *noun*

the female head of a family or group

Grandma Lena always has strong opinions and is definitely the **matriarch** of our clan.

maturation (măch´ə-rā'shən) *noun*

the process of becoming fully grown

Fawns lose their spots during **maturation**.

Vocabulary

metamorphosis (mĕt′ə-môr′fə-sĭs) *noun*

a change; transformation

Caterpillars go through **metamorphosis**, eventually turning into butterflies.

methodical (mə-thŏd′ĭ-kəl) *adjective*

systematic; in a step-by-step manner

The **methodical** shopkeeper sweeps the front steps every morning, even if they're clean.

milling (mĭl′ĭng) *verb*

moving about randomly or in confusion

The sheep were **milling** nervously around the pen, fearful of the strange dogs.

mind (mīnd) *verb*

to take care of; watch closely

Throughout the cold night, Deb was careful to **mind** the fire so it would not go out.

mobile (mō′bəl) *adjective*

capable of moving from place to place

Jeremy will be more **mobile** after the doctor removes the cast from his foot.

musings (myōō′zĭngz) *noun*

deep thoughts

Every night, she writes down her daily **musings** in a journal.

nuisance (nōō′səns) *noun*

something that is annoying or bothersome

The dog's constant barking was a **nuisance** to the neighbors.

oblivious (ə-blĭv′ē-əs) *adjective*

lacking awareness

With the headphones blaring in her ears, Kerry was **oblivious** to her brother's shouts.

opponent (ə-pō′nənt) *noun*

a person who takes the opposite side in a game or contest

Tavaris shook hands with his **opponent** after the wrestling match was over.

optics (ŏp′tĭks) *noun*

instruments that use, modify, or enhance light

The police used night-vision **optics** to search for the lost boy.

orator (ôr′ə-tər) *noun*

a public speaker

The event's main **orator** gave a speech about the history of Memorial Day.

organic (ôr-găn′ĭk) *adjective*

biological; related to living things

The space probe found no plants or other **organic** material on the desert planet.

passive (păs'ĭv) *adjective*

accepting without struggle

During the American Revolution, some colonists were **passive**, while others took up arms and fought the British soldiers.

pathos (pā'thŏs) *noun*

a quality that brings out feelings of tenderness or sorrow

The speaker's sad story used **pathos** to convince the audience to build the clinic.

peculiar (pĭ-kyōol'yər) *adjective*

unusual; odd; eccentric

The cheese he brought home from France had a **peculiar** smell.

pedagogue (pĕd'ə-gŏg') *noun*

a teacher

Mr. Benitez is considered the strictest **pedagogue** in our high school.

peddle (pĕd'l) *verb*

to sell things

The guitarist in our band asked me to **peddle** our music CDs after school.

personified (pər-sŏn'ə-fīd') *verb*

represented an idea; embodied

To many Americans, President Lincoln **personified** honesty and courage.

phenomenon (fĭ-nŏm'ə-nŏn') *noun*

an unusual event; marvel

A shooting star is an amazing **phenomenon** that occurs when an object from space enters Earth's atmosphere.

pour (pōr) *verb*

to move liquid

Tori asked Lou to **pour** her some lemonade from the pitcher.

predominates (prĭ-dŏm'ə-nāts') *verb*

has control over; overpowers

In most children's books, good **predominates** over evil.

prodigy (prŏd'ə-jē) *noun*

an exceptionally talented child or youth

A child **prodigy**, Mozart wrote his first opera when he was about 13.

promote (prə-mōt') *verb*

to support; encourage

Our coaches **promote** exercise and good eating habits.

pulses (pŭls'ĕz) *noun*

regular or rhythmic surges

The windows shook from the **pulses** of music from the car stereo.

recipient (rĭ-sĭp'ē-ənt) *noun*

one who receives

Carmelo is this year's **recipient** of the college scholarship.

Vocabulary

recital (rǐ-sīt'l) *verb*

a formal performance in front of an audience

Our whole family saw Angel perform at the dance **recital**.

reiterated (rē-ĭt'ə-rāt´ĭd) *verb*

said or did repeatedly

The teacher **reiterated** the importance of studying for the test.

reluctantly (rǐ-lŭk'tənt-lē) ad*verb*

unwillingly; hesitantly

Reluctantly, Max picked up his skateboard when he saw the "No Skateboarding" sign.

repetitive (rǐ-pĕt'ĭ-tǐv) *adjective*

done again and again

Blowing up 300 balloons is a **repetitive** job.

resist (rǐ-zǐst') *verb*

to oppose; fend off

Nat found it hard to **resist** the urge to take another cupcake, even though he'd already eaten three.

reverberated (rǐ-vûr'bə-rāt´ĭd) *verb*

echoed

The sound of the trumpet **reverberated** in the empty gymnasium.

reverence (rĕv'ər-əns) *noun*

great admiration; respect

Jill showed her **reverence** for the old woman by bowing her head.

righteous (rī-'chəs) *adjective*

guiltless; morally justified

Kaliyan felt **righteous** after finishing her homework and doing all her chores.

rummaged (rŭm'ĭjd) *verb*

searched by sorting through things

Ellie **rummaged** through her backpack to find her purple pen.

savored (sā'vərd) *verb*

tasted or smelled with pleasure

Francisco **savored** the delicious soup.

script (skrĭpt) *noun*

handwriting

Mustafa wrote in his grandma's birthday card using his finest **script**.

segregated (sĕg'rĭ-gāt´ĭd) *adjective*

divided or separated according to type

Some schools used to be **segregated**, with boys and girls in different classes.

self-sufficiency (sĕlf´sə-fĭsh´ən-sē) *noun*

the ability to provide for one's self; independence

The pioneers prided themselves on their resourcefulness and **self-sufficiency**.

serene (sə-rēn´) *adjective*

calm; peaceful

The lake became **serene** after the wind and waves calmed down.

signals (sĭg´nəlz) *noun*

basic messages

Coach Martinez used hand **signals** to communicate with her players.

signify (sĭg´nə-fī´) *verb*

to indicate; show

Stop signs and traffic lights use the color red to **signify** "stop."

stalked (stôkt) *verb*

walked angrily

Justin **stalked** off the field after his team's third straight loss.

stamina (stăm´ə-nə) *noun*

endurance

It takes a lot of **stamina** to run a long-distance race.

subject¹ (sŭb´jĭkt) *adjective*

likely to; expected to

If it rains tomorrow, the schedule of baseball games is **subject** to change.

subject² (sŭb´jĭkt) *adjective*

prone; having a tendency toward

Her little sister is **subject** to catching colds during the winter.

supervise (sōō´pər-vīz´) *verb*

to oversee; manage

When a teacher is ill, a substitute is called in to **supervise** the day's lessons.

tambourine (tăm´bə-rēn´) *noun*

an instrument made up of a drumhead with jingly disks attached to the sides

During the sing-along, Albert beat the **tambourine** in time to the music.

tantalizing (tăn´tə-līz-īng) *adjective*

tempting; teasing

The chapter ends with **tantalizing** clues about what happens next.

tenacity (tə-năs´ĭ-tē) *noun*

determination; persistence

Kendra's **tenacity** makes her a tough opponent.

tenement (tĕn´ə-mənt) *noun*

a low-rent and often rundown apartment building

Brenda's family lives in a two-bedroom apartment in that **tenement**.

tentatively (tĕn'tə-tĭv-lē) ad*verb*

cautiously; hesitantly

During Darren's first driving lesson, he put the car in gear and **tentatively** pulled out of the parking lot.

thesis (thē'sĭs) *noun*

a proposed explanation; theory

The **thesis** of Jack's paper is that music education benefits schools and communities.

turbines (tûr'bīnz) *noun*

machines that produce power

The **turbines** at Hoover Dam provide electricity for much of Las Vegas.

uncivilized (ŭn-sĭv'əl-īzd) *adjective*

barbarous; primitive

The cabin was very **uncivilized**, with no sink and garbage all over the floor.

unquenchable (ŭn-kwĕnch'ə-bəl) *adjective*

unable to be put out; unstoppable

Akeelah is a remarkable student with an **unquenchable** desire to learn.

verdant (vûr'dnt) *adjective*

green; covered with green plants

The gray sands of the desert contrasted strongly with the **verdant** rain forest.

villain (vĭl'ən) *noun*

a bad person; scoundrel

The **villain** in the book is often cruel to people, but she is nice to animals.

visualize (vĭzh'ōō-ə-līz') *verb*

to form a mental image; imagine

Visualize yourself in a spaceship, and imagine flying to Mars.

women (wĭm'ĭn) *noun*

adult females

The **women** of the ancient tribe made clay pots and hunted small game.

Signal Words Based on Bloom's Taxonomy

Category	Meaning	Location
Remember Units 7–8	Retrieve relevant knowledge from long-term memory	
list	state a series of names, ideas, or events	Unit 7
locate	find specific information	
name	label specific information	
recognize	know something from prior experience or learning	
state	say or write specific information	
describe	state detailed information about an idea or concept	Unit 8
recall	retrieve information from memory to provide an answer	
repeat	say specific infomation again	
retrieve	locate information from memory to provide an answer	
Understand Units 9–12	Construct meaning from instructional messages, including oral, written, and graphic communication	
conclude	arrive at logical end based on specific information	Unit 9
define in your own words	tell the meaning of something in one's own words	
illustrate	present an example or explanation in pictures or words	
predict	foretell new information from what is already known	
tell	say or write specific information	
identify	locate specific information in the text	Unit 10
paraphrase	restate information in somewhat different words to simplify and clarify	
summarize	restate important ideas and details from multiple paragraphs or sources	

Category	Meaning	Location
categorize **classify** **discuss** **match** **sort**	place information into groups organize into groups with similar characteristics talk about or examine a subject with others put together things that are alike or similar place or separate into groups	Unit 11
compare **contrast** **explain**	state the similarities between two or more ideas state the differences between two or more ideas express understanding of an idea or concept	Unit 12
Review **Remember** and **Understand** levels		Unit 12
Apply Units 13–15	Carry out or use a procedure in a given situation	
generalize **infer** **use**	draw conclusions based on presented information draw a logical conclusion using information or evidence apply a procedure to a task	Unit 13
show	demonstrate an understanding of information	Unit 14
Review **Apply** level		Unit 15
Analyze Units 16–18	Break material into its constituent parts and determine how the parts relate to one another and to an overall structure or purpose	
distinguish **select**	find differences that set one thing apart from another choose from among alternatives	Unit 16
arrange **organize** **outline**	organize information arrange in a systematic pattern arrange information into a systematic pattern of main ideas and supporting details	Unit 17
Review all levels		Unit 18

Category	Meaning	Location
Evaluate Units 19–21	Require judgments based on criteria and standards	
assess	determine value or significance	Unit 19
justify	prove or give reasons that something is right or valid	
critique	examine positive and negative features to form a judgment	Unit 20
judge	form an opinion or estimation after careful consideration	
Review **Evaluate** level		Unit 21
Create Units 22–24	Assemble elements to form a whole or product; reorganize elements into a new pattern or structure	
compose	make or create by putting parts or elements together	Unit 22
design	devise a procedure to do a task	
plan	devise a solution to solve a problem	
hypothesize	formulate a possible explanation; speculate	Unit 23
revise	modify or change a plan or product	
Review all levels		Unit 24

Book D contains these terms. Unit numbers where these terms first appear follow each definition.

1-1-1 pattern to Attribute

1-1-1 pattern. See **Spelling conventions.**

Abbreviation. A shortened form of a word. Examples: *Dr.*, Doctor; *Oct.*, October; *CA*, California (postal abbreviation). (Unit 12)

Abstract noun. See **Noun.**

Adding -es. See **Spelling conventions.**

Adjective. A word used to describe a noun. An adjective answers the questions which one? how many? or what kind? A prepositional phrase may also be used as an adjective. Example: ***Six new*** *kids* ***from the school*** *won the* ***big*** *game.* Adjectives can also signal a comparison between nouns or pronouns depending on their ending. **Comparative adjective.** Compares two nouns or pronouns by adding **-er** to the adjective and using the word *than.* Example: *He was* ***shorter than*** *his brother.* **Superlative adjective.** Compares three or more nouns by adding **-est** to the adjective. Example: *She was the* ***shortest*** *member of the band.* See **Prepositional phrase, Participle.** (Units 6, 14)

Adverb. A word used to describe a verb. An adverb answers the questions when? where? and how? A prepositional phrase can also be used as an adverb. An adverb can be moved within a sentence. Examples: *Julio ran in the park* ***yesterday.*** ***Yesterday,*** *Julio ran* ***in the park****.* See **Prepositional phrase.** (Units 4, 5, 6)

Antonym. A word that means the opposite of another word. Examples: *above/below; dead/alive; happy/sad.* (Unit 2)

Apostrophe. Punctuation mark (') that signals singular possession when used with the letter **-s** or the replacement of letters removed to make a contraction. Examples: the *man's* *map, Ann's pan, I'm.* (Units 2, 7)

Appositive. A noun phrase that follows a noun or a pronoun. It renames and tells more about the noun or pronoun that it follows. It is usually set off with commas. Example: *King Tut,* ***an ancient pharaoh,*** *was buried in a pyramid.* (Unit 17)

Assimilation. Where the last letter of a prefix changes or sounds similar to the first letter of the base of a word. Examples: *in + legal = illegal; con + bine = combine; dis + fuse = diffuse.* (Unit 17)

Attribute. A characteristic or quality, such as size, part, color, or function. Examples: *A windmill is* ***tall****. A windmill has a* ***base and blades.***

*Windmills are **narrow**. Windmills catch wind energy to make electric energy.* (Unit 5)

Biography. A type of literature that tells the story of someone's life. Example: **"Leonardo da Vinci: The Inventor."** (Unit 14)

Blend. A consonant sound pair in the same syllable. The consonants are not separated by vowels, and each consonant sound is pronounced. **Initial blends** are letter combinations that represent two different consonant sounds at the beginning of a word. Examples: **bl**-, *black, blink*; **br**-, *bring, brought*. **Final blends** are letter pairs that represent two different consonant sounds at the end of a word. Examples: **-nd**, *band, land*; **-st**, *last, mast*. **Clusters** consist of three or more consonants in the same syllable. The consonants are not supported by vowels. Each consonant is pronounced. Examples: **spr**-, *spread, spray*; **str**-, *stress, stray*. (Units 8, 11)

Business letter. A letter that is written to someone the author does not know or who is a position of authority, such as a government agency, teacher, or minister. Also called a formal letter. Business letters are usually typed; paragraphs are not indented. (Unit 16)

Capital letters. Uppercase letters used at the beginning of all sentences. Examples: *The cat sat. Where did it sit? It sat on my lap!* (Unit 1)

Cluster. See **Blend.**

Comma. A punctuation mark (,) used to signal a pause when reading or writing to clarify meaning. Commas separate phrases at the beginning of sentences (e.g., *At the end of the song, Juan clapped*), adjectives of the same kind (e.g., *The big, black cat sat*), appositives from their modifiers (e.g., *Sam, my pet cat, is black*), the day from the year in a date (e.g., *December 1, 2008*), the city from the state in an address (e.g., *Denver, CO 80020*), and the greeting and the closing from the body of a letter (e.g., *Dear Uncle Tran, Thank you!*). (Unit 5)

Common noun. See **Noun.**

Compound predicate nominative. Can be compared with the conjunctions **and**, **or**, and **but**. Example: *The exits were the fire escape **and** the stairs.* **Compound predicate adjective.** Example: *The detective's work was dangerous **and** hazardous.* (Unit 22)

Compound word. A word made up of two or more smaller words. There are three types of compound words: (1) **closed**, which are written without a space between the words (e.g., *downhill*); **open**, which are written with a space between the words (e.g., *jump shot*); and (3) **hyphenated**, which are written with a hyphen between the words (e.g., *left-hand*). (Units 3, 13)

Concrete noun. See **Noun.**

Conjunction. A word that joins words, phrases, or clauses in a sentence. Can also join sentences. **Coordinating conjunction.** Conjunctions that connect words that have the same function. Examples: *and, but, or.* The conjunction *and* relates two similar ideas. Example: *Ellen **and** her friends rested.* The conjunction *but* signals contrasting ideas. Example: *The hurricane hit land, **but** the people escaped.* The conjunction *or* signals an alteration or choice. Example: *An artist can carve **or** sculpt stone.* (Units 7, 10, 11)

Consonant. A closed sound produced using airflow restricted or closed by the lips, teeth, or tongue. Letters represent consonant sounds. Examples: *m̲, s̲, t̲, b̲.* (Unit 1)

Context cues. See **Vocabulary strategies.**

Contractions. Two words combined into one word. One or more letters are left out and are replaced with an apostrophe ('). Examples: **is + no/t = isn't; I + w/o/u/l/d = I'd; It + w/i/ll = It'll.** (Units 7, 9, 10)

Degrees of Meaning. Levels of words that relate to the context in which they are used. Antonyms can be on either end of the scale. The words along the scale are related by degrees. Examples: *cold* vs. *chilly* vs. *room temperature* vs. *warm* vs. *hot.* (Unit 19)

Digraph. Two letters that represent one sound. Examples: / *ch* / as in ***chop, such***; / *sh* / as in ***shop, dish***. (Unit 8)

Direct object. A noun or pronoun that receives the action of the main verb in the predicate. Answers the question who or what received the action? Example: *Casey visits **granddad**.* **Compound direct object.** Two direct objects joined by a conjunction. Example: *The bugs infest **crops and animals***. (Units 3, 4, 9)

Double consonants. See **Spelling conventions.**

Doubling rule. See **Spelling rules.**

Drama. A literary genre, it is a story written to be acted by characters, such as a play, a musical, or an opera. Example: **"These Shoes of Mine."** (Unit 15)

Exclamation point. Punctuation mark (**!**) used to signal heightened expression or strong emotion. (Unit 1)

Expository text. Text that provides information and includes a topic. Facts and examples support the topic. It is organized using main ideas and supporting details. Expository text can be found in textbooks, newspapers, magazines, and encyclopedias. Example: **"Batty About Bats!"** Also called **informational text** and **nonfiction**. (Unit 1)

Expressions. A common way of saying something. They are similar to idioms. Expressions do not have a specific form. Examples: *all wet* = mistaken; *odds and ends* = leftovers. (Unit 7)

Final silent e. See **Spelling conventions.**

First-person account. A type of literature, either fiction or nonfiction, in which the narrator recalls his or her own personal experiences. Example: **"King Tut: Egyptian Pharaoh."** (Unit 17)

Folktale. A type of narrative text characterized by fictional, everyday people, set in an imagined place and time. Example: **"The Spider's Thread."** (Unit 7)

Helping verb. See **Verb.**

Homophones. Words that sound the same but have different meanings. Examples: *there/their/they're*; *our/hour*; *write/right*. (Unit 7)

Idiom. A common phrase that cannot be understood by the meanings of its separate words—only by the entire phrase. It cannot be changed, or the idiom loses its meaning. Examples: *be in hot water* = be in serious trouble; *hold your horses* = slow down. (Unit 4)

Indefinite pronouns. Pronouns that refer to unspecified or unknown people or things. They do not have antecedents. Example: *Ramdas believes that someone with an injury should not play.* (Unit 23)

Indirect object. A noun or pronoun often placed between the main verb and the direct object. It tells to whom or for whom the action was done. If a sentence has an indirect object, it must also have a direct object. Example: *Nikko gave granddad a gift.* (Unit 17)

Informal letter. A letter that is written to someone the author knows well, such as a friend or relative. Also called a friendly or personal letter. Informal letters can be handwritten or typed; paragraphs are indented. (Unit 16)

Informational text. See **Expository text.**

Irregular verb. See **Verb.**

Legend. A type of narrative text characterized by a particular person and a particular time and place in history. Example: **"Floki: Sailor Without a Map."** (Unit 2)

Letters. See **Informal letter, Business letter**.

Linking verbs. Verbs that connect, or link, the subject of the sentence to a word in the predicate. (Unit 19)

Meaning cues. See **Vocabulary strategies.**

Metaphor. A figure of speech in which a word or phrase implies a comparison or identity. Example: *Life is just a bowl of cherries.*

Myth. A type of narrative text characterized by supernatural beings and superheroes, set in a time before recorded history. Describes how the world, creatures, and people came to be the way they are. Example: **"Mythical Heroes."** (Unit 15)

Narrative text. Text that tells a personal story of the writer. The writer uses "I" to tell the story. Narrative text includes a message, often a lesson learned from the experience that the author is writing about. The story has a beginning, middle, and end. Narrative text can be found in novels, anthologies, and magazines. Example: **"One Sport I Like!"** Also known as **Personal narrative.** (Units 7, 8)

Nominative pronoun. See **Pronoun.**

Nonfiction. See **Expository text.**

Noun. A word that names a person, place, thing, or idea. Examples: *children, campus, lemon, method.* **Abstract noun.** A word that names an idea or a thought that we cannot see or touch. Examples: *love, Saturday, sports, democracy.* **Common noun.** A word that names a general person, place, or thing. Examples: *man, city, statue.* **Concrete noun.** A word that names a person, place, or thing that we can see or touch. Examples: *teacher, car, pencil.* **Possessive noun.** Indicates ownership or possession. Formed by adding an apostrophe (') and an -**s** to signal singular possession. Examples: *Stan's stamps, the man's cap.* Formed by adding -**s** and an apostrophe (') to signal plural possession. Examples: *boys' cards, dogs' bowls.* **Proper noun.** A word that names a specific person, place, or thing. Examples: *Mr. West, Boston, Statue of Liberty.* (Units 1, 2, 3, 11)

Object of a preposition. A noun or pronoun that ends a prepositional phrase. Examples: *in the **cab**; during the **game**.* (Unit 4)

Object pronoun. See **Pronoun.**

Onomatopeoia. A literary device created when a word's sound suggests its meaning. Examples: *bam, bang, buzz, crash.* (Unit 16)

Paragraph. A group of sentences. Each sentence in the paragraph has a specific job. **Topic sentence.** Tells what the paragraph is about. Example: *Regular exercise benefits people's health in two important ways.* **Supporting details.** Give facts or reasons about the topic. Example: *One benefit is that exercise improves people's physical health.* **Transition words.** Link one supporting detail to the next. Examples: *one, also.* **E's, or elaborations (explanations, examples, evidence).** Sentences that support the topic and supporting details and add interest for the reader. Example: *It makes people feel better about themselves and calms them down when they are angry or stressed.* **Conclusion.** Ties the parts together. It often restates the topic. Example: *When people regularly do physical activities they enjoy, their bodies and minds stay fit, happy, and healthy.* **Introductory paragraph.** States the topic for an entire report. Example: *Exercise can benefit your health in two ways. Regular exercise improves your physical health and is good for your mind.* **Body paragraph.** Tells more about the topic. It often begins with a transition topic sentence and includes E's that support the topic sentence. **Concluding paragraph.** Links to the introductory paragraph and ties the whole report together. Example: *It is clear that exercise is great for both the body and the mind. The benefits of exercise are just too important to ignore.* (Unit 7)

Participle. The verb form used with the helping verbs **have**, **has**, or **had** to indicate present or past perfect. **Present participle.** Ends in the **-ing** form of a verb and can be used as an adjective to describe nouns. Examples: *The sun is **shining**; The **shining** sun is hot.* **Regular past participle.** Ends in the **-ed** form of the verb and can be used as an adjective to describe nouns. Examples: *The athlete **injured** his foot; The **injured** athlete used crutches.* Many irregular past participles end in **-en**. Example: *eaten.* (Unit 16)

Parts of a story. The elements that make up a story, including setting, characters, and plot.

Perfect tense. Verb phrases with forms of **have** that signal time in special ways. **Present perfect.** Verbs that always include the helping verb **has** or **have**. They tell about events that took place at some unspecified time in the past. Example: *My sister **has** planted a big garden.* **Past perfect tense**. Verbs that always include the helping verb **had**. They tell about events that took place before another event happened in the past. Example: *Before she planted this garden, she **had** only grown beans in a planter.* **Future perfect tense**. Verbs that always include the helping verb pair **will have**. They are used to tell about an action that will be completed before another actions happens in the future. Example: *By July she **will have** harvested her first crop of peas.* (Unit 21)

Period. Punctuation mark (.) used at the ending of all sentences or an abbreviation. Examples: *The cat sat. Mr. Jones came to the door.* (Unit 1)

Personal narrative. See **Narrative text.**

Personification. Figurative language that assigns human characteristics to an idea, animal, or thing. Example: **"Roberto Clemente: The Heart of the Diamond"** (Unit 16)

Phrasal verb. Consists of a verb and a word whose form looks like a preposition. The second word does not function as a preposition; instead, it is part of the meaning of the phrasal verb. The meaning of the phrasal verb is usually different from the meanings of its individual words. Example: *He ran into the store. He ran into the store with his car.* (Unit 22)

Phrase. A group of words that does the same job as a single word. Examples: *in the house; with a bang.* (Unit 4)

Plot. The sequence of events in a story. Includes conflict, climax, resolution, and conclusion.

Plural. A term that means more than one. Nouns are usually made plural by adding -**s**. Examples: *bats, acts, cabs.* Nouns ending in -**s**, -**z**, -**x**, -**chv**, -**sh**, and -**tch** use -**es** to make them plural. Examples: *dresses, fizzes, boxes, riches, dishes, matches.* (Units 1, 7)

Possession. Indicates ownership of something. **Singular possession.** One person or thing that owns something. Adding **'s** (apostrophe and the letter **s**) to a noun signals singular possession. Examples: *Stan's stamps, the van's mat, the man's cap.* **Plural possession.** More than one person or thing that owns something. Adding the suffix -**s'** (letter **s** and an apostrophe) to a noun signals plural possession. Examples: *boys', girls', dogs'.* (Units 2, 11)

Possessive noun. See **Noun.**

Possessive pronoun. See **Pronoun.**

Predicate. The second of two main parts of a sentence. It contains the main verb of the sentence, describes the action, usually comes after the subject, and answers the question what did they (he, she, it) do? Example: *The man ran.* **Simple predicate.** The verb that tells what the subject did. Example: *The class clapped during the song.* **Complete predicate.** The simple predicate and all its objects and modifiers. Example: *The class clapped during the song.* **Compound predicate.** Two simple predicates joined by a conjunction. *The class sang and clapped.* (Units 2, 8)

Predicate adjective. Follows a linking verb and describes the subject. Example: *Kokopelli's music is beautiful.* (Unit 20)

Predicate nominative. The noun that follows the form of **be** as the main verb. Example: *The girl is a runner.* (Unit 19)

Prefix. A word part added to the beginning of a word that can add to or change the meaning of a word. Prefixes include: **un-, pre-,** and **non-.** Examples: *unplug; preset; nonsense.* (Units 13, 14, 15, 16, 17, 18)

Preposition. A function word that begins a prepositional phrase. Prepositions show relationship. Most prepositions show a position in space (e.g., *inside, over, under*), time (e.g., *during, since, until*), or space and time (e.g., *after, from, through*). (Units 4, 6)

Prepositional phrase. A phrase that begins with a preposition and ends with a noun or a pronoun. A prepositional phrase is used either as an adjective or as an adverb. Examples: *in the van*; *on Monday*; *to the class*. See **Adjective, Adverb**. (Unit 4)

Pronoun. A function word used in place of a noun. Examples: *I, you, he, me, they.* **Nominative (subject) pronoun.** A function word that takes the place of the subject noun in a sentence. Examples: *I, you, he, she, it, we, they.* **Object pronoun.** A function word that takes the place of the object of a preposition or a direct object. Examples: *me, you, him, her, it, us, them.* **Possessive pronouns.** Pronouns that show ownership. Sometimes a possessive pronoun functions as an adjective, or sometimes the possessive pronoun replaces the noun. Examples: *My desk is a mess. Mine is a mess.* (Units 4, 6, 7)

Pronoun referent. See **Vocabulary strategies**.

Proper noun. See **Noun**.

Punctuation. Marks that indicate the ending of a sentence (period, question mark, and exclamation point), a pause within a sentence (comma), or possession (apostrophe accompanied by the letter <u>s</u>). Examples: *The cat sat. Where did it sit? It sat on my lap! Yesterday, school was cancelled. Sam's map.* See **Apostrophe, Comma, Exclamation point, Period, Question mark.** (Units 2, 5, 7)

Question mark. Punctuation mark (**?**) used at the end of a sentence to indicate that a question has been asked. Example: *Where did the cat sit?* (Unit 1)

Regular verb. See **Verb**.

Report. A piece of nonfiction writing that focuses on one topic. The body paragraphs tell different points about the topic. Each point is stated in a transition topic sentence. A report does not include any personal details.

Root. The basic meaning of a word. It carries the most important part of a word's meaning. The root usually needs a prefix or suffix to make it into a word. Example: *ex • tract.* (Unit 20)

Schwa to Spelling conventions

Schwa. A vowel phoneme in an unstressed syllable that has reduced value or emphasis. The symbol for schwa is / ə /. Example: *lesson* = / lĕssən /. The **o** in *lesson* is reduced to **schwa**, which sounds like / ŭ / but is more reduced. If a syllable is not stressed, the vowel is usually reduced to schwa. An **a** that begins or ends a word is often reduced to schwa. Example: *alike* = / ə-līk /. In a multisyllable word, the second syllable is often reduced to schwa. Example: *multiply* = / mul'tə-plī /. (Unit 13)

Science fiction. A type of text characterized by fantastic or futuristic people and places. Example: **"Podway Bound: A Science Fiction Story."** (Unit 13)

Sentence. A complete thought that answers the questions who (what) did it? and what did they (he, she, it) do? Examples: *The cat sat. The players talked. Sam acted.* **Simple sentence.** A complete thought that contains one subject and one predicate. Examples: *The man ran. Casey batted. The bird hopped.* **Compound sentence.** Two sentences joined by a conjunction. Example: *Julio walked **and** Dan ran.* **Topic sentence.** States the topic of the paragraph. It is often the first sentence. Example: *"Batty About Bats"* explains facts about bats. (Units 1, 2, 10)

Simile. A figure of speech that makes a comparison. A simile always uses the words *like* or *as*. Examples: *as smart **as** Einstein; as artistic **as** Picasso.* (Unit 14)

Singular. A word that means one of something. Examples: *bat, act, cab.* (Unit 1)

Spelling conventions. Tips that help us remember how to spell words. **Words with v or s + e.** Almost no word ends with the letter **v**. The letter **v** is almost always followed by **e**. Examples: *have, give, live.* Often the **e** follows a single **s** at the end of the word. The **e** does not signal a long vowel. Examples: *promise, purchase.* **Double consonants.** Use double letters -**ss**, -**ff**, -**ll**, -**zz** at the end of many words, in many one-syllable words, or after one short vowel. Examples: *pass, stiff, will, jazz.* **Ways to spell / k /.** The sound / k / is spelled three ways. The position of / k / in the word signals how to spell it. First, use **c** at the beginning of words before the vowel **a**. Example: *cat.* Second, use **k** at the beginning of words before the vowel **i**. Example: *kid.* Third, use -**ck** after one short vowel in one-syllable words: Examples: *back, sick.* **Adding -es.** Nouns and verbs endings in **s**, **z**, or **x**, add -**es** to form plural nouns or singular present tense verbs. Examples: *dresses, boxes, presses, waxes.* **Using ch- or -tch.** The sound / ch / is represented two ways. The position of / ch / in a word helps you spell it. Use **ch-** at the beginning of words. Use **-tch** after a short vowel at the end of one-syllable words, with four exceptions: *much, such, rich, which*. / *ŭ* / **spelled o**. Some words keep an Old English spelling for the / *ŭ* / sound. In these words, the vowel sound is spelled with the letter **o**. Examples: *front, shove, ton*. **Final silent e**. The **e** at the end of the word is a signal to use the long vowel sound. The final **e** is silent. Examples: *mane, pine*. (Units 3, 4, 5, 7, 8, 9, 10)

Spelling rules. Can help us add endings to words. **Advanced Doubling Rule**. First, double the final consonant in a word before adding a suffix beginning with a vowel when (1) the word is more than one syllable, (2) the final syllable is stressed, and (3) the final syllable has one vowel stressed followed by one consonant. Example: *begin + ing = beginning*. Second, when adding a suffix to a final consonant + **le** syllable, (1) if the suffix begins with a vowel, drop the **e** from the base word (Example: *puzzle + ing = puzzling*) and (2) if the suffix begins with a consonant, do not drop the **e** the base word. Example: *puzzle + ment = puzzlement*. **Doubling rule.** This is also known as the **1-1-1 pattern**. When a one-syllable word with one vowel ends in one consonant, double the final consonant before adding a suffix that begins with a vowel. Examples: *ho**pp**ing, sto**pp**ing*. Do not double the consonant when the suffix begins

with a consonant. Example: *slowly*. **Drop e rule.** When adding a suffix to a final silent **e** word, if the suffix begins with a vowel, drop the **e** from the base word. However, if the suffix begins with a consonant, do not drop the **e** from the base word. Examples: *hope + **ing** = hoping; hope + **ful** = hopeful*. **Words ending in o rule.** For words ending in a consonant plus **o**, add **-es** to form plural nouns and singular present tense verbs. The **-es** keeps the **o** sound long. Examples: *her**o** +**es** = heroes; g**o** + **es** = goes*. For words ending in a vowel plus **o**, add **-s** to form plural nouns. Example: *vide**o** + **s** = videos*. **Change y rule.** When a base word ends in **y** preceded by a consonant, change **y** to **i** before adding a suffix, except for **-ing**. Examples: *tr**y** + ed = **tried**; tr**y** + ing = **trying***. (Units 6, 10, 22)

Subject. The first of two main parts of a sentence. The subject names the person, place, thing, or idea that the sentence is about. Examples: ***The man** made a map. **The map** helped the man*. **Simple subject.** The noun that the sentence is about. Example: *The blue **egg** fell from the nest*. **Complete subject.** The simple subject and all its modifiers. Example: ***The blue egg** fell from the nest*. **Compound subject.** Two subjects joined by a conjunction. Compound subjects require plural verbs. Example: ***Ellen and her friends** rested*. (Units 2, 7, 8)

Substitutions. See **Vocabulary strategies.**

Suffix. A word part added to the end of a word that can add to or change the meaning of a word. Suffixes include: **-ly.** Example: *quickly.* (Unit 17) **Inflectional suffix.** These suffixes are used to change number, possession, comparison, and tense. They are: **-s, -es, -ing, -ed, -en, -er,** and **-est.**

Summary. Tells the most important ideas from a text selection. **Simple summary.** Uses only the main ideas. Example: *"Batty About Bats!" explains facts about bats. Bats can fly. They eat a lot. Bats "see" with sound.* **Expanded summary.** Uses main ideas and some supporting details. Example: *"Batty About Bats!" explains facts about bats. Bats can fly. They are the only mammals that fly. Bats eat a lot of things each day. Bats "see" with sonar and other sound clues.* (Unit 1)

Syllable. A word or word part that has one vowel sound. Examples: *map, bend, ban • dit.* There are seven syllable types: (1) **closed,** which ends with a consonant sound. Examples: *dig, trans • mit;* (2) **r-controlled,** which ends with a vowel followed by **r.** Examples: *car, mar • ket;* (3) **open,** which ends with a vowel sound. Examples: *she, my;* (4) **final silent e,** which is a syllable type and a spelling pattern in which the final **e** is silent and whose function is to signal a vowel change from short to long. Examples: *de • fine; ath • lete;* (5) **vowel digraph,** which is a syllable that contains a vowel digraph. Examples: *rain, see, boat;* (6) **final consonant + le,** which is a syllable pattern that is only at the end of mulitsyllable words. Examples: *a • ble, ea • gle, puz • zle;* and (7) **vowel diphthong,** which is a syllable that contains a vowel diphthong. Examples: *oil, boy, out, cow.* (Unit 3)

Syllable patterns. Vowels and consonants follow certain rules when dividing into syllables. Divide VC/CV syllables between the consonants. Example: ***ban + dit** = bandit.* Divide V/CV syllables after the first vowel if the vowel is long. Example: ***si + lent** = silent.* Divide VC/V syllables after the second consonant if the vowel is short. Example: ***rob + in** = robin.* With VR/CV syllables, if the first vowel is followed by an **r,** the syllable is **r**-controlled. Example: ***mar + ket** = market.* With V/V syllables, divide the syllables between the two vowels. Example: ***ne + on** = neon.* (Units 3, 5, 15)

Syllable stress. Words can look the same but be pronounced two different ways by shifting the syllable stress. Shifting the stress changes the meaning and function of the word. Example: *pro' duce* vs. *pro duce'.* (Unit 13)

Synonym. A word that has the same meaning as, or a similar meaning to, another word. Examples: *big/large*; *slim/thin*; *mad/angry*. (Unit 3)

Tense. A category for verbs that expresses differences between periods of time. **Present tense.** A verb that shows action that is happening now. The **-s** or **-es** at the end of a verb signals present tense. Examples: *hops, drops, stops, wishes, pitches.* **Past tense.** A verb that shows action that is finished. Adding **-ed** signals past tense. The suffix **-ed** represents three sounds: (1) / *t* / after a sound that is not voiced. Examples: *blessed, chipped*; (2) / *d* / after a voiced sound. Examples: *spelled, checked*; and (3) / *ĭd* / after / *t* / and / *d* / so that we can hear the suffix. Examples: *ended, shifted.* **Future tense.** A verb that indicates future time. The verb **will** signals future tense. Examples: *will adapt*; *will connect*; *will finish.* **Progressive tense.** A verb form that indicates ongoing action in time. **Present progressive tense.** The **-ing** ending on a main verb used with **am**, **is**, or **are** signals the present progressive. Examples: *I am sitting. She is picking. We are sitting.* **Past progressive tense.** The **-ing** ending signals the past progressive verb form when proceeded by **was** or **were**. Examples: *was brushing*; *were brushing; were cutting.* **Future progressive tense.** A verb that indicates the action is ongoing in future time. Examples: *will be passing, will be skating, will be camping.* (Units 4, 5, 7, 8, 9, 10)

Text features. Used by writers of expository text to provide clues to the topic and other important information. Examples: title, headings, pictures and captions, margin information, maps, charts, graphs. Also used by playwrights to guide the people who direct and act in the play. Examples: preface, list of characters, set, props, costumes, bold names, and parenthetical references. (Units 1, 15)

Trigraph. Three-letter grapheme that represents one sound. Example: *-tch*. (Unit 8)

Types of conflicts. A conflict drives the plot of a story. Many stories are based on one of six basic conflicts: (1) Character with a personal problem or goal. A character may solve a problem, reach his goal, or change his attitude or feelings. Examples: **"A Game of Catch"**; **"Satyagraha: Power for Change"**; (2) Boy meets girl. A boy and a girl encounter problems that they need to solve. Example: **"The End of Ali"**; (3) Character vs. Nature. A character confronts and battles an aspect of nature. Example: **"The Call of the Wild"** (Book E); (4) Lost and found. A person or object has disappeared, but is finally found and returned; (5) Good Guys v. Bad Guys. Good guys fight to defeat the bad guys and usually win. Example: **"The Treasure of the Sierra Madre"** (Book E); and (6) Mystery and solution. Characters solve mysteries or crimes, and the bad guys are punished. Examples: **"The Disappearing Man"**; **"The Tell-Tale Heart."**

Using ch- or -tch. See **Spelling conventions.**

/ ŭ / spelled o̱. See **Spelling conventions.**

Verb. A word that describes an action (e.g., *run, make*) or a state of being (e.g., *is, were*) and that shows time. Singular verbs are used with singular subjects, and plural verbs are used with plural subjects. Examples: *sits* (present tense; happening now), *is fishing* (present progressive; ongoing action), *acted* (past tense; happened in the past). **Helping verb.** A secondary verb that comes before the main verb in a sentence. Forms of **be** can be used as helping verbs when used with different personal pronouns to achieve subject-verb agreement in sentences. Examples: *I **am** looking. You **are** looking. He **is** looking.* **Regular verbs.** These verbs form the past tense by adding *-ed*. Examples: *I passed. You passed. They passed.* **Irregular verbs.** These verb forms do not end in *-ed* and have different endings and spellings. Examples: *be = was, were; say = said; bring = brought.* (Units 1, 4, 5, 8, 9)

Verb phrases. A group of words that does the same job as a single verb. It has two parts: (1) helping verb. Examples: *am, is, was, were, will*; and (2) main verb. Example: *the bus **is stopping.*** (Unit 9)

Verb, Be. Helping verb that takes the following forms: *am, is, are, was, were, be.* Different forms of **be** are used with different personal pronouns to achieve subject-verb agreement. Examples: *I **am** packing; **he is** packing; **she was** packing; **they were** packing.* (Unit 5)

Verb, Do. A verb that functions as a main verb or helping verb. Different forms of **do** are used with different personal pronouns to achieve subject-verb agreement. **Do** has these forms: *do, does, doing, did.* Examples: *I **do** my homework; **he is doing** his homework; **he was doing** his homework; **they were doing** their homework; **he did** his homework.* (Unit 2)

Verb, Have. A verb that functions as a main verb or helping verb. Different forms of **have** are used with different personal pronouns to achieve subject-verb agreement. **Have** has these forms: *have, has, having, had.* Examples: *I **have** a secret; **he has** a secret; **I will be having** a secret; **he had** a secret.* (Unit 3)

Visual information. See **Vocabulary strategies.**

Vocabulary strategies. Context clues to figuring out the meaning of unknown vocabulary words. **Meaning cues.** These words provide cues to the definition of a word in context. Examples: *is/are, it means, which stands for, can be defined as.* **Substitutions.** Words or phrases that rename nouns. They are often synonyms or distinctive features of the noun. Example: *The Internet links, or connects, computers around the world.* **Pronoun referents.** Use pronouns to identify meaning clues to define unknown vocabulary words in context. Example: *Oliver Zompro is an entomologist. He is a scientist who studies insects.* **Context cues.** Clues to the meaning of an unfamiliar word. Example: *It is a movie review. The writer gives an opinion about a new movie.* **Visual information.** Pictures, charts, and other visual information that accompanies the text to help demonstrate the meaning of new vocabulary words. (Unit 7)

Vowel. An open sound produced by keeping the airflow open. Letters represent vowel sounds. Examples: **a**, **e**, **i**, **o**, **u**, and sometimes **y**. The sounds can be short (e.g., / ă / as in *cat*) or long (e.g., / ā / as in *cake*). The long vowel sounds for **a**, **e**, **i**, and **o** are the same as the names of the letters that represent them. The long vowel sound for **u** can be pronounced two ways: (1) / $\overline{oo}$ / as in *tube*, and (2) / $y\overline{oo}$ / as in *cube*. (Unit 1)

Words with y. See **Spelling conventions.**

Ways to spell / k /. See **Spelling conventions.**

y as a vowel. The letter **y** represents different vowels in different positions in words. At the end of a word, **y** represents a long vowel. At the end of a single-syllable word, the vowel sound is / ī /. Example: *deny.* At the end of a word of more than one syllable, the vowel sound is / ē /. Example: *happy.* In the middle position, **y** often represents / ĭ /. Example: *myth.*

conventions
    spelling, H14–H16
    writing, H114, H116, H118
coordinating conjunctions, H61–H62
costumes, for plays, H79

descriptive writing. *See also* stories
    draft paragraphs, H105
    key to, H104
    questions to ask, H104
digraphs, H5
direct objects, H37, H66, H70–H71
do, correct use of, H50, H51
double consonants, H14
doubling rules, H16–H15

e
    drop, rule, H17
    final silent, H16
    words ending with, H14
-ed, adding, H22, H23
-en, adding, H23
-er, adding, H21
E's (explanations, examples, evidence), H90, H94
-es, adding, H15, H18
    to make plural nouns, H19
    to singular present tense verbs, H22
Essential Words
    Unit 19, H120
    Unit 20, H121
    Unit 21, H122
    Unit 22, H123
    Unit 23, H124
    Unit 24, H125
-est, adding, H21
evidence, H90, H94
examples, H90, H94
expanded summary, H87
explanations, H90, H94
expository text, H77

expressions
    defined, H28
    examples, H28
    idioms and, H28

family, history of word, H31
fluency, of sentences, H114, H116, H118
future progressive phrases, H48
future tense verbs, H45

grammar and usage, H33–H74. *See also*
    sentences
    adjectives, H21, H54–H56, H68
    adverbs, H57, H66–H67
    apostrophes, H73
    conjunctions, H61–H62
    mechanics and punctuation, H73–H74, H116
    multiple functions of words and, H62–H63
    prepositions, H58
graphic organizers, H86

have, correct use of, H50
heading, of informational text, H78
homophones, H29

ideas and content, of writing, H114, H115, H118
idioms
    chart of, H28
    defined, H28
imaginative literature, H77
indefinite pronouns, H61
indirect objects, H38
inflectional suffixes, H26
informal letters, H112
informal outlines, H86
informational (nonfiction) text, H78

personal narratives, H100–H103
phrasal verbs
    chart of, H41
    defined, H41
phrases
    commas in, H73
    future progressive, H48
    past progressive, H47
    perfect tense, H49
    prepositional, H58
    present progressive, H46
    verb, H40, H45–H49
pictures and captions, of informational text, H78
plays, text features of, H79
plot, of story, H106
plural nouns, H19, H20, H34
plural possessive nouns, H20, H35
possessive pronouns, H60
predicate adjectives
    compound, H71
    defined, H51, H56
predicate nominatives
    compound, H71
    defined, H38, H51
    nouns as, H38, H51
predicates
    complete, H53
    compound, H70
    defined, H52
    expansion with adverbs, H66
    expansion with direct object, H66
    simple, H53
    writing sentences with, H88
preface, of play, H79
prefixes
    assimilation of, H24
    chart of, H11, H24
    defined, H24
prepositional phrases, H58
prepositions
    defined, H58
    objects of, nouns as, H39
    showing relationship, H58
present progressive phrases, H46
present tense verbs, H42

progressive form, of verbs, H46–H48
pronouns
    antecedents, H59
    defined, H59
    indefinite, H61
    meaning clues from, H76
    object, H60
    possessive, H60
    subject (nominative), H59
pronunciation keys
    consonants, H119
    vowels, H119
proper nouns, H33
props, for plays, H79
punctuation and mechanics, H73–H74, H116

questions
    answering, H80–H81
    multiple-choice questions, H81
    open-ended questions, H80
    signal words for, H80, H82–H83
quotation marks, H74

reports
    body paragraphs, H96–H97, H99
    concluding paragraph, H96–H97, H99
    introductory paragraph, H96–H97, H98
    opinion essays and, H101
    parts of, H96–H99
    personal narratives compared to, H100–H103
revising paragraphs, H117–H118
roots, H12
    chart of, H12, H26
    defined, H26
-s, adding
    to make plural nouns, H19, H34
    to singular present tense verbs, H22
    subject/verb agreement, H65
    to words ending in o, H18

Sources

Unit 19

Early Olympic Speeders

Elliott, Sheila. 1984. "Riverdale Girl 1st With Gold." *The Times*, July 30, 1984. http://www2.sls.lib.il.us/RDS/Community/BettyRobinson/riverdalegirl.html (accessed October 13, 2004).

Encyclopaedia Britannica Online. 2004. "Thunberg, Clas." Encyclopaedia Britannica Premium Service. http://www.britannica.com/eb/article?tocId=9125273 (accessed October 13, 2004).

Hickok, Ralph. 2000. "Biography: Ethelda Bleibtry." http://www.hickoksports.com/biograph/bleibtry.shtml (accessed October 13, 2004).

International Olympic Committee. 2004. "Elizabeth Robinson: The Runner Who Returned from the Dead." http://www.olympic.org/uk/athletes/heroes/bio_uk.asp?PAR_I_ID=47512 (accessed October 13, 2004).

International Swimming Hall of Fame. 1967. "Ethelda Bleibtrey." http://www.ishof.org/67ebleibtrey.html (accessed October 13, 2004).

Wikipedia. 2004. "Betty Robinson." http://en.wikipedia.org/wiki/Betty_Robinson (accessed October 13, 2004).

Chart Sources

BBC Sport. 2002. "Statistics: Speed Skating: Women's 5000m." http://news.bbc.co.uk/winterolympics2002/hi/english/static/winter_olympics/statistics/events/speed_skating_results.stm (accessed October 13, 2004).

Official Website of the Athens 2004 Olympic Games. 2004. "Swimming: Women 100m freestyle results." http://www.athens2004.com/en/SwimmingWomen/results?rsc=SWW011101&frag=SWW011101_C73A1 (accessed October 13, 2004).

———. 2004. "Athletics: Women 100m final results." http://www.athens2004.com/en/AthleticsWomen/results?rsc=ATW001101&frag=ATW001101_C73A (accessed October 13, 2004).

Fiber Optics: High-Speed Highways for Light

Day, Nancy. 1996. "High-Speed Highways for Light: Optical Fibers," adapted from *Odyssey* (February 1996) "Telescope Technology: Clearing the Air" ©1996 Carus Publishing, 315 Fifth St., Peru, IL 61354. All rights reserved. Reprinted with permission.

Grise, William, and Charles Patrick. 2002. "Passive Solar Lighting Using Fiber Optics." *Journal of Industrial Technology*, vol. 19, no.1. www.nait.org.

Korenic, Eileen. 1994. "Zooming In on Light Speed," adapted from *Odyssey* (April 1994) "Frontiers in Flight" ©1994 Carus Publishing, 315 Fifth St., Peru, IL 61354. All rights reserved. Reprinted with permission.

O'Meara, Stephen James. 1996. "Space-Time and the 'Ether' Bunny," adapted from *Odyssey* (December 1996) "Cosmic Puzzles" ©1996 Carus Publishing, 315 Fifth St., Peru, IL 61354. All rights reserved. Reprinted with permission.

Raymond's Run

Bambara, Toni Cade. 1971. "Raymond's Run," copyright ©1971 by Toni Cade Bambara, from GORILLA, MY LOVE by Toni Cade Bambara. Used by permission of Random House, Inc.

A Slow Take on Fast Food

American Dietetic Association. 2004. "Fast Food and Slow Food." American Dietetic Association. http://www.eatright.org/Public/NutritionInformation/index_17822.cfm (accessed May 18, 2004).

Britannica Concise Encyclopedia. 2004. "Kroc, Ray." Encyclopaedia Britannica Premium Service. http://www.britannica.com/ebc/article?tocId=9369449 (accessed May 18, 2004).

Chadwick, Benjamin. 2002. "The Slow Food Movement Takes on Fast Food Culture." *E/The Environmental Magazine Online*. http://www.enn.com/news/enn-stories/2002/11/11152002/s_48688.asp (accessed May 17, 2004).

Dorfman, Marjorie. 2002. "Fast Food Versus Slow Food: Are You Dancing as Fast as You Can." http://www.ingestandimbibe.com/Articles/fastfood.html (accessed May 18, 2004).

Hodgman, Ann. 2004. "What's for Dinner?" *The Atlantic Online* (June 2004). http://www.theatlantic.com/doc/prem/200406/hodgman (accessed June 18, 2004).

International Slow Food Movement. 2004. "All About Slow Food." http://www.slowfood.com/eng/sf_cose/sf_cose.lasso (accessed May 17, 2004).

Johnson, Jennifer. 2003. "In Our Hectic Lives, Can We Make Room for the Slow Food Movement?" *NYC24*, vol. III, issue 1. http://nyc24.jrn.columbia.edu/2003/issue1/story3/page3.html (accessed May 18, 2004).

Manhattan User's Guide. 2004. "Fast Food/Slow Food." *Charlie Suisman's Manhattan User's Guide*. http://www.manhattanusersguide.com/archives_content.php?contentID=020204&category=food (accessed May 18, 2004).

Voyatzis, Diane. 2002. "Not So Fast…" *The Tufts Daily*, October 7, 2002. http://nutrition.tufts.edu/news/matters/2002-10-07.html (accessed May 18, 2004).

The Tortoise and the Hare: A Fable

Childhood Reading.com. 2004. "The Tortoise and the Hare: One of Aesop's Fables." http://childhoodreading.com/Arthur_Rackham/Tortoise_and_the_Hare.html.

Mooney, James. 1900. "How the Terrapin Beat the Rabbit." *Myths of the Cherokee*. New York: Dover Publications, Inc.

Word History

American Heritage Dictionary (Fourth ed.). 2000. Boston: Houghton Mifflin. http://www.yourdictionary.com/ahd/s/s0620700.html (accessed November 29, 2004).

Unit 20

Nash's Bashes: Word Play

Nash, Ogden. "The Eel" copyright 1941; "The Rhinoceros" copyright 1935; "The Cow" copyright 1942; "The Termite" copyright 1942; "The Wasp" copyright 1942; "The Lama" copyright 1932; "The Ostrich" copyright 1956 by Ogden Nash, renewed. Reprinted by permission of Curtis Brown, Ltd.

The Marble Champ

"The Marble Champ" from BASEBALL IN APRIL AND OTHER STORIES, copyright ©1990 by Gary Soto, reprinted by permission of Harcourt, Inc.

A Game of Catch

Wilbur, Richard. 1953. A GAME OF CATCH, copyright 1953 by Richard Wilbur, reprinted by permission of Harcourt, Inc. Originally appeared in *The New Yorker*, 1953.

Yo-Yo Ma Plays the World

CultureConnect. 2004. "Cultural Ambassadors: Yo-Yo Ma." http://cultureconnect.state.gov/?p=YMBiography (accessed November 18, 2004).

Green, Aaron. 2004. "Yo-Yo Ma: World Class Cellist." Classical Music: About.com. http://classicalmusic.about.com/od/performerbiographies/p/yoyoma.htm (accessed November 18, 2004).

Jong, Mabel. 2003. "Yo-Yo Ma: Family Is the Best Investment." Bankrate.com. http://www.bankrate.com/brm/news/investing/20030821a1.asp (accessed November 18, 2004).

Tassel, Janet. 2000. "Yo-Yo Ma's Journeys: Making Music with Humanity, from Sanders to the Silk Road." *Harvard Magazine* (March–April), vol. 102, no. 4. http://www.harvardmagazine.com/issues/ma00/yoyoma.html. By permission of the author.

Young Playwright on Broadway: Lorraine Hansberry's *A Raisin in the Sun*

Atkinson, Brooks. 1959. "A Raisin in the Sun," from *The New York Times*, March 12, 1959 ©1959 *The New York Times*. All rights reserved. Used by permission and protected by the Copyright Laws of the United States. The printing, copying, redistribution, or retransmission of the Material without express written permission is prohibited.

eNotes.com. 2004. "Profile of Lorraine Hansberry." http://www.enotes.com/raisin-sun/4870 (accessed November 18, 2004).

Hambleton, Vicki. 2001. "A Raisin in the Sun," adapted from *Footsteps* (May/June 2001) "American Negro Theatre" ©2001 Carus Publishing, 315 Fifth St., Peru, IL 61354. All rights reserved. Reprinted with permission.

Hughes, Langston. 1994. "Harlem (2)," copyright 1951 by Langston Hughes, from THE COLLECTED POEMS OF LANGSTON HUGHES by Langston Hughes, edited by Arnold Rampersad with David Roessel, Associate Editor. Used by permission of Alfred A. Knopf, a division of Random House, Inc.

Unit 21

Plant Families

Calgary Allergy Network. 2004. "Botanical List of Food Families." http://www.calgaryallergy.ca/Articles/botanical.htm (accessed November 22, 2004).

Flora of North America Association. 2004. "Flora of North America." http://www.efloras.org/flora_page.aspx?flora_id=1 (accessed November 22, 2004).

Watson, L., and M. J. Dallwitz. 2000. "The Families of Flowering Plants: Descriptions, Illustrations, Identification, and Information Retrieval." http://biodiversity.uno.edu/delta (accessed November 22, 2004).

A Family in Hiding: Anne Frank's Diary

Frank, Anne. 1995. From THE DIARY OF A YOUNG GIRL, THE DEFINITIVE EDITION by Anne Frank, edited by Otto H. Frank and Mirjam Pressler, translated by Susan Massotty, copyright 1995 by Doubleday, a division of Random House, Inc. Used by permission of Doubleday, a division of Random House, Inc.

The Anne Frank Center USA. 2003. "Anne Frank: Life and Times." http://www.annefrank.com/0_home.htm (accessed November 19, 2004).

My Side of the Story

Bagdasarian, Adam. 2002. "My Side of the Story," from FIRST FRENCH KISS AND OTHER TRAUMAS by Adam Bagdasarian. Copyright ©2002 by Adam Bagdasarian. *Reprinted by permission of Farrar, Straus, and Giroux, LLC*.

Bringing Up Baby: Family Life in the Animal World

Brewer, Duncan. 2003. "Parental Care in Mammals." *1000 Things You Should Know About Mammals*. MasterFILE Premier database (accessed November 19, 2004).

Cheater, Mark. 2001. "Granny Knows Best." *National Wildlife* (August/September), vol. 39, no. 5. MasterFILE Premier database (accessed November 17, 2004).

Churchman, Deborah. 2000. "All in a Mother's Day." *Ranger Rick* (May), vol. 34, no. 5. MasterFILE Premier database (accessed November 17, 2004).

Digital Library Project. 2004. "Threespine Stickleback--Gasterosteus aculeatus (Linnaeus)." http://elib.cs.berkeley.edu/

kopec/tr9/html/sp-threespine-stickleback. html (accessed November 19, 2004).

Ehrlich, Paul R., D. S Dobkin, and D. Wheye. 1988. "Precocial and Altricial Young." http://www.stanfordalumni. org/birdsite/text/essays/Precocial_and_ Altricial.html. (accessed November 19, 2004).

Goodman, Susan. 1996. "A Father's Day Top Ten." *National Wildlife* (June/ July), vol. 34, no. 4. MasterFILE Premier database (accessed November 17, 2004).

Grace-Pedrotty, Barbara, and Alan MacBain. 1995. "Fabulous Fathers." *Jack & Jill* (June), vol. 57, no. 4. MasterFILE Premier database (accessed November 17, 2004).

Johnson, Genevieve. 2003. "Sperm Whales and Elephants." PBS Online. http://www.pbs.org/odyssey/ odyssey/20030425_log_transcript.html (accessed November 19, 2004).

Kranking, Kathy Walsh. 1994. "Ranger Rick: Let's Hear it for Dad!--Animal Fathers." http://www.findarticles.com/ p/articles/mi_m0EPG/is_n6_v28/ai_ 16829042 (accessed November 21, 2004).

Mason, Jeffrey Moussaieff. 1999. *The Emperor's Embrace: Reflections on Animal Families and Fatherhood*. New York: Pocket Books.

MSN Encarta. 2004. "Maximum Life Span of Some Plants and Animals." *Microsoft Encarta Online Encyclopedia*. http://encarta.msn.com/media_ 461516708/Maximum_Life_Span_ of_Some_Plants_and_Animals.html (accessed November 22, 2004).

———. 2004. "Animal." *Microsoft Encarta Online Encyclopedia*. http:// encarta.msn.com/encyclopedia_ 761558664_2_67/Animal.html (accessed November 22, 2004).

Morales, Manuel. 2004. "Ant-Pubilia Mutualism." http://mutualism.williams.edu/ Research/ (accessed November 22, 2004).

Milius, Susan. 2004. "The Social Lives of Snakes." *Science News* (March 27), vol. 165, no. 13. MasterFILE Premier database (accessed November 17, 2004).

Petfish.net. 2004. "How Fish Spawn." http://www.petfish.net/how.htm (accessed November 20, 2004).

Current Science. 2002. "Lion Adopts Antelope." *Current Science*, April 12, 2002, vol. 87, no. 15. MasterFILE Premier database (accessed November 17, 2004).

Taflinger, Richard F. 1996. "Taking Advantage: Endnotes for Human Cultural Evolution." http://www.wsu.edu:8080/ ~taflinge/notes.html (accessed November 19, 2004).

Wikipedia. 2004. "Bird." http:// en.wikipedia.org/wiki/Bird (accessed November 20, 2004).

———. 2004. "Three-spined stickleback." http://en.wikipedia.org/ wiki/Three-spined_stickleback (accessed November 21, 2004).

———. 2004. "Cichlid." http:// en.wikipedia.org/wiki/Cichlid (accessed November 21, 2004).

———. 2004. "Insects." http:// en.wikipedia.org/wiki/Insects (accessed November 22, 2004).

Woodland Park Zoo. 2004. "Animal Fact Sheets: African Elephant." http://www. zoo.org/educate/fact_sheets/elephants/ africel.htm (accessed November 19, 2004).

World Book, Inc. 2002. "Fish." *World Book*. Chicago: World Book, Inc.

Who Cares About Great-Uncle Edgar?

Unit 22

How To Make a Crossword Puzzle

Eliot, George. 2004. "Introducing Crossword Puzzles: This is a Puzzling World." American Crossworld Puzzle Tournament. http://www.crosswordtournament.com/more/wynne.html (accessed November 22, 2004).

Frantz, Christine. 2004. "The History of the Crossword Puzzle." *Information Please*. Pearson Education, Inc. http://www.infoplease.com/spot/crossword1.html (accessed November 22, 2004).

Pearson Education, Inc. 2004. "History of the Crossword Puzzle." *Information Please*. http://www.infoplease.com/ipa/A0856331.html (accessed November 22, 2004).

A Collection of Puzzling Tales

Shannon, George. 1985. *Stories to Solve: Folktales From Around the World*. New York: HarperCollins. TEXT COPYRIGHT ©1985 BY GEORGE W. B. SHANNON. Used by permission of HarperCollins Publishers.

———. 1982. *True Lies: 18 Tales for You to Judge*. New York: HarperCollins. TEXT COPYRIGHT ©1982 BY GEOERGE W.B. SHANNON. Used by permission of HarperCollins Publishers.

The Disappearing Man

Asimov, Isaac. 1985. "The Disappearing Man," from *The Disappearing Man and Other Mysteries*. Text copyright ©1985 by Isaac Asimov. "The Disappearing Man" appeared in *Boys' Life*, June 1978 copyright ©1978, Boy Scouts of America. All rights reserved. Published by permission of The Estate of Isaac Asimov c/o Ralph M. Vicinanza, Ltd.

Puzzle People

Anecdotage.com. 2004. "Puzzling Question: Margaret Farrar Anecdotes," originally published in *The New Yorker* ©1959. http://www.anecdotage.com/index.php?aid=1328 (accessed November 19, 2004).

Bellis, Mary. 2004. "Rubik's Cube--Rubik and the Cube: The History of Rubik's Cube and Inventor Erno Rubik." About.com. http://inventors.about.com/library/weekly/aa040497.htm (accessed November 19, 2004).

CBS News. 2004. "A Maze: The World's Latest Craze." CBS Broadcasting. http://cbsnews.com/stories/2004/09/08/earlyshow/living/travel/main641936.shtml (accessed November 19, 2004).

CrosswordTournament.com. 1998. "A Puzzling Occupation: Will Shortz—Enigmatologist." American Crossword Puzzle Tournament. http://www.crosswordtournament.com/1998/art01.htm (accessed November 19, 2004).

Encyclopaedia Britannica. 1999. "Farrar, Margaret Petherbridge." Encyclopaedia Britannica's Women in American History. http://search.eb.com/women/articles/Farrar_Margaret_Petherbridge.html (accessed November 19, 2004).

———. 2004. "Farrar, Margaret." Encyclopaedia Britannica Premium Service. http://www.britannica.com/eb/article?tocId=9125716&query=%22margaret%farrar%22&ct=eb (accessed November 19, 2004).

———. 2004. "Rubik, Erno." Encyclopaedia Britannica Premium Service. http://www.britannica.com/eb/article?tocId=9001210&query=rubik&ct=eb (accessed November 19, 2004).

Frost, Caroline. 2004. "Tetris: A Chip Off the Old Bloc." BBC Online. http://news.bbc.co.uk/1/hi/magazine/3479989.stm (accessed November 19, 2004).

Rosinsky, Natalie. 2002. "The Puzzling Business of Sam Loyd & Erno Rubik," adapted from *Odyssey* (October 2002) ©2002 Carus Publishing, 315 Fifth St., Peru, IL 61354. All rights reserved. Reprinted with permission.

The Rosetta Stone: A Linguistic Puzzle

Brier, Bob. 1999. "Napoleon in Egypt." *Archaeology* (May/June), vol. 52, no. 3, EBSCOhost database (accessed January 17, 2005).

The British Museum. 2005. "The Rosetta Stone." http://www.ancientegypt.co.uk/writing/rosetta.html (accessed January 17, 2005).

———. 2005. "Cracking Codes: The Rosetta Stone and Decipherment." http://web.archive.org/web/20030608203320/http://www.thebritishmuseum.ac.uk/egyptian/ea/ccodes/decipher.html (accessed January 17, 2005).

Dyke, Daniel J. 2005. "Chapter IV: Language and Writing." http://www.dabar.org/Rawlinson/Raw-Ch4/RAE-p57.html (accessed January 17, 2005).

Egyptology Online. 2005. "Rosetta Stone." Astra Corporation. http://www.egyptologyonline.com/rosetta_stone.htm (accessed January 17, 2005).

Encyclopaedia Britannica. 2005. "Hieroglyphic Writing." Encyclopaedia Britannica Premium Service. http://www.britannica.com/eb/article?tocId=53614 (accessed January 17, 2005).

Geocities.com. 2005. "Napoleon in Egypt: A Short Account." http://www.geocities.com/athens/styx/3776/Nap.html (accessed January 17, 2005).

KingTutShop.com. 2005. "Rosetta Stone." http://www.kingtutshop.com/freeinfo/rosetta-stone.htm (accessed January 17, 2005).

KMT Communications. 1996. "Giants of Egyptology: Jean Francois Champollion." *KMT: A Modern Journal of Ancient Egypt* (Winter 1995–1996), vol. 6, no. 4, http://www.egyptology.com/kmt/winter95_96/giants.html (accessed January 17, 2005).

Millmore, Mark. 2005. "Hieroglyphs." http://www.eyelid.co. uk/hiero1.htm (accessed January 17, 2005).

Sproat, Richard. 2005. "Decipherment." http://catarina.ai.uiuc.edu/L403C/decipherment.html (accessed January 17, 2005).

Strachan, Richard A., & Kathleen A. Roetzel. 1997. "Ancient Egyptian Culture." *Ancient Peoples: A Hypertext View.* http://www.mnsu.edu/emuseum/prehistory/egypt/hieroglyphics/rosettastone.html (accessed January 17, 2005).

Wikipedia. 2004. "Rosetta Stone." http://en.wikipedia.org/wiki/Rosetta_Stone (accessed January 17, 2005).

The Dust Bowl

Roop, Peter. 1983. "Living in the Dust Bowl," adapted from *Cobblestone* (December 1983) "Making and Breaking the Soil" ©1983 Carus Publishing, 315 Fifth St., Peru, IL 61354. All rights reserved. Reprinted with permission.

Unit 23

Horsepower

Casey-Meyer, Brigid. 1982. "Horsepower Helped," adapted from *Cobblestone* (October 1982) "Erie Canal" ©1982 Carus Publishing, 315 Fifth St., Peru, IL 61354. All rights reserved. Reprinted with permission.

The International Museum of the Horse. 2005. "The Domestication of the Horse." http://www.imh.org/imh/kyhpl1b.html (accessed January 24, 2005).

WebCars! 2001. "What Is Horsepower?" http://www.web-cars.com/math/horsepower.html (accessed January 24, 2005).

Wikipedia. 2005. "James Watt." http://en.wikipedia.org/wiki/James_Watt (accessed January 18, 2005).

Zaaaaaaap!

Fermilab. 2007. "Questions About Physics." http://www.fnal.gov/pub/inquiring/questions/lightning3.html (accessed December 19, 2007).

Google Answers. 2007. "Lightning as Energy." http://www.answers.google.com/answers/threadview?id=765667 (accessed December 19, 2007).

"How Much Energy?" 2007. http://library.cma.gov.cn/publications/tx/2000tx/00.08/english.htm (accessed December 19, 2007).

National Aeronautics and Space Administration (NASA). 2007. Kennedy Space Center Frequently Asked Questions. "Can lightning be harnessed as a source of power?" http://www.nasa.gov/centers/kennedy/about/information/science_faq.html#1

Ratliff, Jennifer A. 2004. "Zaaaaaaap!" adapted from *Odyssey* (April 2004) "Future Power" ©2004 Carus Publishing, 315 Fifth St., Peru, IL 61354. All rights reserved. Reprinted with permission.

Reucroft, Stephen and John Swain. 2007. *The Boston Globe*. October 29, 2007. "Ask Dr. Knowledge: Why can't we capture lightning and convert it into usable electricity?" http://www.boston.com/news/globe/health_science/articles/2007/10/29/why_cant_we_capture_lightning_and_convert_it_into_usable_electricity/ (accessed December 19, 2007).

Singapore Science Centre. 2007. "ScienceNet – Physical Sciences – Magnetism/Electricity. Question No. 19343." http://www.science.edu.sg/ssc/detailed.jsp?artid=5001&type=6&root=5&parent=5&cat=57 (accessed December 19, 2007).

Smith, Chris. 2007. "How do Thunderstorms Work?" The Naked Scientists. http://www.thenakedscientists.com/HTML/articles/article/howdothunderstormswork-2/ (accessed December 19, 2007).

Satyagraha: Power for Change

Carter, Alden R. 2001. "Satyagraha" by Alden R. Carter, copyright ©2001 by Alden R. Carter, text, from ON THE FRINGE, edited by Donald R. Gallo. Used by permission of Dial Books for Young Readers, A Division of Penguin Young Readers Group, A Member of Penguin Group (USA) Inc., www.penguin.com. All rights reserved.

Mohandas Gandhi: Soul Force

Beck, Sanderson. 2003. "Gandhi's Nonviolent Revolution." http://www.san.beck.org/GPJ20-Gandhi.html (accessed January 14, 2005).

Falk, Richard. 2004. "Gandhi, Nonviolence and the Struggle Against War." Transnational Foundation for Peace and Future Research. http://www.transnational.org/forum/Nonviolence/2004/Falk_GandhiNonviolence.html (accessed January 14, 2005).

Oldenburg, Veena Talwar. 1993. "Mahatma Gandhi and the Untouchables of India," adapted from *Faces* (February 1983) ©1983 Carus Publishing, 315 Fifth St., Peru, IL 61354. All rights reserved. Reprinted with permission.

Blackout!

Kowalski, Kathiann M. 2004. "Blackout!" adapted from *Odyssey* (April 2004) ©2004 Carus Publishing, 315 Fifth St., Peru, IL 61354. All rights reserved. Reprinted with permission.

Word History

Roget's II: The New Thesaurus (Third ed.). 1995. Boston: Houghton Mifflin. http://www.yourdictionary.com/ahd/thes/p/p1158300.html (accessed February 8, 2005).

Unit 24

Dream While You Sleep

Brynie, Faith Hickman. 2002. "The Brain Never Sleeps," from *Odyssey* (January 2002) ©2002 by Faith Hickman Brynie. Reprinted with permission of the author.

Dream Moods. 2005. "Dream Research: The Sleep Cycle." http://www. dreammoods.com/dreaminformation/ dreamresearch.htm (accessed January 14, 2005).

Saleeby, J. P. 2003. "Sleep: The Often Ignored Guardian of Wellness." *JIVE Magazine*. http://www.jivemagazine.com/ column.php?pid=945 (accessed January 14, 2005).

Dreaming the Night Away

Herbst, Judith. 1985. Reprinted with permission of Atheneum Books for Young Readers, an imprint of Simon & Schuster's Children's Publishing Division. "The Great Shut-Eye Mystery," from *BIO AMAZING: A Casebook of Unsolved Human Mysteries* by Judith Herbst. Copyright ©1985 by Judith Herbst. All rights reserved.

Dream Team

Jones, Ron. 1976. "Winning," from *The Co-Evolution Quarterly* (Summer). By permission of the author. Copyright 1976 by Ron Jones.

Pursuit of a Dream

Eaglesham, Barbara. 2002. "Out of Her Hands: The Woman Who Didn't Win the Nobel Prize," adapted from *Odyssey* (February 2002) "Science Feuds" ©2002 Carus Publishing, 315 Fifth St., Peru, IL 61354. All rights reserved. Reprinted with permission.

Maddox, Brenda. 2002. *Rosalind Franklin: The Dark Lady of DNA*. New York: Perennial.

Piper, Anne. 1998. "Rosalind Franklin: Light on a Dark Lady." Contributions of 20th Century Women to Physics. http:// cwp.library.ucla.edu/articles/franklin/piper. htm (accessed January 14, 2005).

The San Diego Supercomputer Center. 2005. "Rosalind Elsie Franklin." Women in Science. http://www.sdsc.edu/ ScienceWomen/franklin.html (accessed January 14, 2005).

Martin Luther King, Jr.: The Freedom Dreamer

Haskins, Jim. 1994. "Timely Leader," adapted from *Cobblestone* (February 1994) "Martin Luther King, Jr. and the Civil Rights Movement" ©1994 Carus Publishing, 315 Fifth St., Peru, IL 61354. All rights reserved. Reprinted with permission.

King, Martin Luther, Jr. 1963. "I Have a Dream." Reprinted by arrangement with The Heirs to the Estate of Martin Luther King Jr., c/o Writers House as agent for the proprietor, New York, NY. Copyright 1963 Dr. Martin Luther King, Jr.; Copyright renewed 1991 Coretta Scott King.

Roop, Peter. 1983. "Five Leaders for Freedom," adapted from *Cobblestone* (February 1983) "Black History Month: The Struggle for Rights" ©1983 Carus Publishing, 315 Fifth St., Peru, IL 61354. All rights reserved. Reprinted with permission.

Whitman, Sylvia. 1994. "To the Promised Land: The Civil Rights Years," adapted from *Cobblestone* (February 1994) ©1994 Carus Publishing, 315 Fifth St., Peru, IL 61354. All rights reserved. Reprinted with permission.

Word History

American Heritage Dictionary (Fourth ed.). 2000. Boston: Houghton Mifflin. http://www.yourdictionary.com/ahd/n/ n0104100.html (accessed January 14, 2005).

Photo and Illustration Credits

Cover

Illustration

©Jonathan Till/Martin French

Unit 19

Photographs

4: ©IOC/Olympic Museum Collections.
5: Sports Museum of Finland.
7: ©Brandxpictures. 7: ©PhotoDisc.
23: ©Kai's Power Photos.

Illustrations

3: ©Martin French/Morgan Gaynin Inc.
6: Steve Clark. 9–19: Lea Lyon. 20–21:
Steve Clark. 25–28: Karen Lee.

Unit 20

Photographs

29: ©1999–2004 Getty Images, Inc.
30: ©Bettmann/Corbis. 45: ©1999–2004
Getty Images, Inc. 45: ©2001 Cylla
von Tiedmann 49: The Minneapolis
Institute of Arts. 51: t. ©Underwood
& Underwood/Corbis 51: ©Bettmann/
Corbis. 53: ©Bettmann/Corbis.

Illustrations

32–38: Alan Flinn. 39–43: Dennis Balogh.

Unit 21

Photographs

57: ©Bob Torrez/Getty Images.
.59: ©2005 Jupiter Images. 60: ©2003
Getty Images. 60: ©2003 Getty Images.
67: ©1999–2005 Getty Images, Inc.
74: ©Comstock, ©Kai's Power Photos,
©Digital Vision, and ©Photo Disc.
76: ©1999–2005 Getty Images, Inc.
77: ©1999–2005 Getty Images, Inc.
80, 86: ©Comstock Images.
83: ©Bettmann/Corbis. 84: ©Royalty-
Free/Corbis.

Illustrations

58–59, 78: Steve Clark. 69, 72: Jing
Tsong.

Unit 22

Photographs

87: ©Digital Vision. 91–95: ©2005
Jupiter Images. 96–100: ©2005 Jupiter
Images. 103: ©Jason Hawkes/Corbis.
108: ©2005 Jupiter Images. 109: ©2004
Jupiter Images. 105–107, 110: ©Artville.

Illustrations

88–91, 96–100: Steve Clark. 102:
David Danz. Use of Rubik's Cube® is by
permission of Seven Towers Ltd.
104: David Danz.

Unit 23

Photographs

111: ©PhotoDisc. 120: ©Royalty-Free/
image100. 123: ©2005 Jupiter Images.
124: ©2005 Jupiter Images. 126:
©Bettmann/Corbis. 128: ©Comstock
Images. 131: ©Bettmann/Corbis.
133: ©Bettmann/Corbis. 136: ©2005
Jupiter Images 139: ©Andrew
Lichtenstein/Corbis.

Illustrations

112: ©2005 Jupiter Images.
113–119, 136–137: Steve Clark.

Unit 24

Photographs

142: ©Royalty-Free/Corbis.
148: courtesy Dr. Stephen La Berge.
150: ©Getty Images, Inc. 155: ©Photex/
W. Smith/Masterfile. 161: ©1999–2004
Getty Images, Inc. 163: detail ©National
Portrait Gallery, London. 165: Norman
Collection on the History of Molecular
Biology. 166: A. Barrington Brown/©2005
Photo Researchers, Inc. 168: ©Hulton-
Deutsch Collection/Corbis. 169–174:
©2003 Getty Images.

Illustrations

141: Steve Clark. 143: Becky Malone.
145: ©1999–2004 Getty Images.
149: ©1999–2004 Getty Images. 163:
©Royalty-Free/Corbis. 165: Steve Clark.